the interior design intern

fb

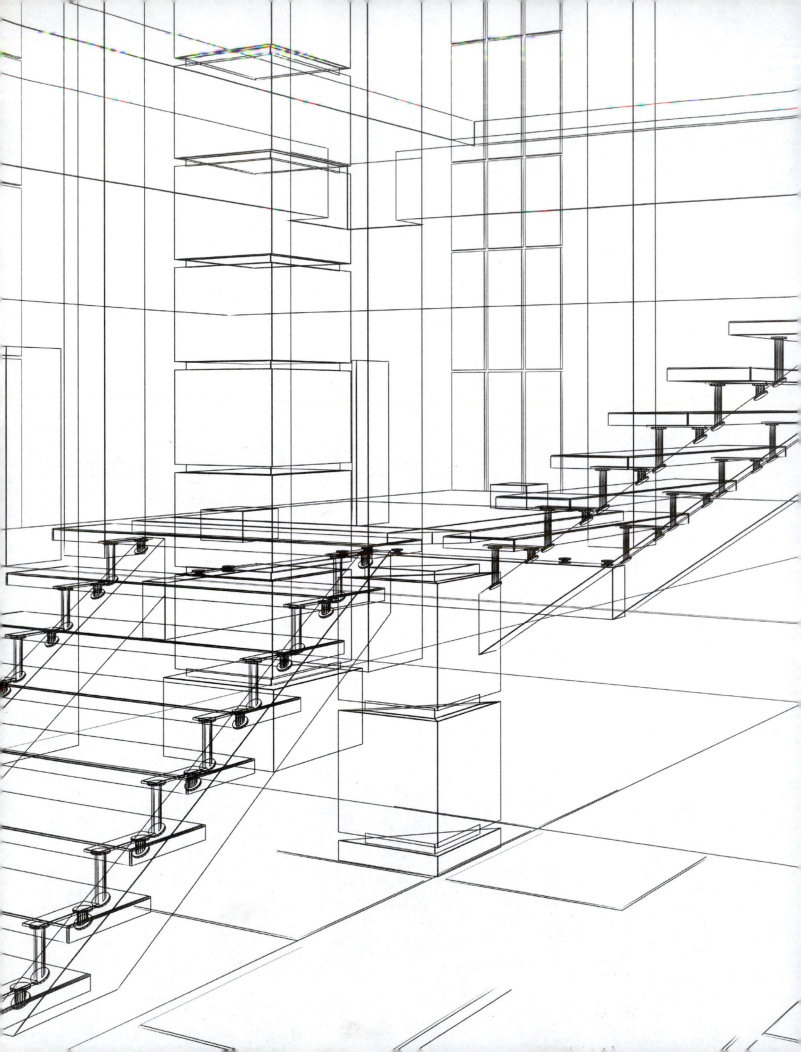

the interior design intern

LINDA L. NUSSBAUMER, Ph.D., CID, ASID, IDEC

South Dakota State University

FAIRCHILD BOOKS

New York

To the students and
site supervisors who
provided personal insight
for future interns.

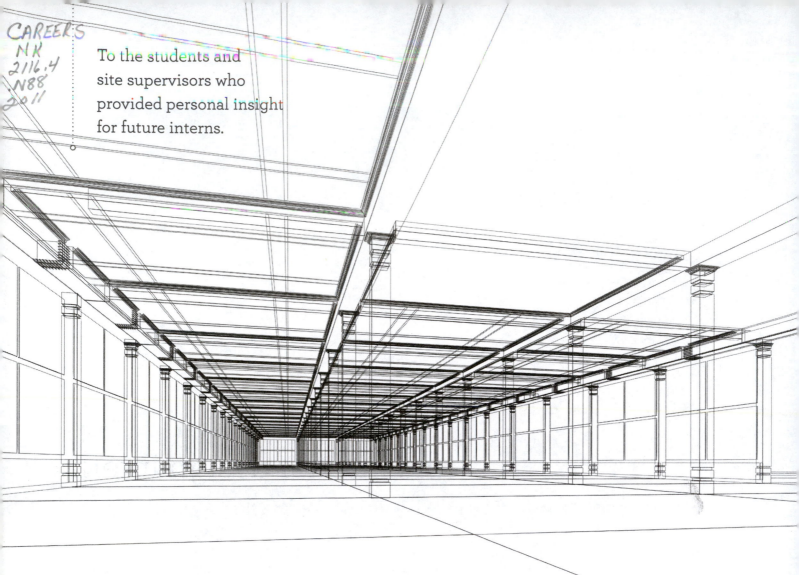

Executive Editor: Olga T. Kontzias
Assistant Acquisitions Editor: Amanda Breccia
Editorial Development Director: Jennifer Crane
Development Editor: Rob Phelps
Creative Director: Carolyn Eckert
Production Director: Ginger Hillman
Production Editor: Andrew Fargnoli
Copyeditor: Susan Hobbs
Ancillaries Editor: Noah Schwartzberg
Cover and Text Design: Katie Craig
Cover Art: Courtesy of iStockphoto/zilli (front);
© Beau Lark/Corbis (back)

Art Credits: Courtesy of iStockphoto/Roman Sakhno (p. ii);
Courtesy of iStockphoto/Roman Sakhno (p. iv); Courtesy of
iStockphoto/Roman Sakhno (Part 1); Courtesy of iStockphoto/
Feng Yu (Chapter 1); Courtesy of iStockphoto/Plesea Petre
(Chapter 2); © The Print Collector/Alamy (Chapter 3); Courtesy
of iStockphoto/Pali Rao (Chapter 4); Courtesy of iStockphoto/
Dmitry Goygel-Sokol (Chapter 5);: Courtesy of iStockphoto/
Chad McDermott (Chapter 6); Courtesy of iStockphoto/Mustafa
Deliormanli (Part 2); Tim Klein/Getty Images (Chapter 7);
Courtesy of iStockphoto/Petro Feketa (Chapter 8); © National
Geographic Image Collection/Alamy (Chapter 9); Courtesy
of iStockphoto/Roman Sakhno (Part 3); © paulasfotos/Alamy
(Chapter 10); Courtesy of iStockphoto/victor zasto (Appendices)

Library of Congress Catalog Card Number: 2009940162
ISBN: 978-1-56367-907-0
GST R 133004424
Printed in the United States of America

TP09

contents

extended contents

appendices

cd-rom contents

foreword

I have always been grateful for the assistance that I received from my college professors who mentored me through a terrific internship, which turned out to be one of the best events in my career. They helped me prepare for the job interviews, and they choreographed the work experience to ensure that my employer offered me a variety of opportunities. I chose an internship in a commercial firm where I learned about the realities of the design process. I developed strong working relationships that still exist today.

My internship gave me the confidence to search for a firm that provided meaningful design solutions after I graduated from Iowa State University. I had a mission and a passion and knew that I wanted to design with a purpose. It took patience and persistence before I found LHB, Inc., where I not only found a firm with a soul but also a wonderful mentor.

I have had the joy of being both an intern and now a mentor for other interns. I was fortunate to work with wonderful people as an intern, and my goal as a mentor is to inspire students just as I was inspired.

As a student I served on the ISU College of Design's Design Council with students from other design disciplines, and we were the liaison between the faculty leadership and the design students. As a representative of the interior design students I felt fortunate to have this leadership opportunity and have continued to serve others in leadership positions throughout my career. My favorite groups to work with are those that interact with students. I encourage you to engage with professionals in these situations. It can be a rewarding experience for everyone.

Volunteer leadership leads to professional leadership. By the time I was 30 years old I was elected president of the American Society of Interior Designers (ASID) Minnesota chapter and I was promoted to project principal at LHB, Inc. I am one of the founding members of the U.S. Green Building Council (USGBC) Minnesota chapter, where I served as liaison between the board of directors and the Emerging Green Builders, my favorite group in USGBC. I have served two terms on the Minnesota Board of Architecture, Engineering, Land Surveying, Landscape Architecture, Geoscience, and Interior Design, a position appointed by the governor. My experience on the licensing board included reviewing applications for certified interior designers where we evaluated education, work experience, and required the passage of the National Council for Interior Design Qualification (NCIDQ) exam. Using the Interior Design Experience Program (IDEP) process, as outlined in Chapter 10 of this book, is an excellent way for a young professional and supervisor to work together to find opportunities for the variety of experience required. I am currently serving a two-year term on the ASID National Board of Directors. All of these leadership positions have introduced me to wonderful mentors from all over the world, each one of them adding to my interior design toolbox and deepening my passion for sustainable design and a desire to promote the next generation.

I love to learn and I love to teach and I try to live by Hannover Principle #9—"Seek constant improvement by the sharing of knowledge"—published in 2000 for The World's Fair in Hannover, Germany. Each one of us can choose to make the world a better place with every decision we make, and each one of us can share our experiences with others to seek constant improvement. The work we do will change someone's life.

On Earth Day 2007, my business partner and I launched Studio 2030. The launch of this business is the culmination of almost 20 years of design, learning, teaching, management, leadership, research, and mentorship. Our life experiences provide the opportunity to grow a practice founded on the conviction that environmental and economic objectives are not mutually exclusive, that there is no need to compromise ethics in the pursuit of aesthetic or functional goals. We believe the ideals of sustainability—resource conservation, energy efficiency, and pollution prevention—are fully compatible with design excellence: work that is highly original, high performance, and sublimely beautiful. We believe design professionals are accountable for the well-being of those who interact with their work. We believe buildings should be capable of evolving over time, in line with changing conditions and uses. And we believe that every project is a process of discovery, an opportunity to realize solutions that are smarter, offer a better human experience, and produce less waste than what has come before.

I am thrilled to introduce you to Linda Nussbaumer and her book. I met Linda when I was giving a presentation on indoor air quality and she was working on her Ph.D. Her

research on multiple chemical sensitivity (MCS) and indoor air quality has combined with my experience designing a house for a woman with MCS and developed into a wonderful relationship. Linda often shares her research, which continues to inform the work that I do. She teaches her students the importance of research and how to incorporate research into design solutions, and she connects students to firms that also integrate research into their design practice when searching for internship opportunities.

Linda, as the program coordinator at South Dakota State University, has devoted her career to teaching and research. She has raised the bar in her department by promoting and achieving the standards set by the Council for Interior Design Accreditation (CIDA). She was one of the first interior design professors to introduce sustainability to her students, and she continues to challenge them to integrate their knowledge into projects and to seek more from their internship. She succeeds in building connections among interior design practitioners, academic researchers, and students with the hope that students will find a passion that will influence their design career. Linda fosters inspiration and encourages the students to challenge themselves.

It is her devotion to teaching and research that Linda brings to this book; her thorough approach to planning for, carrying out, and evaluating the design internship will prove as valuable to your future career as I found my internship experience did for my own.

Your internship is a chance to try something new: to work with incredibly talented people, to work in an office that mentors emerging professionals, to experience interior design from the client perspective, to experience life in other parts of the world. This is your opportunity to take a risk, to explore a city that you are curious about, to experience projects that you think you may someday want to design, and to expand your interior design connections. If you plan early in your college career, have an open mind, and start your contact network early, you could potentially even have three to four internship experiences before you graduate.

Your internship can be one of the most rewarding experiences of your college career. I urge you to set a vision and goals for what you want to achieve during your internship. Through determination, courage, and persistence, you can create a memorable and life-changing adventure.

RACHELLE SCHOESSLER LYNN
FASID, CID, LEED AP BD+C
Partner, Studio 2030 Inc.

preface

An internship is designed as a learning experience that generally takes place during the student's academic career. Sometimes students obtain an internship but become disappointed with a lack of opportunities and find themselves spending most of their time in a resource library. To remedy this situation, a well-considered plan of preparation can provide the student with an organized and enriching internship experience.

The purpose of this book is to provide information that prepares students for the interior design internship; it will help them put together their own organized plan to gain a variety of experiences during their internship. Because an internship educates students through field experiences during their academic career, it is important for each student to develop an organized plan to prepare, complete, evaluate, and reflect upon their internship. Ultimately, they will benefit from a greater learning experience in this way.

Typically, when books in our field include discussion on obtaining employment, this topic becomes integrated into the overall business of interior design. One such textbook briefly covers internships whereas another covers information on obtaining the entry-level position. No book has been written specifically for the interior design intern until now.

This book provides students with guidelines to develop an organized plan to prepare for, carry out, and evaluate their interior design internship after its completion in order to plan for their future careers. It provides organizational tools and annotated examples of successful résumés and portfolios on a companion CD-ROM. It also explores the international internship and shares quotes from interns and site supervisors to provide insights to the reader.

cd-rom

Accompanying *The Interior Design Intern* is a PC- and Macintosh-friendly CD-ROM, which can be found on the inside front cover of the book. This feature provides electronic forms to help students develop their own cover letters, résumés, and internship reporting tools—Microsoft Word and Excel documents that can be saved onto the student's computer and printed out or used electronically. The Read Me document offers tips on how best to use the CD-ROM with the book. The CD-ROM also features examples of traditional, digital, and website-based portfolios, each of which includes a final page of descriptive notes that point out, page-by-page, important elements of each example for students to adapt into their own portfolios. Throughout the book, a special icon marks a feature that you can access on the CD-ROM:

preparing for the internship

Internships generally take place when students reach the upper division level and most often in the summer between the junior and senior years. By this time, students have completed a business course related to interior design and possibly other business courses for a minor. Therefore, students are expected to have a basic understanding of various interior design firms and their business operation prior to their internship.

Before their internship, students will have read this text and completed a set of goals—professional and personal, organized a job search, considered an international internship, applied for an internship, prepared for an interview, and been interviewed.

getting the most from the internship experience

When the student intern is hired, the internship supervisor will be informed of the student's academic expectations for learning experiences and have read the chapter on reporting the internship, which is designed to enhance the learning experience. Though the reporting process may seem tedious and cumbersome to some students, those who have completed these reports state that they have gained more from the internship, not only from goal setting and topical assignments but also from the reflective journaling. Students report to their academic supervisor on a weekly basis in addition to reporting to an internship supervisor at the firm. They are also expected to respect the firm's process of problem solving. The internship supervisor is required to honestly evaluate the intern, discuss this feedback with the student, and send it along to the interior design program. Such feedback is intended to provide information to the students and the program regarding the student's performance.

organization of the book

The organization of this book follows the process as previously outlined—from preparation for the internship; through reporting, analyzing, and positive adjustment-making during the ongoing internship; to post-internship reflection in order to gain the most from the experience and plan for the future.

The book is divided into three parts: Part I: "Preparation"; Part II: "The Internship"; and Part III: "Drawing Conclusions for Your Career."

Part I includes Chapters 1 through 6. In Chapter 1, "Getting Started" students learn about setting goals that focus on profession and personal goals to enhance the internship experience. This chapter also discusses personality types and helps students evaluate their own personality so they can become better team players during their internship and throughout the design world. In Chapter 2, "Organizing the Job Search," students learn how to search for and locate an internship that is appropriate for them. Chapter 3, "The International Internship," provides students with background information on searching and preparing for an international internship. In Chapter 4, "Preparing to Apply for an Internship," students learn about résumés, cover letters, and portfolios, and are directed to the CD-ROM for examples that demonstrate the ability to communicate through the written word and graphics. These full-color portfolios illustrate a variety of methods for students to design a portfolio. In Chapter 5, "Preparing for the Interview," students learn about researching the firm where they will interview and preparing for the interview. In Chapter 6, "Preparing for the Internship," students learn about the forms that need to be completed if it is a paid internship. Students also learn to investigate the firm's organizational type to be prepared for the way they work and the appropriate wardrobe needed. In the process of looking for housing, students are directed to learn about the community and how to be comfortable and safe during the internship.

Part II: "The Internship" includes Chapters 7 through 9. In Chapter 7, "During the Internship," students are reminded about professional conduct such as ethics, etiquette, netiquette, and handling conflicts. In Chapter 8, "Reporting the Internship," students learn that reporting their internship will enhance the learning experience. In Chapter 9, "Evaluating the Internship," students learn how to evaluate what they have learned and to bring this new knowledge into their professional career.

Part III: "Drawing Conclusions for Your Career" consists only of Chapter 10. In Chapter 10, "Pathways to Success: From Internship to Career," students explore the connections between education and their internship and between their education/internship and their career. They will learn about the IDEP program and the value and variety of career-related certifications.

Integrated throughout each chapter, former interns and site supervisors share experience and advice in their own voices.

from internship to successful career

This book is geared for higher-education interior design programs that require internships. Because most, if not all, interior design programs at the college level require internships and no single textbook or manual has covered the entire internship process until now, these programs should find this textbook to be an essential manual. It has been designed for easy reading and easy referencing. Additionally, firms should have copies so that the site supervisor knows the academic expectations for the intern.

Through a thorough preparation for and reporting of an internship, students will gain a greater learning experience that will enhance the final academic year and ultimately their career.

acknowledgments

Resources addressing or preparing students for an internship are few. Although the following resources are also referenced throughout the book, I'd like to offer a special note of appreciation to the following: *Designing Your Business* by Gordon Kendall, *The Fashion Intern* by Michele Granger, *Professional Practice for Interior Designers* by Christine Piotrowski, *The Survival Guide to Architectural Internship and Career Development* by Grace Kim, and *World Wise: What to Know Before You Go* by Lanie Denslow.

Condé Nast Publications and Fairchild Books are publishers who have once again provided guidance and encouragement. These professionals include Executive Editor Olga Kontzias, Editorial Development Director Jennifer Crane, and Development Editor Rob Phelps. A special thanks goes to Rob for his great work as a reviewer and editor. I would also like to thank the talented production and art team of Creative Director Carolyn Eckert, Production Director Ginger Hillman, and Production Editor Andrew Fargnoli. I am also grateful for the review and constructive criticism of proposal reviewers Erin Speck, The George Washington University at Mt. Vernon Campus; Michele Granger, Missouri State University; LuAnn Nissen, University of Nevada, Reno; Gwendolyn Fisher, IADT, Orlando; Adair Bowen, Baylor University; Beth Miller, Mississippi State University; and development reviewers Gwendolyn Fisher, IADT, Orlando; Susan Ray-Degges, North Dakota State University; and Diane Bender, Arizona State University.

Thanks to students and site supervisors who contributed to my book in a very special way. Through comments on questionnaires, many student interns and site supervisors provided insight and advice that will help many future interns. These comments, which are quoted throughout the book, provide a special personal touch for the reader. Thank you to student reviewer and South Dakota State University interior design student Michelle Ralston, who reviewed and edited the manuscript from a student's perspective. Especially, thank you to students who permitted their résumés and portfolios to be published within the book.

Many firms open their doors to interns, and many site supervisors patiently work with interns. They especially deserve credit for helping students make a transition from the classroom to employment.

Thank you also to Jane Hegland, department head, and to Laurie Nichols, former dean of the College of Family and Consumer Sciences and presently the provost and vice president of Academic Affairs, both at SDSU, for their continued encouragement and support. Thank you also to my friends and family who supported this endeavor. Especially, thank you to my husband, Jerry, who continually encourages my endeavors. Without his encouragement and support, this book would not have been possible.

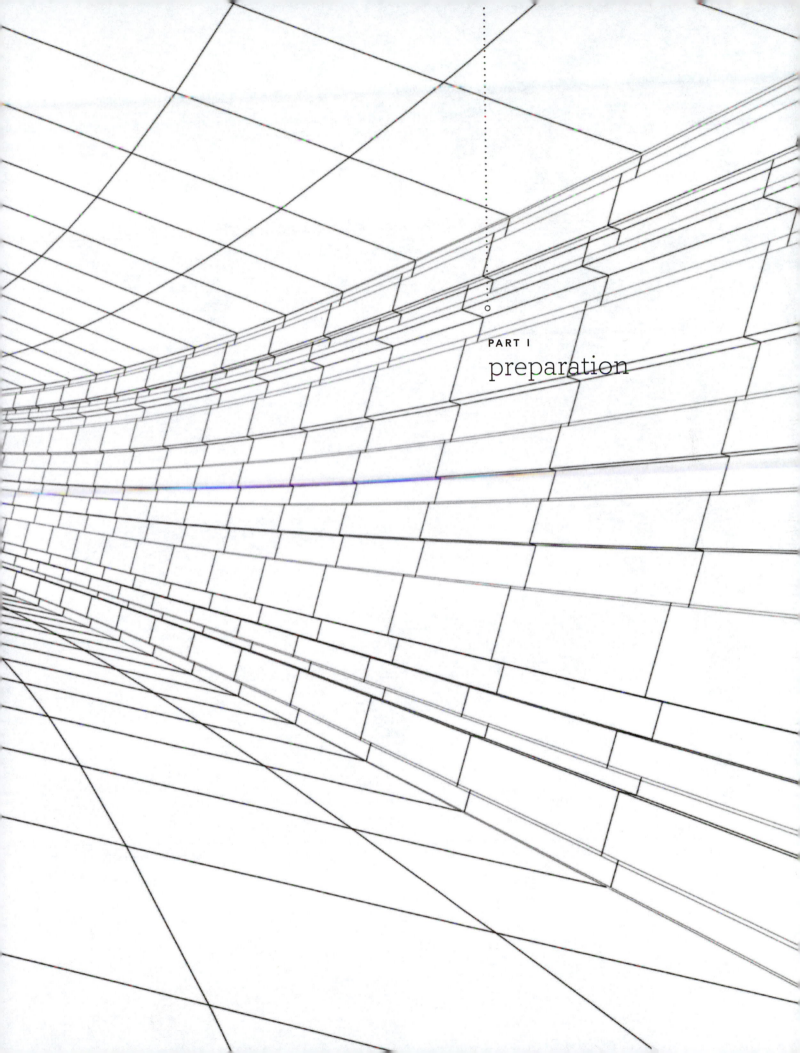

PART I

preparation

1 getting started

"My internship goals were to work hard to make a good name for myself in the field, take on as many different responsibilities as possible to get a wide variety of learning, and become confident in asking to go do hands-on projects with the designer."

—*K.S., who completed an eight-week internship at a retail establishment that provided design services.*

OBJECTIVES

- Establish professional and personal goals.
- Develop personal goals to prepare and manage time better.
- Determine priorities.
- Examine energy levels.
- Develop a daily time-management schedule to fit priorities and energy levels.
- Identify and understand your personality type.

The purpose of this book is to help you develop your own organized plan to prepare for, carry out, and evaluate your internship in order to set both career and personal goals for your future.

So let's get started.

what is an internship?

An **internship** is a supervised work experience within a profession (*Business Dictionary*, 2008). For an interior design internship, the work experience most often takes place in a design firm, design studio, showroom in a design center, retail establishment, or design-related firm. It provides opportunities for interaction between the student, a firm, and the university. At most higher educational institutions, students are required to complete an internship for specific number of work hours or on-the-job training for credit hours.

Most importantly, an internship is designed to assist the student in the transition from theory or hypothetical scenarios to professional interior design practice. However, before you, the student, begin an internship, you must choose where you want to transition these theories and hypothetical scenarios—in short, all that you are learning in your academic programs—into your future professional life. To make this decision, you must consider your future goals, both professional and personal.

goals

A **goal** is an objective, a target, or an aim; it is a plan to do something today or at sometime in the future (*The Free Dictionary*, 2008). An interior design student's professional goal may be to work for a firm that designs healthcare facilities or start his or her own

interior design firm in the future. For this last long-range goal, steps must be established to reach it—one that may seem like a vision to the future. A **personal goal** may relate to the achievement of a skill such as running in a major marathon. Again, steps to meet this goal must be established.

Setting Goals

Norman Vincent Peale, author of *The Power of Positive Thinking,* once stated, "If you want to get somewhere you have to know where you want to go and how to get there. Then never, never, never give up." Thus, if you want to get somewhere, you must establish a set of goals.

Of course, it is risky to set goals; setting goals demands effort and promises no guarantee for success. Goals require commitment of time and energy as well as a mental process to carry them out. They also involve a potential fear of failure. However, not achieving a goal does not actually amount to failure. It only means that the goal is unattainable at the present time for some reason or another (Piotrowski, 2007). For example, not attaining a goal may mean that you need to take a different direction because you are not quite ready to achieve that goal. Maybe something got in the way, such as illness or a family situation. It may be that the goal was simply set too high (Piotrowski, 2007).

Regardless, it is important to set goals or you will achieve nothing. So, before discussing goal setting further, take the self-quiz to discover your ability or need to set goals (see Table 1.1; also available on the CD-ROM as Appendix A). This will help you set the goals that are the most realistic for you to achieve.

YES   NO

TABLE 1.1 (ALSO APPENDIX A)

Self-Quiz: Setting Goals

If you answer *yes* to these questions, you manage your time well.
Answering *no* means you have some work to do in time management.

QUESTIONS

1 During the past year, have you logged the way you spend time for at least one week?

2 Do you write out a weekly time plan that includes objectives, activities, priorities, and the time estimated to complete them?

3 Can you find large blocks of uninterrupted time when you need it?

4 Do you prepare a daily activity list that identifies priorities and the time estimated to complete them?

5 Do you control interruptions and drop-in visitors rather than allowing them to control you and your time?

6 Do you meet all deadlines and finish all your work on schedule?

7 Do you start projects on time without procrastinating or put them off until the last minute?

8 Is your desk well organized and free of clutter?

9 Do you avoid getting involved in other people's work, such as solving their problems, doing things they could—or should—be doing for themselves?

Why Set Goals?

Setting goals is a common, effective method to manage and motivate one's own performance and productivity as well as improve one's professional competencies and accomplishments. It is also useful as a practicing designer to structure your career development whether you are an employee or an employer (Nussbaumer & Isham, 2009). This is why goals are incorporated into the internship experience described in Chapter 8.

As suggested earlier, setting goals also involves thinking and planning ahead. You might ask yourself these three questions:

1. How do I see myself in the future?
2. How do I want others see me?
3. What might I do to achieve these results?

Writing a Personal Success Story

An exercise in thinking ahead is to write a personal success story. Such a story might be printed in a newspaper upon your retirement or appear in an announcement of your attaining a professional position or achieving a noteworthy accomplishment. Whether or not it is ever used for such purposes, writing a personal success story at the outset of your career can help you focus your goals. This story must show where you *want to be* and *would be*, and what you *want to achieve in a lifetime*. Writing it down solidifies those goals.

Before and while you write your personal success story, keep asking yourself the three previous questions about visualizing and planning for your future; this will keep your story focused and help you come up with the details. By focusing on these questions, you may just find your story writing itself.

Establishing Your Goals

To achieve long-term goals, you will need to set goals for daily achievement as well as for weekly, monthly, quarterly, and yearly benchmarks. Completing Table 1.2, "Establishing My Goals—Part 1," will help you see into your future by thinking ahead for each of these time frames and establish your goals. (This document is also available on the CD-ROM as Appendix B.)

You should then establish a second list of goals that you can turn into a to-do list. (To-do lists are discussed later in this chapter.) However, at this point, use Table 1.3, "Establishing My Goals—Part 2," to set daily, weekly, monthly, quarterly, and yearly goals. (Table 1.3 is also available on the CD-ROM as Appendix B.)

Professional Goals

Professional goals may relate to where you want to be in your career in a year or in several years. These goals may involve the type of firm in which you would like to work (e.g., an architectural firm, a healthcare design firm, a residential interior design firm, or any other type of firm). They may concern a professional achievement, such as taking and passing the NCIDQ, becoming LEED certified, or becoming a registered or certified interior designer. Other goals may be related to achieving a particular position within a firm, taking a leadership position in the ASID or IIDA, or completing a master's or doctoral degree. Some of these goals may seem rather lofty, but all are attainable through goal setting.

Specific Tasks

You may also set goals for the completion of specific tasks. In interior design, defining specific tasks begins with the initial client meeting. At this meeting, designer and client establish their goals and schedules for the project. Based on these goals, the designer plans and assigns specific tasks.

TABLE 1.2 (ALSO APPENDIX B)

Goal Setting: Establishing My Goals—Part 1

As you establish goals, give yourself permission to have some fun!

Communicate your goals to anyone you want to be part of your support system.

By doing so, you will have just completed the first step toward reaching your goals!

MY MOST IMPORTANT **ACADEMIC** GOAL

....
....
....

MY MOST IMPORTANT **CAREER** GOAL

Upon graduation ....

In 3 years ....

In 5 years ....

MY MOST IMPORTANT **LEADERSHIP** GOAL

During College ....

During Career ....

In my Community ....

MY MOST IMPORTANT **FAMILY/HOME** GOAL

Current ....

In 3 years ....

In 5 years ....

MY MOST IMPORTANT **LEISURE** GOAL

Current ....

In 3 years ....

In 5 years ....

MY MOST IMPORTANT **SELF-TIME** GOAL

Current ....

In 3 years ....

In 5 years ....

TABLE 1.3 (ALSO APPENDIX B)

Goal Setting: Establishing My Goals—Part 2

To complete this list in establishing goals, answer the following questions:

- Daily goals: What tasks must be completed and in what order (prioritized)?

- Weekly goals: What must be accomplished during a specific week, and on what day must it be completed?

- Monthly goals: What needs to be accomplished this month? What day must it be completed? How long will it take? (Allow for emergencies, other work, or the unforeseeable.)

- Quarterly goals: Ask yourself questions similar to those for the monthlies.

- Yearly goals: Look ahead!

DAILY GOALS:

WEEKLY GOALS:

MONTHLY GOALS:

QUARTERLY GOALS:

YEARLY GOALS:

For you, the student, this method of goal setting can also be used to achieve a systematic completion of a project in your academic program or during your internship. For example, a reasonable goal for an intern would be to answer questions about one's future career. In a recent post-internship interview, one student stated that his goal was to better understand the business of interior design: the processes, relationships, and techniques. Another student's goal related to her place in the industry. She stated that an internship could help determine where she best fit within the field of design, such as residential design or commercial design. Her goal was to make that determination (Box 1.1).

Personal Goals

As you begin to set professional goals, you must often set and achieve some personal goals. For example, as a student, you must first consider an academic goal, which is to obtain a degree that you could reasonably expect would lead to your future employment.

The internship must be completed prior to the attainment of either of these goals. Thus, setting a goal for locating the appropriate internship is important. This is a personal goal that rests on the edge of a professional goal; for example, work in an interdisciplinary team (architects, engineers, and interior designers) or participate in a post-occupancy evaluation. To achieve this goal, you will need to determine the type of design or design-related firm where you would like to work. Then, you need to determine the skills you have and those you need to improve to obtain the internship position. Now you have goals that will help you attain an internship. However, goals still need to be set to attain an internship such as creating a résumé, developing an internship portfolio, determine the area or city, locating

a variety of firms, creating a list of firms to contact, preparing a cover letter for each, sending cover letter and résumé, and sending portfolio (if requested).

Personal goals can also be viewed in a different sense (i.e., leisure activities, health and wellness achievements, and more). Though these types of achievements are very personal, they often affect your professional and other personal goals and must be considered in goal setting (see Table 1.2, also Appendix B—Establishing My Goals Part 1, which you can access, print, and fill out from the CD-ROM).

Internship Goals

Much of what is known now about goal setting resulted from studies carried out by the psychologist Edwin Locke and his associates (1970). These pioneering researchers developed a theory of goal setting that states the following: (1) difficult goals result in a higher level of performance than do easy goals, and (2) specific goals result in a higher level of performance and assumes that the higher and more specific a person's goals, the harder the person will try and the higher his performance will be. Locke (1968) also found that when individuals are given low, medium, and high goals, it is those with high goals who are consistently the most productive. This assumes, however, that the goals are attainable and are not unreasonably high.

During your internship, your goals may be preset by your academic supervisor, or you may establish your own goals. Such goals should progress from the simple low-level performance to the complex higher-level performance that will enhance the learning process. See Chapter 8 for suggested goals to achieve during the internship.

Through questionnaires, students commented on the goals they hoped to accomplish during their internship (see Box 1.1).

setting goals

The following interns responded to the question below:

E.J. completed an eight-week internship at an interior architectural firm. She graduated from a private university in a large Southern city.

J.E. interned at an interior design firm specializing in high-end residential interiors and hospitality design. She graduated from a private college in a large Midwestern city.

J.F. completed a paid four-month internship at a development company that specialized in both residential and commercial interior design by constructing high-end, single-family homes, condos, and commercial spaces. She graduated from a private college in a large Midwestern city.

J.H. completed a 12-week unpaid internship at a residential design firm in Buenos Aries, Argentina. She graduated with a double major of interior design and Spanish from a large public university in the Midwest. She went through Cultural Diversity Success (CDS) International, which required two weeks of Spanish classes followed by a ten-week internship.

J.L. completed a two-and-a-half-month, full-time internship at a commercial design firm. She graduated from a private college in a large Midwestern city. She is also an experienced business professional with two prior degrees and 19 years of practice in executive positions with major global corporations.

K.B. completed a paid eight-week internship at a commercial design firm that focused on healthcare interiors. She graduated with a degree in interior design from a private university in a large Southern city.

K.S. completed an eight-week unpaid internship at a retail establishment that provided design services. She graduated with an interior design degree from a large public university in the Midwest.

M.A. completed a paid two-month internship at a high-end kitchen cabinetry manufacturer. She graduated from a large public university in a Southwestern city.

M.R. completed a seven-week paid internship at an architectural firm between her junior and senior years. She graduated from a large university in a Midwestern city.

M.S. completed an unpaid two-and-a-half-month part-time (20 to 30 hours per week) internship at furniture dealership. She graduated from a private university in a large Southern city.

S.M. completed an unpaid five-month internship at a high-end residential firm. She graduated from a private college in a large Midwestern city.

BOX 1.1 (CONTINUED)
setting goals

What goals did you hope to accomplish during your internship?

E.J.: "I hoped to gain work experience but also to learn more about hospitality design."

K.B.: "Going into the internship with experience only in residential design, I was not sure what type of interior design I was really interested in. My primary goal was to gain a better understanding of my interests through the internship."

J.E.: "My goal was to gain both experience in the field as well as knowledge that could not be taught in the classroom."

In reading these goals, it is clear that each intern set goals specifically based upon their personal desires. Already having set goals prior to their internships, the students came into the experience with direction. This added meaning to their learning experiences.

J.F.: "To get a better understanding of the industry and a more hands-on experience with day-to-day operations of an interior design business."

J.H. (*international intern*): "To gain more knowledge of international business and a better professional Spanish vocabulary. I also wanted to meet with clients, be active in design charettes, network, and learn new computer programs. Being in a foreign city, I also planned to go on site tours and generally get to know the city and its culture."

J.L.: "To experience a commercial design firm, its culture, and its design process as well as to understand how my [two prior degrees and 19 years of business experience working in executive positions with major global corporations] might fit within an interior design firm environment."

K.S.: "To work hard and make a good name for myself in the field, take on as many different responsibilities as possible to get a wide variety of learning, and be confident about asking to do hands-on projects with the designer."

M.A.: "I wanted to work for a large, well-known company, work on a LEED project, and build relationships that could potentially get me a job in the future. I also wanted to further my skills with real-world experience."

M.S.: "To learn more about how furniture dealerships work and to gain real-life experience with a design firm, learn any new programs I could, see how different people deal with their client relations, and gather background knowledge of the industry."

M.R.: "My goals pertained to learning more about product, application, and specification. I wanted to learn about design techniques and what drove designs in the workplace: who made what decisions, why final products were chosen, how much involvement representatives had, and so on.

"I also wanted to know how much professional organizations were involved in day-to-day activities, what information they were able to provide to their members, and the interactivity between all team members in the firm and on the project."

S.M.: "To experience day-to-day work as an interior designer and to add career-related experiences to my resume."

Economic Goals

If you take an internship in the summer, you will probably have additional expenses such as summer housing, food, transportation, and more. Thus, the following goals should be set.

- Determine the amount of money you will need during your internship.
- Determine how you will raise the money prior to or during the internship.

time management

Unexpected events and other interruptions affect time management. These may include phone calls, text messages, friends stopping by to chat, family demands, television shows, and more. To note where there may be problems with time management, keep track of your time to help you determine areas that create demand and then eliminate or lessen these demands. (A Personal Daily Time Record Log, Table 1.10 and Appendix C, can help you manage and make the most of your valuable time. After you have read this chapter, Exercise 5 under "Achieving Chapter Objectives" will show you how to use this tool.)

Prioritizing Means Taking Action

Setting priorities is all about actually doing the tasks that you identified as steps to achieving your goals; when priorities are set, time can be better managed. To set priorities, begin by listing tasks in order of importance by asking the three questions as follows:

1. Does the task need to be done today?
2. Can the task be completed tomorrow?
3. Can the task wait until a future date?

The 80/20 Rule

So often the 80/20 rule comes into play relative to the importance of the task and its pay-off results—timely completion. For 80 percent of the time, the task is urgent but not important, or neither important nor urgent with 20 percent pay off. For 20 percent of the time, the task is important and urgent, or important but not urgent with 80 percent payoff. Thus, because only 20 percent of your time is spent on tasks with 80 percent payoff, it is important to complete tasks that need to be done first to ensure you will be free when those crucial 20-percent tasks come along.

Priorities

The old English proverb, "Poor planning on your part does not constitute an emergency on mine," is a reminder that each individual is responsible for completing his or her own tasks on time—*no one else is responsible*. Thus, setting **priorities** is important, as is evaluating what is important and urgent.

For students, to complete an academic goal of a degree in your chosen field, your top priority should be projects, homework, or other assignments—all of which bring successful completion of this goal. Begin your projects, assignments, readings, and other basic work early. Allow time for the unexpected, and begin the work as soon as it is assigned. Starting early does not mean the day before or the day it is due. When assigned, allow time each day to work on the project. Additionally, all classes require outside work; therefore, it is important to utilize class and studio time to your best advantage to complete tasks on time, if not early.

Remember: *when time is lost, it is gone forever*.

Setting Priorities

Time wasted is not recoverable. For class projects, time may be made up with all-nighters, but mistakes happen when you are tired, work may not be your best, or work may be incomplete. Thus, to set priorities, perform a risk and value analysis by asking three questions:

1. What is the risk or the consequences if the task is not completed?
2. What is the value of the task? High importance; high impact?
3. Does the completion of the task support my overall goal?

Here are guidelines to help answer these questions.

1. The greater the risk, the greater the value.
2. For a student, high risk; high value items are grades, deadlines, or anything important to the successful completion of a degree.
3. If the deadline is past, it is a low priority, if a priority at all.
4. If it is in the present or future, it is a priority.

Prioritize the task in the following manner:

1. Highest Impact: Vital—*Do first*
   - Serious consequences if not completed
   - Examples: schoolwork—assignments, projects, readings, study for test
2. Moderate Impact: Important—*Nice to get done*
   - Could wait until later or even tomorrow
   - Examples: e-mail or Facebook a friend
3. Low Impact: Has some value—*don't do first*
   - Important, but can wait a day, week, month, or more
   - Examples: shopping, cleaning out your closet

Energy Levels

Most people have one or two times a day when their **energy level** is at its highest. So, as you read the following, think about the times of the day when your energy level is at its peak, as in each of these categories:

- 100 to 80 percent—Highest energy level (the two-for-one energy level)
- 80 to 60 percent—High energy level
- 60 to 40 percent—Tackle the difficult but familiar tasks
- 40 to 20 percent—Tackle the routine, familiar tasks (the mundane tasks)
- 20 to 10 percent—Low energy level

At the peak or highest energy level, you will get two for the price of one. In other words, you are at your best. This is when learning, studying, and/or problem solving is at its peak. It is also a time to accomplish tasks that you dread, but are important, because you can do your best. This is not the time to socialize; this is the time to tackle the difficult tasks.

Smart Scheduling

Along with noting your highest level of energy, the following are tips for scheduling time:

- Decide a time to do the task.
- Find a block of time to do the task—identify tasks that involve more work and take longer periods of time.
- Use your highest energy level time wisely. This is when you can do your best work.
- Use the 80/20 rule.
- Write daily to-do lists.
- Use the salami method (complete a big task with *one slice at a time*).
- Or use the sandwich method (complete a big task *one bite at time*).
- Complete the hardest task first when your energy level is at its highest.

Listing goals can be turned into to-do lists of daily, weekly, monthly, quarterly, and yearly goals. For example, the daily goals are tasks to complete that day; turn this into the to-do list for that day. Weekly goals are tasks that need to be accomplished that particular week; these can be noted by which day the task should be completed. Then, when a particular day approaches, the goal is again turned into the to-do list.

personality types

Knowing and understanding yourself can help you in many ways. For example, it can help you recognize work that is most satisfying and help you discover your strengths (Myers & Briggs, n.d.). It can also help you function and interact more positively with others. One way to gain this understanding is to know your personality type. Your personality makes you similar to or different from other people, and you can classify yourself based on your preferences. The Myers-Briggs Type Indicator® (MBTI) is frequently used and is a highly regarded personality test (Innovative Training Concepts, 2005). The knowledge gained from the MBTI inventory can be applied to a variety of situations in your everyday life (Myers & Briggs).

The MBTI® uses four categories: energy, information gathering, decision making, and lifestyle (Innovative Training Concepts, 2005). These four categories are then separated into two areas: mental processes of gathering information and making decisions, and mental orientations of energy and lifestyle. Thus, "your personality type is determined by how you are energized (Extraverted or Introverted), how you gather information (Sensing or Intuition), how you make decisions (Thinking or Feeling), and your lifestyle (Judging or Perceiving)" (Innovative Training Concepts, 2005). From the interaction of preferences, four different personality types emerge as

shown in Table 1.4 (Innovative Training Concepts, 2005; Myers & Briggs; Reinhold, 2006).

Four Personality Categories

According to Innovative Training Concepts (2005), you will use all personality types at different times; however, within each of the four categories, you will feel more comfortable and natural with one preference than the other. This is what determines your personality type. The following are descriptions of these areas.

Energy (Extroversion or Introversion)

The energy orientation takes two forms of energy consciousness—outward or inward. Extroverts are drawn to the outside world as source of energy (e.g., people, places, things, activities, and more). Introverts draw energy from inward sources of information (e.g., ideas, thoughts, or other reflections) (Reinhold, 2006).

Information Gathering (Sensing or Intuition)

As part of the mental processes, people gather or take in information (perceive) through sensing or intuition. People who prefer sensing perception like clear, tangible information that relates to the here and now. People who prefer intuition perception like to gather information from more abstract and conceptual ideas or possibilities for the future (Reinhold, 2006).

Decision Making (Thinking or Feeling)

As part of the mental processes, these preferences identify how people make judgments or decisions. People who prefer *thinking* judgment make decisions through logical, analytical, and objective means. They place emphasis on the task and the results. People who use *feeling* judgment make decisions in a global manner and are concerned about a decision's impact on others (Reinhold, 2006).

Lifestyle (Judging or Perceiving)

This fourth preference refers to the mental orientation of lifestyle (or outer world orientation). People who prefer *judging* will rely on their preference for making decisions (thinking or feeling) to manage their outer world or lifestyle. These peoples prefer closure, are organized and scheduled, and make lists. People who prefer *perceiving* rely on their preference for gather information (sensing or intuition) to manage their outer world or lifestyle. This often results in a more flexible, open, adaptable style, where a lack of closure is tolerated (Innovative Training Concepts, 2005; Reinhold, 2006). Table 1.5 lists these and more descriptors. Table 1.6 combines the paired categories into symbols (first letter of each pair) that signify the 16 different personality types. Table 1.7 lists each category with the name of celebrity as an example.

TABLE 1.4

MBTI® Framework

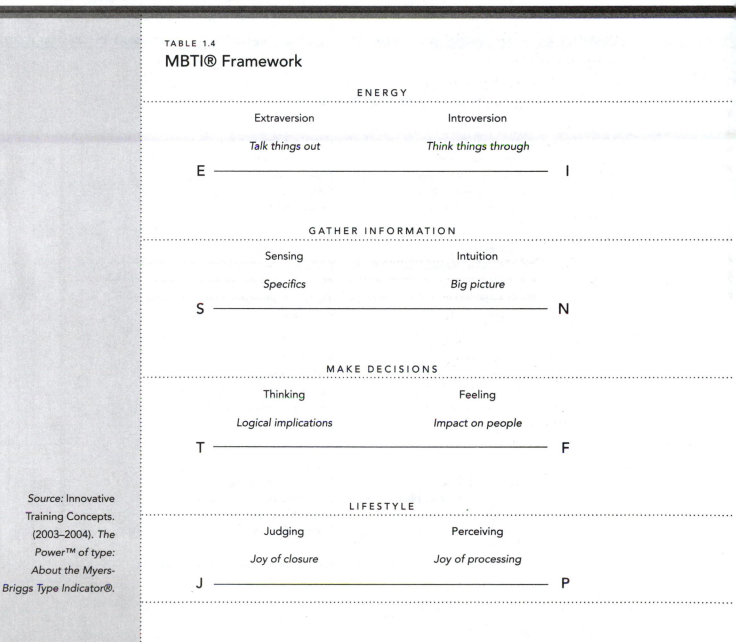

ENERGY

Extraversion	Introversion
Talk things out	*Think things through*

E —————————————————————— I

GATHER INFORMATION

Sensing	Intuition
Specifics	*Big picture*

S —————————————————————— N

MAKE DECISIONS

Thinking	Feeling
Logical implications	*Impact on people*

T —————————————————————— F

LIFESTYLE

Judging	Perceiving
Joy of closure	*Joy of processing*

J —————————————————————— P

Source: Innovative Training Concepts. (2003–2004). *The Power™ of type: About the Myers-Briggs Type Indicator®.*

Identification of Personal Strengths Based on Personality Types

You can get your own personality assessment from the Myers & Briggs Foundation (www.mystersbriggs.org). To take the MBTI® personality assessment online for a fee, you can go to http://www.myers-briggs.org/my-mbti-personality-type/ take-the-mbti-instrument. Without taking the assessment, it will difficult to determine your exact personality type; however, using the descriptors from Table 1.5, you should be able to have a sense of your type. Also, a handout that provides further understanding of your preferences can be downloaded from the following website: www.capt.org/catalog/MBTI-Book-20026.htm.

TABLE 1.5

Myers-Briggs Type Indicator®

ENERGY	**E-EXTRAVERSION** Prefer to talk things out Sociable and expressive Communicate by talking Speak first, then reflect	**I-INTROVERSION** Prefer to think things through More private and contained Communicate by writing Reflect first, then speak
GATHER INFORMATION	**S-SENSING** Prefers specific facts, details Practical application Trusts experience Present-oriented	**N-INTUITION** Prefer the big picture Options, possibilities, ideas Trusts inspiration, hunches Future-oriented
MAKE DECISIONS	**T-THINKING** Prefers logical implications Analytical, objective, fair Tough-minded, reasonable Objective truth	**F-FEELING** Prefers impact on others Sympathetic, relationship driven Tender-hearted, accepting Personal values, harmony
LIFESTYLE	**J-JUDGING** Prefers joy of closure Scheduled, organized, plans Systematic, makes lists Avoids last-minute pressures	**P-PERCEIVING** Prefers joy of processing Spontaneous, flexible, casual Adaptable, open to changes Energized by last-minute pressures

Source: Innovative Training Concepts. (2003–2004). *The Power™ of type: About the Myers-Briggs Type Indicator®.*

TABLE 1.6

MBTI® Type Table: Sixteen Different Personality Types

This table shows the combinations of all four categories into 16 different personality types.

ISTJ	ISFJ	INFJ	INTJ
ISTP	ISFP	INFP	INTP
ESTP	ESFP	ENFP	ENTP
ESTJ	ESFJ	ENFJ	ENTJ

TABLE 1.7

MBTI® Type Table: Examples of Sixteen Different Personality Types

This table shows the combinations of all four categories into 16 different personality types with examples of famous personalities for each type.

ISTJ	ISFJ	INFJ	INTJ
Julia Roberts	Toni Collette	Calista Flockhart	Jill Hennessy
Anthony Hopkins	Kiefer Sutherland	Joe Pantoliano	Cuba Gooding Jr.
Kirk Douglas	Tyne Daly	Madeleine Stowe	Carrie-Ann Moss
Michael Rapaport	William Shatner	Ralph Fiennes	George Lucas
ISTP	**ISFP**	**INFP**	**INTP**
Rowan Atkinson	Matt LeBlanc	D.B. Sweeney	Dustin Hoffman
Kathy Bates,	Julie Delpy	Miguel Ferrer	Gabriel Byrne
Ashley Judd	Trevor Blumas	Gillian Anderson	Stewart Granger
Meg Ryan	Xenia Seeberg	Kevin Costner	John Travolta
ESTP	**ESFP**	**ENFP**	**ENTP**
Peter Falk	Al Pacino	Cher Bono	David Schwimmer
Eric McCormack	Gene Hackman	James Woods	Jamie Lee Curtis
Tommy Lee Jones	Kevin Spacey	Keanu Reeves	Dick Van Dyke
Antonio Banderas	Paul McCartney	Heather Locklear	John Cleese
ESTJ	**ESFJ**	**ENFJ**	**ENTJ**
Bruce Willis	Michael Palin	Michael Douglas	Quentin Tarantino
Angela Lansbury	Geri Halliwell	Kurtwood Smith	Frances Fisher
Brendan Fraser	Eddie Murphy	Amy Locane	Robert Downey Jr.
Jeri Lynn Ryan	Julia Louis-Dreyfus	Patrick Swayze	Steve Buscemi

After completing an assessment or reviewing the preference, review Table 1.5 and ask yourself these questions (Innovative Training Concepts, 2004):

1. What do I see as my personal strengths?
2. What do I see as my challenges?
3. How can I use this information on a daily basis?

Then, consider the locations or type of firm for your internship that would best suit your personality by asking these questions:

1. What strengths or challenges do my preferences bring to an internship?
2. How can I use the information in these tables to choose the most appropriate firm?

Next, think of someone you know (best friend, relative, or others) and ask yourself these questions:

1. What do you think his/her MBTI® preferences may be?
2. How can you use the information in Tables 1.8 and 1.9 to help you with these relationships?
3. How will this information help me work with various people in a firm?

During your internship, you may be asked to do work that you do not prefer or does not seem to fit your personality type. However, your "knowledge and understanding of type can help you discover and use your strengths to accomplish the work" (Myers & Biggs).

common internship questions and answers

When stepping into a new environment, somewhere you've never been before, or even when taking on a new responsibility in perfectly familiar territory, it's natural to feel some anxiety or simply be unsure about practical concerns. The good news is that internships are far from uncharted territory. As the seasoned interior designer turns to precedent students before signing off on a new project, you can learn from those who have interned before you. The following questions, common among students heading into internships, and their subsequent answers will help put any anxiety or uncertainty to rest:

1. What if I do not know what type of design I'd prefer?
2. Where should I intern? What area of the country or city? Should I go abroad? If so, what country should I consider?
3. How many résumés and cover letters should I send?
4. What if they reject me?
5. What if I don't have the right skills?
6. I'm afraid. I've never worked before. What if they don't like me?
7. What are my budget considerations? How much money will I need to support myself during the internship?
8. What are the university requirements for completing an internship?
9. What are some networking options or contacts that have been made in the past?

TABLE 1.8
MBTI® Communication Tips

This table provides tips for communicating with others. For example, if you identify with E, then the "E" tips are important to you; the other columns provide tips to help you communicate with someone in another category.

"E" TIPS

Keep your energy up

Allow them time to talk

Say "tell me more"

Use open-ended questions

Maintain good eye contact

"I" TIPS

Calm your energy

Allow them time to pause and think

Don't interrupt

Use close-ended questions

Send out an agenda prior to a meeting to allow them time to think things through

"S" TIPS

Give enough details and facts

Talk in terms of present moment

Be realistic and practical

Be specific

Give information sequentially and in order of priority

Use concrete examples and facts

"N" TIPS

Talk in generalities, not too many details

Discuss future possibilities

Provide innovative options and ideas

Be prepared for creative bursts of ideas and concepts

Engage their imaginations and creativity

"T" TIPS

Business first

Be logical, rational, analytical

Present an objective, impersonal argument

Be prepared to be challenged

Don't take skepticism or criticism personally

"F" TIPS

Talk in terms of personal values

Use personal pronouns such as we, us, and our

Create an atmosphere of harmony, appreciation

Draw conclusion about what is good and positive

"J" TIPS

Will push for completion

Be time conscious

Be punctual for meetings, appointments or returning phone calls or e-mails

Be scheduled, organized

View planning as vital

"P" TIPS

Allow time for processing

Be spontaneous and flexible

Be adaptable, open to change

Might lose track of time

View rules and controls as limiting and suppressing

TABLE 1.9

Z-Model & MBTI® Tips to Remember

This table provides tips for working with individuals each set of the four categories.

ENERGY

E-EXTRAVERSION

Provide adequate time for discussion
and questions

When working with an E remember:
Energy up

I-INTROVERSION

Written information ahead of time to
think things through

When working with an I remember:
Calm

GATHER INFORMATION

S-SENSING

What currently exists?

Specifics around who, what, when,
where, how?

When working with an S remember:
Details

N-INTUITION

What are the alternatives, options,
and possibilities?

Long-term implications

When working with an N remember:
Generalities

MAKE DECISIONS

T-THINKING

What are the pros and cons, and
objective rationale of options?

Cost-benefit analysis?

Logical consequences?

When working with a T remember:
Logical implications

F-FEELING

Connect logical options to people
and values

How will it impact people?

Invite others to be involved

When working with an F remember:
Impact on others

LIFESTYLE

J-JUDGING

Move to closure, timeframes

Clear, concise plan structure

No surprises

When working with a J remember:
Goal oriented

P-PERCEIVING

Open to new information

Flexible to changes

Builds flexibility into plans

When working with a P remember:
Process oriented

Source: Innovative Training Concepts. (2003–2004). The Power™ of type: About the Myers-Briggs Type Indicator®.

Finding the Answers

These questions may seem strange to some, but they are very real to others and must be addressed.

What if I do not know what type of design I'd prefer?

Evaluate your skills. In what area is your best work—residential or commercial; CAD; hand-drafting; selection of materials; and so on? What piques your interest as you read about or work on various types of design in studio—residential (materials, kitchens, space planning) or commercial (space planning, CAD, material selection for office or other commercial types, conducting code search, writing specifications)?

Where should I intern? What area of the country or city? Or should I go abroad?

Look at multiple possibilities. Where would you like to live for a short period of time or in the future? This may be the opportunity to see if you like the area or city. Do you have relatives or friends who would be willing to house you temporarily? If you need to stay closer to your university, consider all the firms within the city or surrounding area. If you are interested in an international internship, start examining and researching early. These may take a year to obtain.

How many résumés and cover letters should I send?

This depends on the number of firms in the area or city. Do not limit yourself. The more you send, the greater the chance of obtaining an internship and obtaining it early.

What if they reject me?

Turn this around and ask, "What can I learn from this rejection?" Maybe your interview skills need work and the list of possible interview questions should be reviewed. It may be that some design skill(s) may have been missing. If so, determine ways to improve these skills. Maybe this firm is not the right firm and a different type of firm should be considered. An in-depth self-evaluation is important.

What if I don't have the right skills?

Examine your skills: what skills were lacking and can you hone these skills? Or are your skills more appropriate for another type of design firm?

I'm afraid. I've never worked before. What if they don't like me?

Practice mock interviews with professionals, other students, or in your career placement center at your institution. Consider the skills you have and review your projects and know the requirements. Research the firm; know all you can about them. Being well prepared will help boost your confidence level.

What are budget considerations? How much money will I need to support myself during the internship?

The amount of money needed will depend upon where you obtain an internship. At the same time as you are considering various locations, investigate the cost of living: cost of temporary rentals, food, and transportation. You will then be able to determine how much money you will need during that time period.

What are my school's requirements for completing an internship?

Each program is different; therefore, you should begin by visiting your academic advisor to learn the process and requirements.

What are some networking options or contacts that have been made in the past?

Networking among professionals may seem intimidating, but interior design professionals are more than happy to meet, visit, and give advice. Some of these professionals may become your employer or a connection to other employment. So, make a list of contacts—those you have met at seminar, career days, or even visited in their showrooms or other locations. Continue to add to this list as you attend.

recommended timeline for the internship

There is no specific recommended timeline for beginning the process of obtaining an internship nor is there a specified timeline to complete an internship. However, there may be a specific time within your interior design program.

Timeline to Obtain the Internship

Though no specific time is suggested to begin the process of locating an internship, the search could begin as early as seven or eight months ahead. This would involve going through the process of creating the résumé and portfolio and beginning the job search. A reasonable time to start making contacts may be four to six months ahead.

Timeline to Complete the Internship

A recommended timeline for completion is seven to eight weeks at 32 to 40 hours per week (approximately 280 total hours). However, some programs require shorter or longer (e.g., five to eight weeks with 150 total hours at 20 to 30 hours per week or as long as 10 to 15 weeks with 400 total hours). During your internship, you will have an opportunity to observe various phases of design projects. In Chapter 8, a seven- to eight-week timeline is recommended for reporting purposes. Some internship timelines may be longer if hours are between 20 and 32 per week. When reporting is complete, continuing on with the internships is highly recommended. For example, with a summer internship, spending the entire summer (three months, 12 to 15 weeks) would provide the greatest learning experience.

the paid versus unpaid internship

When applying for internship positions, clearly, a paid position is preferred; however, this is not always possible. Some firms are not able or do not budget for interns, whereas others consider the intern an employee and provide compensation through an hourly wage. Some firms provide compensation with a check or a product at the end of an internship. The unpaid internship can be very difficult because of the need to pay for living expenses, internship credits, and college tuition for the coming year. However, it would be unwise to turn down an internship solely on this criterion (see Box 1.2 for legal issues to consider). Such positions can provide a great experience, and although the compensation does not come in the form of pay, you may still find means of support that include:

- Applying for an internship scholarship if available at your school.
- Searching for grants, scholarships, or fellowships available outside your institution. These can often be found through an Internet search.
- Asking for a loan or gift from your parents or a relative. The loan may be without interest; however, you must still pay them back.
- Applying for financial aid through your institution or securing a loan from your local bank or lending institution.
- Obtaining part-time work during the weekends and/or in the evenings while on the internship. This would be easier if the internship is 20 to 30 hours per week. (Granger, 2010)

summer or non-summer internship

Many universities require their students to take internships during the summer; others allow them to take internships at any time of the year. There are advantages and disadvantages to both. With a summer internship, you are able to concentrate on the position; however, this may mean that you are unable to earn your usual summer income. With a full-summer internship, you will be able to follow the progress of projects as an employee. You will also have the opportunity to accept a summer internship that is in a different region (e.g., in another state or an international internship). A non-summer internship allows you to learn during the academic year. It may, however, limit the amount of time you need to devote to projects at school or at the internship.

BOX 1.2
legalities of the unpaid internship

Because job openings have become scarce, an unpaid internship may give you a greater opportunity for work. This has become a common practice among for-profit corporations. Unfortunately, providing an unpaid position may violate labor laws and give the employer unfair advantages over the intern. So, before accepting an unpaid position, you may want to ask the following questions:

- Does the internship violate the minimum wage laws?
- Will employment discrimination laws protect me?
- Will this employer provide the design experience I desire or expect me to only perform menial tasks?
- Will this employer overlook my résumé because of my need to be paid?
- Will the university's or the firm's insurance cover me if I'm injured? (Greenhouse, 2000)

Often the unpaid internship is your only option, especially in slower economic times. In this case, come to the interview prepared to discuss other means of compensation such as merchandise or a lump sum at the end of your term. You might also discuss what you expect to gain from your internship. Ideas from Chapter 8, "Reporting the Internship," will provide a basis for your discussion during the interview as well as give you a greater learning experience during your internship.

summary

An internship is an opportunity for interaction among the student, a firm, and the university. The majority of higher educational institutions require students to complete an internship, and it is an invaluable experience that prepares you for future employment. These internships are designed to help you transition from theory or hypothetical scenarios to professional interior design practice. And as discussed in this chapter, you must consider your future goals—professional and personal—prior to beginning the internship. Goals will help you focus on your future plans. From the CD-ROM, you can download a self quiz and a goal-setting tool, Appendices A and B, to help you establish your goals. You can also download a time-management log, Appendix C, from the CD-ROM.

Evaluating your own personality will also help you understand others and become a better team player during your internship and in the design world. With this knowledge, you can begin researching various firms to find the one(s) that best fit your goals.

TABLE 1.10 (ALSO APPENDIX C)

Time Management: Personal Daily Time Record Log
Recording of Tasks, Energy Levels, and Interruptions

Name:

Day:

Date:

TIME	ACTIVITY	IMPORTANCE	ENERGY LEVEL	INTERRUPTIONS PHONE	OTHER
7:00 a.m.		1 2 3 4 5	H M L		
8:00 a.m.		1 2 3 4 5	H M L		
9:00 a.m.		1 2 3 4 5	H M L		
10:00 a.m.		1 2 3 4 5	H M L		
11:00 a.m.		1 2 3 4 5	H M L		
12:00 p.m.		1 2 3 4 5	H M L		
1:00 p.m.		1 2 3 4 5	H M L		
2:00 p.m.		1 2 3 4 5	H M L		
3:00 p.m.		1 2 3 4 5	H M L		
4:00 p.m.		1 2 3 4 5	H M L		
5:00 p.m.		1 2 3 4 5	H M L		
6:00 p.m.		1 2 3 4 5	H M L		
7:00 p.m.		1 2 3 4 5	H M L		
8:00 p.m.		1 2 3 4 5	H M L		
9:00 p.m.		1 2 3 4 5	H M L		
10:00 p.m.		1 2 3 4 5	H M L		
11:00 p.m.		1 2 3 4 5	H M L		
12:00 a.m.		1 2 3 4 5	H M L		

achieving chapter objectives

Review the Chapter Objectives at the beginning of this chapter. You are now ready to put them into practice.

get started

Complete the following assignments using documents provided.

1. Take the self-quiz (Table 1.1).

2. Write a Personal Success Story. This is a story of your successes as you look at your life from the present to retirement. From this story, you will be able to develop long-range goals.

3. Establish goals (Tables 1.2 and 1.3).

4. Evaluate your time for one week to determine your energy levels and demands on your time. Analyze and develop a method to improve your time management skills. Use Table 1.10 to evaluate each day. Instructions are as follows:

   a. Access the time management log (Appendix C) on the CD-ROM (see Table 1.10).

   b. Enter your name, day of the week, and date.

   c. Record tasks throughout each day in half-hour intervals. Enter information using indicated codes to identify the type of work. Set up a personal code and legend for these codes.

   d. Record the importance of the task: Circle 1, 2, 3, 4, 5 (1 = highest importance).

   e. Record your energy level and indicate with an H, M, or L for High, Medium, or Low.

   f. Record interruptions during tasks: phone, nature (day dreaming), other.

   g. Evaluate yourself: Note peaks and valleys in performance with an eye on strengths and weaknesses in time management.

   h. Write a paragraph to answer the following questions:

      i. Where are your peaks and valleys of energy?

      ii. Are you using those peaks for the difficult or important tasks?

      iii. Where do you need to improve?

REFERENCES

- Business Dictionary (Eds). (2008). "Internship," *Business dictionary*. Retrieved on July 24, 2008, from www.businessdictionary.com/definition/internship.html

- Covery, S. R. (1989). *The 7 habits of highly effective people: Restoring the character ethic*. New York: Simon & Schuster.

- The Free Dictionary (Eds). (2008). "Goal," *The free dictionary*. Retrieved on July 24, 2008, from http://www.thefreedictionary.com/goal

- Granger, M. (2010). *The fashion intern* (2nd ed.). Fairchild Books: New York.

- Greenhouse, S. (2010, April 3). The unpaid intern, legal or not. *The New York Times*. Retrieved on April 6, 2010, from http://www.nytimes.com/2010/04/03/business/03intern.html?emc=eta1

- Innovative Training Concepts. (2005). *The Power™ of type: About the Myers-Brigs Type Indicator®*. Retrieved on November 22, 2008, from http://www.poweroftype.com/mbti.html

- Locke, E. (1968). Toward a Theory of Task Motivation and Incentives. *Organizational Behavior and Human Performance, 3*, 157–89.

- Locke, E., Cartledge, N., & Knerr, C.S. (1970). Studies of the Relationship Between Satisfaction, Goal Setting, and Performance. *Organizational Behavior and Human Behavior, 5*, 135–58.

- Myers & Briggs. (n.d.) *My MBTI Personality type—MBTI Basics*. Retrieved on November 22, 2008, from http://www.myersbriggs.org/my-mbti-personality-type/mbti-basics

- Nussbaumer, L. L., & Isham, D. D. (2009). *Professional practicum student manual: Interior design*. Unpublished manuscript.

- Piotrowski, C. (2007). *Professional practice for interior designers*. New York: Wiley.

- Reinhold, R. (2006). Personality Pathways: Exploring personality types and its application. Retrieved on November 21, 2008, from http://www.personalitypathways.com/MBTI_intro.html

KEY TERMS

- American Society of Interior Designers (ASID)
- corporation
- International Interior Design Association (IIDA)
- networking
- partnership
- practitioners
- sole proprietorships
- teamwork

2 organizing the job search

"Our firm has somewhat of an entrepreneurial spirit and we look for that characteristic in everyone we hire, temporary or not. Candidates should be hard working, dedicated, driven, passionate, eager to learn, and eager to share."

—A.G., an interior designer at Gensler, a Chicago-based interdisciplinary design firm with offices in Europe, Africa, the Middle East, and the United States.

OBJECTIVES

- During your job search, research various businesses and organizational structures.

- Research design firms that use the team approach.

- Observe the teamwork dynamics within various firms during your job search.

- Research the client types of various interior design firms.

- Develop your time-management schedule.

Finding the internship for which you are best suited takes research. Now that you have completed Chapter 1, you have set goals and determined your personality type. You are now ready to identify the firms for which you are best suited. But first, you will need to understand the difference among various firms as well as their specialties (e.g., residential or commercial). You will need to know the team structure and dynamics within the organizations. This type of information helps you understand these firms and where you might fit into these organizations.

To organize your job search, several steps should be taken:

1. Consider your fit to a firm.
2. Consider possible resources to locate internships.
3. Begin locating possible internships.
4. Make a list of possible internships.
5. Research the employers.
6. Set up a timeline to complete your search and move on to developing your documents for application: résumé, cover letter, and portfolio.

matching yourself to the right firm

At this point in your academic career, you have had the opportunity to work on many projects—some real, some hypothetical. These projects have probably shown you where your strengths lie. First, start making a list of skills that are important for interior designers; then, organize the list according to your strengths. You will also want to return to your personality inventory, explored in Chapter 1, and examine your best fit within different types of organizations.

Types of Design Firms

Most design firms are within architectural, interior design, or retail-based operations.

- Architectural: Firms that work on large commercial projects that may be of specific types; for example, corporate offices, hospitality, or retail. Some may include residential projects. Projects require multidisciplinary teams, and the client may include an owner, board of directors, or others with a vested interest. These projects are more complex and affect a great number of people who will use the space.

- Interior design: Firms that focus on residential projects, commercial projects, or both. The size of the project will depend on the firm's size. Some interior design firms are **sole proprietorships** or **partnerships** whereas others are **corporations.**

- Retail-based firms: Firms found in shopping areas and focus on residential design. A showroom of furniture and/or accessories may draw customers into the firm that may require designers to spend time selling as well as providing design services.

Specialties of Design Firms

Generally, design firms specialize in either residential or commercial design projects. Consider the qualifications for residential and commercial designers. Match your strengths and your personality to these qualifications to determine a possible fit. Next, within each category—residential or commercial—consider what areas you prefer and where your skills may lie. Make a list of these preferences and skills.

Preferences and Skills: Residential Design

To help do this, begin by considering the residential designer. Preferences and skills most important for the residential designer include:

1. Being people oriented (i.e., preferring to work with individuals and families).
2. Working with people who may have a difficult time making decisions.
3. Rendering hand drawings more frequently than creating CAD drawings.
4. Presenting information and/or materials—presentations may be informational and usually include materials choices.
5. Selecting materials such as carpeting, wall finishes, or window treatments and applying design theory to your selection.
6. Selecting products such as architectural details, furniture, and household equipment.
7. Designing kitchens and/or bathrooms.
8. Residential space planning.
9. Using accessories as an important part of the overall design.

You might add to this list as you consider work by specific residential designers.

Preferences and Skills: Commercial Design

For commercial designers, some qualifications are similar to those in the previous list; others differ. The following list begins with qualifications, and then moves into various types of design. Important skills include:

1. Being a team player. Teamwork is important in commercial design; team members may include architects, interior designers, engineers, and landscape designers.
2. Working on projects that may take months or years to complete.
3. Conducting deeper research (e.g., fact-finding and evidence-based).
4. Developing CAD drawings.
5. Writing specifications.
6. Making more formal presentations.
7. Focusing material selection on design theory.
8. Selecting material that meets fire codes.
9. Including ADA requirements and possibly Universal Design concepts in space planning.

Once again, you may well find yourself adding to this list as you consider the work of specific commercial designers.

Creating these lists will help you make a decision between residential and commercial design. As you consider your options, it will help you to know what skills, personal characteristics, and duties are expected in various design firms. In Box 2.1, site supervisors share comments about skills that they expect from their interns. Box 2.2 provides comments by site supervisors on personal characteristics they prefer in an intern. Box 2.3 provides expected duties in various firms.

Professional Attributes

To help you focus more sharply on the connection between your personal interests and abilities, and where you might do your internship, you will need to consider some of the attributes or skills required in each firm. (Refer also to Table 10.1.)

- A retail establishment: The *ability to sell* is an important attribute. Interior designers in retail establishments design and sell. This means that an internship may be a combination of design and selling. Thus, an internship provides opportunities to interact with clients and learn selling techniques

site supervisors' advice

BOX 2.1

required skills

The following site supervisors offered advice throughout this chapter:

A.G. is an interior designer at Gensler in Chicago. Gensler is an inter-disciplinary design firm with offices in the United States, Europe, the Middle East, and Africa. It specializes in architecture, interior design, branding and strategy, product design, and sustainability. Its market area is broad-based and includes aviation and transportation, civic and community, office building, education, entertainment, hospitality, and retail facilities.

B.H. is supervisor of creative design services within StarMark Cabinetry. StarMark is a manufacturer of semi-custom cabinets in Sioux Falls, South Dakota, with an in-house design team. Its cabinetry is sold throughout the United States and installed in residential setting such as kitchen, bathrooms, dining rooms, family rooms, and dens.

K.C. is interior design director for Interstate Office Products (IOP) in Sioux Falls, South Dakota. IOP is an office furniture dealership and interior design firm that offers a full range of design services. Its clients include corporate offices, financial institutions, law firms, education, and healthcare. It also designs and specifies products for architectural firms' projects.

K.W. and R.K. are, respectively, interior design director and senior human resources representative for AECOM in Minneapolis. AECOM is a multidiscipline architectural and engineering firm with offices in the United States, Europe, Africa, the Middle East, Australia, and New Zealand. AECOM recently joined with Ellerbe Becket (the century-old firm specializing in architecture, interiors, and engineering) to blend their global reach and local knowledge. The firm is committed to enhancing and sustaining the built, natural, and social environment. It works on a wide range of projects including corporate offices, healthcare, law firms, hospitality, education, cultural and event facilities, and more. Its interior services include interior design, facility programming, and feasibility studies, FF&E, renovation and preservation, adaptive re-use, and workplace consulting.

as well as gain greater knowledge of products and materials. This opportunity may lead to a career as an interior designer and/or a sales position. It may also lead you toward a sales representative for a particular product or material such as a carpet or wall-covering representative.

- A residential design firm: The *ability to work with a variety of people* is an important attribute. Residential designers work with individuals, couples, a nucleus family, large extended families in one space, and more. Thus an internship provides opportunities to observe and work with your

BOX 2.1 (CONTINUED)
required skills

What specific skills does your firm expect of the intern?

TAKEAWAY FROM
site supervisors

Student interns are generally expected to be well-rounded, but not proficient in on-the-job skills. However, some skill-set requirements vary with the type of firm. Comparing your skill sets against the requirements of a firm will help you decide your best fit.

A.G. *(interior designer, Gensler):* "Skill sets can and are expected to vary. We typically look for a baseline of technological skills depending on the area of focus. For example, architects and designers should be well versed in AutoCAD at a minimum. Revit and 3D visualization skills are desirable. Graphic design interns should have a strong command of the Adobe Creative Suite. Hand sketching and collaboration and communication (verbal and visual) skills are all taken into consideration when looking for strong candidates."

B.H. *(supervisor of creative design services, StarMark Cabinetry):* "They should have a general idea of space planning, know how to use the Internet, and be skilled in using software such as Excel, Word, and 20-20."

K.C. *(interior design director, Interstate Office Products):* "Commercial design experience— exposure to codes, such as LEED; knowledge of AutoCAD (or equivalent); and sales skills (ability to sell ideas in a clear and concise manner)."

K.W. and R.K. *(interior design director and senior human resources representative, AECOM):* "We appreciate well-rounded (technical and design-oriented) skill sets. We do not expect a high level of proficiency."

supervisor in various situations. This opportunity may lead to working in a residential design firm, or with experience; you may choose to form your own firm.

- A kitchen and bath design firm: The *abilities to apply knowledge of construction, draw details, and be precise in measurements* are important attributes. Kitchen and bath designers also work with a variety of clients, but their skills must also relate to cabinet construction design and the understanding of millwork. An internship provides opportunities to not only work with clients but also to measure spaces, design and draw in detail the plans, sections, and elevations. Along with the knowledge and understanding of construction, an interior designer employed in the kitchen and bath design business must understand the interface of cabinetry to mechanical and electrical systems. Additionally, this type of work deals with a product that is not flexible and must be precisely measured and designed. An internship experience might lead you to become a full-time kitchen and/or bath designer who will also study and take the qualifying exam through the National Kitchen and Bath Association (NKBA). A certification indicates specific knowledge

BOX 2.2
personal characteristics

TAKEAWAY FROM
site supervisors

Personal characteristics that site supervisors expect in interns include a professional work ethic and a willingness to learn. (For more on professional ethics, refer to Chapter 7.)

Refer to Box 2.1 for background on each site supervisor who offered advice throughout this chapter.

What personal characteristic does your firm expect of the intern?

A.G. *(interior designer, Gensler)*: "Candidates should be hard working, dedicated, driven, passionate, eager to learn, and eager to share."

B.H. *(supervisor of creative design services, StarMark Cabinetry)*: "An intern should be a self-starter and need minimal supervision. They should be friendly, outgoing, and willing to do things such as filing along with the other more exciting tasks that are part of the whole job experience."

K.C. *(interior design director, Interstate Office Products)*: "Interns must have organizational skills, people skills, and a willingness to learn and take direction from superiors."

K.W. and R.K. *(interior design director and senior human resources representative, AECOM)*: "We're looking for patience and flexibility as well as enthusiasm and a willingness to learn."

BOX 2.3
duties

TAKEAWAY FROM
site supervisors

Although site
supervisors' expectations
may vary regarding
duties that interns
should perform, there is
an underlying theme—
they all expect interns
to assist, accompany,
observe, learn, and
participate in specific
tasks. They also want
their interns to come
prepared to get the
most out of their
experience regardless of
their expected duties.

Refer to Box 2.1 for
background on each site
supervisor who offered
advice throughout this
chapter.

What duties do you generally expect of your interns?

A.G. *(interior designer, Gensler)*: "We like our interns to get the most out of their experience here and the best way for them to do that is to hit the ground running. Of course there is a lot of training, but the faster someone can get embedded into a project, the greater their knowledge curve will be. Interns will often help with preparing presentations (renderings, graphics, etc.), assist with documents by picking up redlines, or even get out into the field for site surveying and construction observation. The broader and deeper their skill set upon entering, the greater the opportunities. Also the more they are willing to take on and take ownership of, the more they will take away."

B.H. *(supervisor of creative design services, StarMark Cabinetry)*: "We expect our interns to:

- Attend formal product training offered by our internal trainers.
- Attend employee orientation and safety class to prepare for working in operations area.
- Work in operations for a day—real hands-on experience.
- Measure existing displays and identify the cabinets that are used in each, draw them by hand (to scale), and then duplicate them on 20-20 design software
- Accompany sales staff to a jobsite to observe a "measure."
- Observe a cabinet installation.
- Process paperwork for incoming design requests.
- Generate invoices for design fees.
- Check acknowledgements for cabinet orders.
- Find and print specifications and installations for appliances being used in kitchen designs."

K.C. *(interior design director, Interstate Office Products)*: "Assist in client projects, such as pulling finishes; writing specs; and creating plans, 3D, or rendered drawings. Perform miscellaneous tasks, such as field verification, inventory, library maintenance, and purchase order documents."

K.W. and R.K. *(interior design director and senior human resources representative, AECOM)*: "We expect our interns to be capable of working in a team environment. They should expect to be ready to participate in all phases of the design process."

related to cabinetry, mechanical and electrical systems, construction, and more. Other career possibilities within this area include those who provide workshop or educational seminars for new designers.

- An office systems franchise or facilities mangers within a corporate office: The *ability to work with office systems and furniture on a large scale* is an important attribute. Interior designers in a franchise generally work with one product manufacturer whereas the facilities manager may choose to work with more than one. However, the similarity is that both design office spaces and most projects are more complex and may last several months. An internship for a franchise or within a corporate office will aid your understanding of one or more furniture and office systems in which repetition may occur. As an interior designer in a franchise, your clients vary whereas a facilities manager generally designs and reconfigures offices for one particular office. Such position may lead from the entry-level interior designer to managerial positions such as a director of design.

- An architectural firm (large or small): The *ability to work in teams and with designers from a variety of disciplines* is an important attribute. Interior designers in an architectural firm often work in teams that include architects, engineers, landscape designers, and graphic designers. An internship within an architectural firm aids your understanding of teamwork as well as other design areas. Design projects may run a few months long but the majority will take a year or more. Some firms specialize in areas such as healthcare, hospitality, office, or retail, whereas others may work

with a variety of design types. An internship in an architectural firm may lead you to a firm that specializes or works on a variety of design types. Within large architectural offices, there will be opportunities to advance to a managerial level or work within specialized areas such as a specifications writer or code specialist.

resources for researching internships

There are many sources of information that will help you locate an internship. One of the most important sources will be faculty (your instructors) who may be able to provide a list of firms; however, there are other important resources such as professional organizations; people you know including interior designers and people who know interior designers, Internet listings, the telephone directory, and so on. There are a variety of resources to help locate a firm to which you would be suited. These include:

- Magazines: Advertisements by or articles about firms may be found in design magazines such as *Interior Design*, *Interiors and Sources*, and *Metropolis*.

- Faculty: The faculty at your institution will receive requests for interns from various firms in your region. Ask them about these requests.

- Alumni: Learn who some of the alumni are and where they are employed and make a contact.

- Friends and family: Find out if any of your friends or family members know or have worked with an interior designer.

- Fellow students: Ask your upper classman who have completed their internship where they found the position and suggestions they may have. These students have had the most recent experience and can be an excellent source for firms.

- Career service or placement department: Most higher education institutions have a department that continually receives information about positions and internships. Contact them and place your name on file.

- Direct contact with preferred employer: If you know a reputable firm and would like to intern in that firm, they should be at the top of your list.

- Design marts (merchandise mart or regional marts throughout the country): Located throughout the country, design marts are filled with showrooms that include furniture, office systems, fabrics, floor coverings, and more. Some examples include Arizona Design Mart in Scottsdale; San Francisco Mart; The Merchandise Mart in Chicago; International Market Square in Minneapolis; and New York Design Center. For more, refer to the Interior Design Centers' directory (www.i-d-d.com/interior_design_centers.htm).

- Internet: Searching the Internet is another method by which a firm may be located. In your favorite search engine, entering "interior design firms" or "architectural firm" with the city and state will provide websites of some firms in that vicinity. Further information is provided in "The Internet as a Tool" later in this chapter.

- Telephone directories (Yellow Pages): Look up Interior Designers or Architecture whether in the phone book or online. Generally, designers who are certified or affiliated with a professional organization includes this information in the advertisement.

- Newspaper, classifieds section: Some design firms will advertise in the classifieds section of the newspaper. Though the ads will most likely be for full-time positions rather than interns, it is still a good practice to review ads on a weekly basis. Even though a firm may prefer a full-time employee, an intern may also be needed. Therefore, the classifieds are still worth checking.

- Contacts: Business associates that may have worked for a particular firm, including, contractors, and other staff members affiliated with a particular firm are also good contacts. Though they may or may not know if an intern is needed, this source may also give you an "in" to an interview.

- Volunteer work with professional organizations: This effort will place you among the design professionals who will know and observe your work and involvement. This also becomes a great networking tool.

- Networking: There are many ways to network; the best way is to interact with professional designers or those connected with the design industry (Kendall, 2005; Piotrowski, 2002). This may occur during expositions, seminars, meetings, or even simply by visiting showrooms.

- Seminars or guest speakers that come to your university: Visiting with guests who come to your university will provide another network of new contacts.

- Professional organizations (ASID, IIDA): Often opportunities may present themselves in a variety of categories. For example, being involved with a professional organization will give you a greater chance to network and to do volunteer work in which you can make a good impression.

Professional Organizations

One of the best resources is a professional organization such as **American Society of Interior Designers (ASID)** and **International Interior Design Association (IIDA).** If you are involved in either of these organizations as a student, you have the opportunity to visit with **practitioners,** or professional interior designers, whether you are attending a professional meeting, seminar, or visiting a design mart.

Many organizations hold career expos for interior design students. During such expos, you will have many opportunities to network— to meet and visit with professionals and make a good impression. Ask about the firm, collect business cards from its representatives, and learn all you can about the firm and staff.

Professional organizations also create a directory. If you are a student member, you have access to these professionals. Their name, affiliation, firm name, address, phone number, and website will be part of this listing. Though generally the listing does not separate residential from commercial designers, the firm name provides a source. From this point, you should be able to find a website if they have one.

The Internet as a Tool

The Internet is a great tool to locate firms who may be interested in an intern. To locate a firm, there are several ways to do so. Here are a few examples:

1. Interior Design Directory (www.i-d-d.com) provides a list by state of interior design firms. This list is rather small at present, but over time, it should grow. If residential design is your interest, this will be an important beginning source. Additionally, you may find this information by locating their credentials, locate the firm's website, advertisement, or listing within ASID.

2. American Society of Interior Designers (http://asid.org) provides information specifically for students. Look for links related to students.

3. International Interior Design Association (http://www.iida.org) provides information specifically for student. Look for links related to students.

4. University of Dreams (www.summer internships.com/interior-design-internships) provides college students with internship placement in cities such as New York, Los Angeles, Chicago, San Francisco, Washington, D.C., and San Diego, as well as offering international opportunities.

5. Inside Arch (www.insidearch.org/home.php) provides an inside view of firms in the profession. If you would like to work in an architectural firm that is a large and well-known organization, you will find them through this website. For example, Perkins+Will is on the list. It will not provide openings for interns, but it will provide names from which to conduct further research.

Other Resources for Researching Internships

Appendix D lists many major national architectural design firms with interior design services or departments. For interior design firms that focus only on interior design, you will want to examine the ASID or IIDA websites. Appendix E lists firms by categories—commercial, residential, and interior architecture. (You can also access Appendices D and E on the CD-ROM.)

After you have located a variety of firms, research the firms' websites to learn more.

A design firm's website may list position openings. Though an internship position may not be listed, it should not deter you from adding the firm to your list and making a contact.

locating internship positions

Using the resources provided, locate and begin a list of the firms that you are interested in contacting. This will help you organize your search. Using an Excel spreadsheet, the following information should be included for each firm:

1. Name of firm and name of owner
2. Mailing address
3. Phone number
4. E-mail
5. Website (if there is one available)
6. Name and title of contact person (owners, secretary, or receptionist)
7. Information about the firm such as their specialty or how they work
   a. Specialty or target market (health-care, hospitality, or high-end residential clients)
   b. Commercial, residential, or retail
8. Other information specific to the firm
9. Leave space for later information such as any correspondence, phone calls, interviews, follow-up meetings or calls

In Box 2.4, site supervisors share how their firms prefer to be contacted.

researching firms

The next step is to research several firms in greater depth. Begin by prioritizing your list. This could be by city, state, residential or commercial, design specialty, or other. Of those that interest you, research the firm in greater depth. You may need to add columns to your spreadsheet as you locate information. Use as many resources as possible to keep the field open. This is not the time to eliminate; rather, it is time to keep your options open.

Your research may have begun through an Internet search from which you found a firm's website. Generally, a website provides a great background of information: about the firm, types of projects, design and support staff, specialties, contact information, and more. To further research the firm, you may look for articles in design magazines or even on the Internet that describe one of the firm's projects. If you live in the same city, consider viewing a project via an open house event. Ask your faculty members, friends, or family if they are familiar with the firm.

teamwork within firms

Teamwork is an important part of design, especially in commercial architectural and interior firms where projects involve several professionals working together to complete a project. These professionals include other interior designers as well as architects, engineers, and landscape architects. In an architectural firm, various disciplines work within the firm. In a smaller interior design firm, several interior designers may work together on each project; in addition to this, the firm will hire architects, engineers, electricians, and others as needed to work on a project. As you review your personality type and preferences, you need to review the best way for you to work as a team member—not only knowing yourself, but understanding others and being able to work with team members. With this knowledge and understanding, you will be an asset to your team and the firm.

BOX 2.4

contacting the firm

If students are interested in a summer internship, when should they contact your firm?

A.G. *(interior designer, Gensler)*: "All of our internship info is online at www.gensler.com. This is the best way for a candidate to keep in touch and learn of application deadlines."

B.H. *(supervisor of creative design services, StarMark Cabinetry)*: "They should contact us in the fall of the previous year, when we are submitting budgets for the following year."

K.C. *(interior design director, Interstate Office Products)*: "Contact anytime with a clear date they are available."

K.W. and R.K. *(interior design director and senior human resources representative, AECOM)*: "Our internships run all year long and coincide with the school terms. I would suggest initiating contact six weeks prior to a term."

What type of contact do you prefer? Should the intern begin by calling, e-mailing, or mailing a cover letter and résumé?

A.G. *(interior designer, Gensler)*: "All correspondence should go through the online process."

B.H. *(supervisor of creative design services, StarMark Cabinetry)*: "Mailing a cover letter and résumé is best for initial contact. A follow-up e-mail is fine as well."

K.C. *(interior design director, Interstate Office Products)*: "We prefer a phone call and follow up with an e-mail résumé, cover letter, and references. We like to see a portfolio and examples of design work experience included with the résumé."

summary

Finding the internship for which you are best suited takes research. Research includes understanding the differences between firms and knowing the structure and dynamics of the firm. Understanding the various types of firms will help you determine in which you will fit or where you will fit within the firm.

This chapter discussed the steps to consider in selecting firms where you would feel most comfortable. Your greatest consideration should be your fit to a firm. To determine the appropriate firm, review resources for locating internships, begin locating possible internships, make a list of possible internships, research the employers, and finally, set up a timeline to complete the search. Appendix D lists major national architectural design firms with interior design services or departments. Appendix E lists firms by commercial, residential, and interior architecture categories. You can also access both appendices on the CD-ROM.

All of this must be completed in order to take the next step of writing the résumé and cover letter.

achieving chapter objectives

Review the Chapter Objectives at the beginning of this chapter. You are now ready to put them into practice.

organize your job search

Research employers (firms or other types of businesses):

1. Prepare an Excel document as suggested earlier in this chapter.

2. List as many firms as possible in which you would be interested by using the various sources suggested in this chapter. This list may relate to a preferred location or several locations, or it may relate to a design type such as residential, health care, hospitality, or others. Remember to keep your options open by considering as many firms as possible at this point.

3. Select a minimum of 15 firms.

4. Fill in the Excel document with information for each firm.

5. Prioritize the list.

6. Select eight to ten firms from the list.

7. Research each of these firms in greater depth.

time management

Set a timeline to organize your search. If you intend to complete an internship in the summer, begin planning early in the fall semester. Start by making lists using the suggestions provided earlier in this chapter; then place a start and end date for each of the following steps:

1. Examine your skills and desire.

2. Match to firm types.

3. List resources to use.

4. Begin searching these resources.

5. Start a list of possible firms using the suggested resources.

6. Prioritize the list of firms, but do not eliminate any from the list (only prioritize).

7. Research the top eight to ten on your list.

8. Complete the Excel document.

RESOURCES

- American Society of Interior Designers (ASID) (http://asid.org)
- International Interior Design Association (IIDA) (http://iida.org)
- Inside Arch (www.insidearch.org/home.php)

REFERENCES

- Kendall, G. T. (2005). *Designing your business.* New York: Fairchild Books.
- Piotrowski, C. M. (2002). *Professional practice for interior designers.* New York: Wiley.

KEY TERMS

- British Institute of Interior Designers (BIID)

- Commonwealth of Independent States (CIS)

- Cooperative Center for Study Abroad (CCSA)

- European Union (EU)

- Inhwa

- globalization

- Guanxi

- Interior Designers of Canada (IDC)

- passport

- visa

- Wa

3 the international internship

"To do an internship abroad you **must** have prior knowledge of the language of the country to make the internship as successful as possible. I would have hated this experience if I didn't know Spanish."

—J.H., who completed a 12-week internship at a residential design firm in Buenos Aires.

OBJECTIVES

- Explore the possibilities of learning about other cultures through an international internship.

- Understand the concept of globalization and the implications of conducting the practice of design within a world market through an international internship.

- Develop background knowledge about countries throughout the world that may be possible internship destinations.

- Research a variety of interior design businesses and organizations that may include international firms such as for-profit, nonprofit, publicly versus privately held, hierarchical, and flat.

- Develop a time management schedule for an international internship.

The greatest challenges to embarking on an international internship are planning ahead and locating one, understanding the foreign country's cultures, and having all paperwork completed before departure. Though it will take more time and effort than a domestic internship, however, an international internship is sure to give you a "once in a lifetime" experience.

globalization

Many businesses have moved from local and national markets to markets around the world. With this change, we are now a global community with international trade and cultural exchanges. For centuries, products from around the globe have been specified for design projects. But in more recent times, some design firms have established international offices so they can work on projects around the globe. This means that you may be able to work on projects anywhere. This also means that you have the opportunity to learn more about other cultures. **Globalization** also brings challenges in being comfortable and able to work with people from other cultures whose customs are very different from yours. An international internship experience gives you a better understanding of global work and another culture.

is an international internship right for you?

Before you begin to search for an international internship, you must first consider your reasons for obtaining international work experience. Is it really right for you?

Ask yourself the following questions:

- Do you want the experience of living in a foreign country? If so, which country?
- Do you want to obtain specific skills (CAD, client contact, or other)? If so, which skills? And would cultural or language barriers impede this goal?

- In what type of firm do you want to work (architectural, interior design, retail, or other)?
- What type of experience do you want to obtain (project management, sales, or other)?
- Are you prepared to be on your own, or even feel isolated due to a language or cultural barrier?

locating the international internship

An international internship may seem impossible, but you have options, even if you don't recognize them at first. Some students may already have international experience from either working on international projects within an American design firm or from actually working abroad. But if you don't, there are several ways to obtain this experience. The easiest way is to locate a firm that has regional offices abroad. For example, HDR (www.hdrinc.com), whose corporate office is located in Omaha, Nebraska, has international offices in Canada, the United Arab Emirates, and the United Kingdom.

Locating Firms Based in Other Countries

Knowing a foreign language (being bi- or multilingual) increases your opportunity to work abroad. If you are interested in working internationally, locating firms within other countries may be a bit more challenging and will take advanced planning and research.

Research should begin with people you know, such as professors, friends, family, or others. You may be pleasantly surprised at their connections. Contact your university's alumni association or career service, which might have a list of alumni living abroad (Kim, 2006, p. 212). Though they may not work at a design firm, they may know people who do or have other connections. They also may know their way around and what it takes to live in a specific city, such as how to obtain a visa and finding housing (Kim, 2006, p. 212) or ascertain the cost and location of public transportation, cost of living, and other expenses.

study abroad programs

A good option to help you locate an international internship is the study abroad program. Some of these programs may be supported by your university whereas others may not. It would be wise to contact your university's international offices to make this determination. Additionally, some

field experience

BOX 3.1

an international intern

The following interns responded to all Field Experience questions in this chapter:

A.H. completed her three-month unpaid internship in a nonprofit organization in Juan Comalapa, Guatemala. She graduated from a large public university in the Northwest. She located her internship through IE3 Global Internships.

J.H. completed a 12-week unpaid internship at a residential design firm in Buenos Aires, Argentina. She graduated with a double major of interior design and Spanish from a large public university in the Midwest. She went through Cultural Diversity Success (CDS) International, which required two weeks of Spanish classes followed by a ten-week internship.

What process did you go through to locate your international internship?

A.H.: "There wasn't really a process. I knew I wanted to go abroad and when I read the mission statement of [the nonprofit where she interned called] Long Way Home, I was hooked."

J.H.: "I searched online for international internships available, and a company called CDS International came up. They offered internships in Argentina, Germany, Switzerland, and Spain. I immediately chose Argentina because I love South America and couldn't wait to go back to the city of Buenos Aires. I was there a year ago visiting a friend for a weekend. I fell in love with the city and didn't get to know it as well as I wanted to, so I was excited to see that now I possibly had the chance to go again and, even better, put my Spanish to the test and work!

"I then went through the basic e-mails asking, 'Can I please have more information and whom do I need to be talking to and what do I need to do?' I filled out an eight-page application and was accepted about a month later into the actual internship program. From there I had to translate my résumé into Spanish and cover letter as well. Then, I wrote a report about my school and previous travels experiences. I also had to have a phone interview in Spanish and English."

BOX 3.1 (CONTINUED)
an international intern

FIELD EXPERIENCE
Takeaway

J.H. has provided many tips for moving forward the process of an international internship and becoming immersed into another culture. In particular, it is vital to know the language, specifically for design terms.

Did you have prior knowledge of this culture?

A.H.: "Yes. I had traveled through Nicaragua for two weeks a few years prior to my internship and fell in love with the culture of Central America."

J.H.: "I had prior knowledge of the South American culture having been in Venezuela for a year and in Chile for four months. But being in Argentina for four days a year ago didn't make me an expert about it. I knew what to expect in general, but still was aware that things could be different."

What can you share about this type of experience?

A.H.: "This wasn't just an experience for me, it has changed my life. I am still involved with the organization trying to do as much as I can from the States. I am going back to visit and am trying to organize a group of students from Oregon State University to go and volunteer as well."

J.H.: "It was definitely one of the most interesting and hardest experiences abroad that I have ever had. I can tell you to do an internship abroad you must have prior knowledge of the language [and] of the country to make the internship as successful as possible. That may be just my opinion, but I would have hated this experience if I didn't know Spanish.

"I also must say that even if you are still learning the language you can't be afraid to speak up and talk basically. You have to laugh at your language mistakes and be easygoing and open-minded about it. Getting frustrating and crying doesn't help the situation.

"Don't get upset if your internship isn't what you expected. Mine wasn't. I thought they were going to put me into a commercial design firm designing some amazing hotel, but with the economy here and as well as all over the world people just aren't building and it was hard to find an internship for me. I was lucky that my site supervisor was interested and as you know that I ended up in a residential firm running a computer.

"Don't be mad if you don't get the hours that you expected. For instance, I only worked four days a week, four hours a day, whereas other students were only allowed six hours a day, which is the legal limit for interns in Argentina.

"People there are very friendly and they greet each other every morning with a kiss on the cheek— when you arrive and when you leave. When clients came to the door/showroom I had to remember it was custom to kiss on the cheek and to get up off the computer and greet them.

"Immerse yourself into the tea and coffee drinking habits. Every morning they make tea and coffee, and it is custom to sit at our computers and drink our tea and eat crackers or croissants.

"I found it very helpful to learn the Spanish vocabulary that I would be using on a regular basis. That way I understood when my boss talked to me. I got an ear for Portuguese, too, because my boss spoke a mix between Spanish and Portuguese. I can't say that I learned Portuguese, but I definitely started to understand it."

organizations focus on study abroad and internship programs and may or may not be supported by your university. A few examples of these organizations include Intern Abroad, Study Abroad, International Internships, CDS International, and **Cooperative Center for Study Abroad (CCSA).**

Study Abroad Programs: What's on Their Websites?

The Intern Abroad website (www.intern-abroad.com/search.cfm) lists a variety of countries such as China, Spain, Australia, New Zealand, Germany, and Canada. When you select a country, it links you to further information on the internship experience as well as to application details.

The Study Abroad website (www.study-abroad.com/internabroad/) provides you with access to information by country or by subject. You will also find a link to various internship programs. Through this website, opportunities are available in more than 100 countries where various languages are spoken.

The International Internships website (www.international-internships.com) provides access to internships in nine countries—Argentina, Australia, China, France, Germany, Ireland, London, New Zealand, and Scotland, whereas the CDS International website (www.cdsintl.org) provides opportunities for internships in Switzerland, Germany, Argentina, and Spain.

The Cooperative Center for Study Abroad (CCSA, sites.google.com/a/ccsa.cc/ccsa) provides opportunities in English-speaking countries. Having a second language for these internships, therefore, is not necessary. CCSA also has international representatives at work to locate internships that meets student's particular needs; however internships are limited to only a few locations such as Dublin, London, or Sydney.

continental differences

Countries differ in historical and cultural background, which often affects their approach to business. Therefore, understanding cultural differences gives you an advantage and, hopefully, greater success in your internship.

Canada

In many ways, Canada is similar to the United States; however, the differences must be clearly understood by visitors. Here are two examples. First, Canada gained independence from the British through treaties, and yet they are still connected to Britain; the Queen of England remains their head of state (Denslow, 2006). A constitutional monarchy, Canada receives the queen's representation locally by a governor-general and an elected the prime minister—both Canadian (Canada, 2009). Second, English and French are both official languages within the government and throughout the country. Though Canadians speak English, French is the primary language in the Quebec province, which includes cities such as Montreal and Quebec (Denslow, 2006).

Business culture in Canada is similar to the United States where "time is linear . . . [and] punctuality is important and expected" (Denslow, 2006, p. 113). Linear time means work is conducted using a schedule or calendar in which activities take place on a day and time listed on one's calendar. Within the business world, efforts of the individual and equality are important. The differences are in mannerisms. Canadians tend to be "more quiet and introspective than Americans" and do not want to "appear boastful" (p. 113). Additionally, Canadian business rates higher on the 2009 Corruption Perceptions Index (CPI) and are rated at 8.7 on a 10-point scale

(10 = best, 0 = worst) in comparison to the United States, which is rated 7.5 (Table 3.1). One might interpret from these statistics that Canadians have high ethical standards (Transparency International, 2009).

There are also differences in people within the various provinces. For example, people of Quebec are impacted by their French heritage; people of Ontario are more reserved, people of British Columbia are less reserved. Of course, these are generalities and will also vary among individuals.

Creating a Cultural Checklist for Canada

As you look for an internship in Canada, you must remember that Canada is not the United States—this, of course, is true for all foreign lands. After you've done your research on a country's history and culture, keep a mental checklist of the important differences in mind. This can be an informal exercise; the point is to always be aware of the key points to remember. For example, Canadians tend to be more formal in

TABLE 3.1

The Corruption Perceptions Index

The Corruption Perceptions Index (CPI) is maintained by Transparency International (www.transparency.org), an international nonprofit network of more than 90 chapters worldwide dedicated to fight corruption in government, civil society, business, and the media. Transparency International posts this index as a table on its website that ranks and scores more than 80 countries.

The rank shows how one country compares to others included in the index. The CPI score indicates the perceived level of public-sector corruption in a country/territory. The CPI is based on 13 independent surveys. For the latest complete index, go to Transparency International's website and type "Corruption Index" into the search field.

COUNTRY OR REGION	CPI 2009 SCORE
Canada	8.5–9.0
United States	7.5
Latin America	6.7–1.5
Europe	9.3–3.8
Russia and CIS	4.1–1.7
Middle East and the Indian Subcontinent	7.0–1.3

Source: Transparency International, 2009.

business. They are friendly and helpful but are more cautious in the way they sell themselves and their services, and have high ethical standards. Therefore, when applying for an internship, do not overstate your qualifications, and be friendly and helpful but reserved. Behave in a similar fashion when you arrive at the internship. And don't forget to keep adding mental notes to your informal checklist with each new experience you encounter during you internship.

Latin America

Latin America encompasses countries in Central and South Americas as well as the Caribbean. The largest Central American country, Mexico, is the only Latin American country that borders the United States. Brazil, the largest South American country, has grown in influence throughout the world and become a leader among the developing countries (Denslow, 2006). Latin American countries have governments that vary from democracies to dictatorships (History of Latin America, 2009). The majority of these countries use the peso as currency (Peso, 2009).

Language Diversity

Spanish is the dominant language in most of Latin America; however, Portuguese is the dominant language in Brazil, and French is spoken in Haiti, the Caribbean, Guadeloupe, and Martinique. In many of these countries, there are other languages spoken, such as English, Italian, Chinese, and German. Particularly, in some regions, an indigenous language is spoken among the Native Indians (UNESCO, 2008).

A More Relaxed Approach

People in Latin America are friendly, hospitable, and more relaxed. They have very flexible schedules. In contrast, people in the United States maintain rigid schedules and often have difficulty with this flexibility (Denslow, 2006). Examples of the business culture from three Latin American countries include:

- Belize: The pace of life is not regulated by the clock but by events and people.
- Venezuela: The joy of an event or needs of an individual are more important than the demands of a time schedule.
- Paraguay: Time is flexible according to the importance of appointment (Denslow, 2006, p. 133).

Clearly, business in Latin America will differ relative to time as well as dealings with people. Additionally, different classes of people—wealthy, rich, middle class, and poor—impact business dealings. First, initial agreements are made at the top level—with the wealthy and rich. Then, the mid-level managers implement the agreement. Also, business is conducted on the basis of people recognized within a community and who have good character rather than financial backing (Denslow, 2006). However, corruption rankings of businesses vary among the various Latin American countries. Two countries rank above 5.0: Chile at 6.7 and Uruguay at 6.7. The remainder rank below 5.0: El Salvador at 3.4 and Haiti at 1.5 (Transparency International, 2009). This means that there may be a concern for ethical behavior in business in some Latin American countries.

Creating Your Latin American Cultural Checklist

As you look for an internship in a Latin American country, it is important to understand that people are important, schedules are flexible, and business must be conducted with the right people.

Europe

When considering European travel, we frequently think of cities such as Paris, London, Rome, or countries such as Ireland, England, France, Germany, Italy, or Spain. However, Europe is composed of 45 different countries with many cities and towns that range widely in population and culture.

The European Union

In the 1970s, the European Union (EU) was formed with six nations: Germany, France, Luxembourg, Belgium, the Netherlands, and Italy, but today it consists of 27 countries (Denslow, 2006). The website http://europa.eu/abc/european_countries/index_en.htm lists countries in the EU. Fifteen are considered inner countries (countries generally associated with Europe), and the remaining countries were formerly part of the former USSR (Europa, 2008). The only European inner countries not in the EU are Switzerland, Norway, Iceland, and Liechtenstein; however, they are closely tied and involved in economics of the area. It is also important to note that there is freedom of movement between and within countries in the EU (Denslow, 2006), whether by road, train, or plane.

The EU focuses on trade in the region and throughout the world as well as the maintenance of regional peace and positive interactions between people of all EU nations (Denslow, 2006). Additionally, 13 of the 27 countries are united through currency—the Euro. These countries include Austria, Belgium, Finland, France, Germany, Greece, Ireland, Italy, Luxembourg, the Netherlands, Portugal, Spain, and Slovenia (Crown, 2009). Three inner countries—Sweden, Denmark, and the United Kingdom—do not use the Euro (Denslow, 2006).

A Culture of Similarities and Differences

Depending on the country within the EU, the business culture has similarities and differences, and, therefore, businesses within the EU must be flexible. Their similarities relate to key issues such as managing change, technology, work ethic, and more. Another similarity is the use of the English language in business from one country to the next. However, the differences begin with each country having its own language. Other differences can be stated in generalities that may help understand various regions of the EU:

1. The northern populations are linear and work collectively.
2. The southern populations including Spain and Portugal are more emotional.
3. Some of the central populations (those formerly under for USSR dominations) are used to centrally planned economies and are still adjusting to the free market whereas others have adjusted to democratic ways. For example, Czechs work by the book whereas Hungarians are free-wheeling (Denslow, 2006).

Many countries within the EU recognize their regional differences and, therefore, have developed a mutual understanding of one another (Denslow, 2006). Another difference is in the corruption rating. Twelve countries rate higher than the United States, including Denmark, Sweden, Finland, Netherlands, Luxembourg, Germany, Ireland, Austria, and the United Kingdom; however, several rate lower than 5.0 (Transparency International, 2009). Thus, the level of ethical behavior in business varies between countries.

Prioritizing Your Cultural Checklist

With the information previously noted, preparation for an internship in Europe will take research not only into a firm. but also about the EU and the specific countries' customs. For example, concerning the EU, you would do well to prioritize your checklist in the following order,

1. Understand the EU and currency used in the country where you will intern.
2. Understand local customs, both business and traditions.
3. Understand the country's business culture, down to the detail such as the way to present a business card (Denslow, 2006).
4. Understand the importance of relationships between and among people.
5. Be able to speak the language.
6. Be prepared to be isolated due to these differences.

Russia and the Commonwealth of Independent States

Other than Russia or the Russian Federation, the 12 countries within the **Commonwealth of Independent States (CIS)**—Armenia, Azerbaijan, Belarus, Georgia, Kyrgyzstan, Kazakhstan, Moldova, Tajikistan, Turkmenistan, Ukraine, and Uzbekistan—are not well known to Americans. After the breakup of the USSR, these countries became independent and responsible for themselves, which can be difficult for a people who have been dependent a larger government for so long (Wenslow, 2006).

The CIS countries are diverse in size, geography, location, religion, and are within two different continents—Europe and Asia. Though each country's currency is different, they are working toward the adoption of the Russian ruble as their common currency (Stratfor, 2008). When the USSR controlled these countries, religion was suppressed. However, with independence, religion has emerged throughout the region; these include Christianity, Islam, and Judaism, and yet, their governments do not advocate any particular religion (Starovoitova, 1999).

Individual Relationships

A common element in business in the CIS is the relationship between individuals. "You must know someone, be introduced, be patient, and build the connections" (Wenslow, 2006, p. 164). You must have a relationship with someone before you can do business together; therefore, connections are extremely important. It is not clear whether this originates from the early tribal roots or possibly the distrust developed during the Soviet domination. You must understand that "the casual American approach of introducing yourself, doing business first, and building relationships later does not fit in this environment" (Wenslow, 2006, p. 164).

A Different Approach to Time

Businesspeople in the CIS treat their time as flexible and ongoing (i.e., not following a rigid schedule), which means that they tend to be late; and their day begins and ends later than Americans. Additionally, many business procedures or expectations common to American business, such as long-range planning, paying taxes, or making a profit, are not common in these countries. In fact, these are challenges to new businesses in the CIS. Due to the past socialistic (state-controlled) society, citizens have difficulty forming their own businesses. However, entrepreneurial spirit is slowly emerging. Another challenge is the low corruption perception ratings with all countries ranking lower than 5 (from 1.8 to 4.1) (Transparency International, 2009), which means there may be a concern for ethical behavior in business.

Cultural Checklist: The CIS

With this information, preparation for an internship in any CIS country will take research into the firm as well as understanding the way it conducts business. It is important to know that they have a more relaxed way of viewing and conducting business. Also, they feel that it's important to have a good relationship with a person before conducting business.

The Middle East and the Indian Subcontinent

Countries in the Middle East and the Indian Subcontinent include Afghanistan, Bahrain, Bangladesh, Egypt, India, Iraq, Iran, Israel, Jordan, Kuwait, Lebanon, Oman, Pakistan, Qatar, Saudi Arabia, Syria, Turkey, the United Arab Emirates, and Yemen. These countries vary in size, geography, religion, culture, and governments. This is also a region with great political turmoil (Wenslow, 2006).

Family Roots

These cultures began as individual family groups that grew to larger tribes or groups. Because of invasion over the years, these groups gathered and fought to protect their resources and defend themselves when necessary. Many continue to defend themselves, and today, these groups are tightly knit and may be difficult to penetrate (Wenslow, 2006).

India and Pakistan

The British governed India for more than 50 years and left an impact on the region. For example, though 18 official languages are spoken, the English language is used for business and education. Additionally, Pakistan exhibits more subtle cultural influences; bagpipe bands and traditional Scottish Highland clothing may be found among the people (Wenslow, 2006).

Government

Governments of the region are as varied and diverse as the culture and geography. India is a democratic republic, Afghanistan has a provisional government, Jordan has constitutional monarchies, Iran is a theocratic democracy, Iraq is in transition, Syria and Yemen are republics, and the United Arab Emirates is a federation of emirates (Wenslow, 2006). The currency within the region is also diverse; before going to any of these countries, it would be important to know and understand their currency (Mideastweb Middle East, 2009).

Religion

Religion is a powerful and influential force in this region, to such a degree that Iran, Saudi Arabia, Pakistan, and Afghanistan are Islamic theocracies. The three monotheistic religions (Judaism, Christianity, and Islam) began in this region and affect decisions related to dress and food consumption. For example, although this may vary from one country to another, Muslim women generally wear veils over their faces or may be restricted from participating in societal decisions (Wenslow, 2006). On the other hand, India's dominant religion is Hinduism, which affects its peoples' lifestyle from the foods they eat to their behavior toward humans and animals (Hinduism, 2009).

Business Roots

Business in this region relates to tribal roots—family. This cannot be stressed enough. Each tribe has its own customs, dress, and speech; therefore, the highly regarded hierarchy and group decision-making is crucial. With some countries such as India, when born into a tribe or caste, the person remains in that caste for life. Though the caste system has been outlawed, discrimination through the caste system is still significant in politics and business (Wenslow, 2006).

Understanding how people in this region do business takes a great deal of research. Particularly important to understand is the amount of possible corruption in business. For example, even though Qatar (7.0), the United Arab Emirates (6.5), and Israel (6.1) rank high in the region on the Corruption Perception Index, they are lower than the United States (7.5). The majority of the countries in this region rank below 5.0 (Transparency International, 2009).

Yet Another Relationship to Time

In these regions, people are not controlled by time as we are in the Western world. Schedules do not control the business process; rather, it is people's needs that dictate how time is to be spent. This means that people must begin by building a relationship with others through conversation and shared hospitality. It is a slow process; taking time to know people will not only help build a business relationship, but will indirectly help build confidence in the individual (Wenslow, 2006).

Customizing Your Cultural Checklist

With this information, preparation for an internship in any Middle Eastern or Indian Subcontinental country requires not only research into the firm but also demands an understanding of the way they conduct business. Thus, in the business world, it will be especially important to know that time is not the master. Particularly, developing a good relationship with a person and their group is crucial, which must take place before doing business. However, in locating an internship, it would be wise to have a prior connection—knowing someone or a group in the region.

Australia and New Zealand

Australia and New Zealand lie in close proximity to one another but a greater distance from the industrialized countries in Europe and America. Australia is made of two islands—the largest is Australia, and the smallest is Tasmania. Australia's government is similar to that of Canada—a democratic federal state that recognizes the British Monarch as the head of state (Denslow, 2006). Its official language is English, and its currency is the Australian dollar ($A) (Australia, 2009).

New Zealand is also made up of two large islands and includes several smaller ones (Denslow, 2006). New Zealand's government is the same type as Australia's, but its official language is both English and Maori. Currency is the New Zealand dollar (NZ$) (New Zealand, 2009).

Aussies versus Kiwis

Australia is six times larger than New Zealand, but both want to be recognized individually as Australians and New Zealanders, just as Canadians, Americans, or Britons do. Australians refer to themselves as Aussies and New Zealanders as Kiwis (Denslow, 2006).

There are many similarities between New Zealanders and Americans in the way they do business, but differences still exist. People dress differently (Denslow, 2006). New Zealanders' business dress is conservative, but when at work, jackets are often removed (Kwintessential, n.d.). And just as Americans are proud of doing things the American way, New Zealanders are proud of their "Kiwi ingenuity" and prefer to develop their own solutions. They are also one of the leaders in developing entrepreneurships in the world—even greater than in the United States.

Though Australia has fewer entrepreneurial businesses, they have a larger economy and greater opportunity to do business due to its size. Both countries have become places where regional headquarters of multinational companies are located, and both rank higher in the 2004 Corruption Perceptions Index (9.4 and 8.7 respectively) (Transparency International, 2009). Thus, businesses in these countries among the least corrupt in the world.

Equality Rules

Equality is a core value within the Australian and New Zealand culture. This value shows in their business approaches in that they believe in fairness; however, they do not like interference, authority, and people giving orders (Denslow, 2006). Sustainability is also important among Australian and New Zealand business. Similar to nonprofit organizations that promote green environments in America, the Environment Business Australia (EBA) raises awareness about the solutions to environmental challenges affecting their economy and quality of health and wellness (EBA, n.d.). Additionally, peace as well as sustainability is particularly important to New Zealanders because they have declared their country a nuclear-free zone where no ship with nuclear weapons is allowed into their seaports (Denslow, 2006).

Equality, Sustainability, and Peace: Noting Values in Your Cultural Checklist

With this information, preparation for an internship in Australia or New Zealand will take research into the firm as well as towards an understanding of the way its people conduct business. It is important to know that they are very proud of their difference from other English-speaking countries, and because of the greater number of entrepreneurial business, New Zealand will most likely have more proprietary (or single-owner) design firms than in Australia. Thus, the key is to remember they are proud, and support equality, sustainability, and peace.

Asia

Asia is the world's largest continent. It contains China, the most populated nation in the world with more than 1.3 billion people. It also includes Japan and South Korea, two countries with strong economies where many U.S. students find rewarding internships. These three Asian countries are diverse in size, geography, and climate.

A Fluctuating "Openness"

China is a country that has alternated between being open, closed, and open again to the outside world. Japan has also alternated between being open and closed to outsiders and trade (exporting and importing of goods). However, when open, Japan was influenced by outsiders such as China. In today's world, Japan has used knowledge gained from the Western world and become the first non-Western country to industrialize; this helped it become a powerful trading nation.

Korea is currently a nation that has suffered invasions and outside control from China, Japan, and Mongolia—each closing the country to the outside world. Today, Korea is divided between the north and south. North Korea has been a communist government whereas South Korea is democratic (Wenslow, 2006).

Different Countries, Different Cultures

Even though these countries are Asian, each has a different form of government, language, and currency. The Chinese government is a republic with one legislative house, the language is Mandarin Chinese, and its currency is the yuan (Y) (China, 2009). Japan's government is a constitutional monarchy, the language is Japanese, and the currency is the Yen (¥) (Japan, 2009). North Korea is a unitary single-party republic while South Korea is a unitary multiparty republic. However, the language and currency are the same in both North and South Korea, as are the Korean language and the won (W) (North Korea, 2009; South Korea, 2009).

Trade with Asia

Trade with Asia began via the Silk Road, the age-old trade route that connected Asia with Africa and Europe. Today, the exchange of products and knowledge also occurs among Asian countries, the United States, and the rest of the world. Exchange can even bring several cultures together. For example, a French fashion school opened in Shanghai with a German instructor who was educated in London and designed in Paris (Wenslow, 2006).

Religions

Religious beliefs and philosophies influence the culture, behaviors, and designs of these countries. There are a variety of religions; these include Catholicism, Islam, and Eastern religions—Confucianism, Taoism, Buddhism, Shintoism. Particularly, Eastern religions focus on harmony and daily life or even relate to social values such as courage, politeness, and reserve. Religion in this region is intertwined the daily lives of its peoples (Wenslow, 2006) and, therefore, becomes an important concern in the design profession as well as in behavior.

"People Do Business with People They Know"

Although the business culture varies in Asia, personal connections among people are important. This means that before business can be conducted, people must be properly introduced and know something about each other. In other parts of the world,

connections and introductions are important; however, in Asia, it is crucial. "People do business with people they know" (Wenslow, 2006, p. 203).

Philosophical Business Styles

As do many firms within the United States, Asians have different philosophical styles of doing business. These are called **Guanxi, Wa,** and **Inhwa.**

Guanxi: A Chinese philosophy, Guanxi represents a commitment by one to offer assistance to another.

Wa: A Japanese philosophy based on the group and the individual's affiliation, Wa means that membership and group loyalty are critical. Loyalty to the group builds consensus and maintains harmony that consequentially benefits the individual.

Inhwa: A Korean philosophy, Inhwa emphasizes harmony between individuals. This includes harmonious relationships among and loyalty to one another. Even unequals, such as a boss and an employee, are included. For example, in the home, the older takes care of the young, and the young are loyal to the older individuals. (Wenslow, 2006).

Respect Ranks High on an Asian Cultural Checklist

With this information, preparation for an internship in Asia includes research into the firm as well as understanding into the way each country's people conducts business. It will be important to know that there are different philosophies for developing relationships and that building a relationship will take time. Thus, the key is to not only be patient and friendly but also respectful.

Africa

Africa is the world's second-largest continent with the Sahara Desert covering the majority of its northern half. Within Africa, there are 54 countries of varying sizes, cultures, religions, and more. Sudan is the largest, covering 970,000 square miles, and Seychelles is the smallest, covering 175 square miles. Cultures vary from European, Turkish, Arab, Chinese, and Indian to native tribal descendants and many other ethic groups. Religions vary from Muslim, Christian, Hindu, Jewish, Ethiopian Orthodox, and indigenous traditional religions to independent churches that combine African and Christian beliefs (Denslow, 2006).

Tribal Societies

Visitors to Africa must understand the family, group, or tribe and that African countries are "based on tribal societies that are family and relationship oriented" (p. 229). In fact, family is more important than any business dealing and decision-making process. For example, the decision-making process does not occur individually or with the consensus of a managerial group. Rather, "a decision cannot be finalized until the tribal leader gives approval. Only after a tribal leader's agreement can a transaction move forward" (Denslow, 2006, p. 229).

Business in Africa ranges from promising to disappointing. Some areas are impoverished, such as Sudan and Tanzania, wheras others such as South Africa and Uganda show promise and businesses thrive there. For example, Uganda ranks among the top five entrepreneurial countries, which include New Zealand, Chile, Thailand, and Venezuela. South Africa ranks in the medium range along with Germany, Israel, and Switzerland. On the other hand, Sudan and Tanzania are

densely populated with a low life expectancy (median age is 17.9 and 17.6 respectively), in part due to illnesses such as HIV/AIDS (Denslow, 2006). These ranges demonstrate the diversity within the continent of Africa. Some countries experience growth and may have the need for design services whereas others are in greater need of humanitarian aid.

A Relaxed Approach to Business

Business is flexible, and schedules are often not followed. This does not mean a lack of interest. On the contrary, people are polite and interested; they just have a different sense of priorities and time and expect others to be just as flexible. African cultures are similar to Latin American and Asian cultures in which the people develop personal relationships before doing business. Clearly, the focus is to develop a long-term relationship, not a quick transaction. Thus, conversation must be devoid of business until the relationship is formed. Additionally, a higher level of formality is expected among colleagues. It is also important to note that corruption is not uncommon in business and the public sector.

Creating a Cultural Checklist for Africa

With this information, preparation for an internship in any country in Africa requires research into the firm as well as an understanding of the way that country's people conduct business. It is important to understand the language and the culture. Interns within a firm must recognize that a personal relationship must be developed before a transaction is made, and the tribal leaders must agree to the transaction before business can occur.

contacts for international internships

Contact information varies within each country. In some cases, the contact may be through a firm within the United States. In other cases, it is through a professional organization, directly through the international firm, or through individuals who live in that country. Some organizations, such as International Federation of Interior Architects/Designers (IFI), link through its website (www.ifiworld.org) to many design firms throughout the world. IFI provides contact information through its website under Members Directory (IFI, 2006). The following provides contacts information for a few countries.

Canada

If you are interested in an internship in Canada, there are many architectural firms with interior design services. (See Appendix G.) However, many interior designers are members of **Interior Designers of Canada (IDC)** or IIDA, and each website will become an important resource. The directory from IDC website provides a link to each province's website. In these websites, you will find a list of registered members; however, contact information is not provided (IDC, 2007). You may want to search the Internet's Yellow Pages, Google, or another search engine for interior designers who are members in IDC or IIDA.

Latin America: Mexico

Interior designers in Mexico have the opportunity to become members of IIDA. To find an internship in Mexico, begin by locating the contact information from either Mexico City or Guadalajara chapters on the IIDA website (www.iida.org/i4a/pages/index.cfm?pageid=302).

Europe

If you are interested in an internship in Europe, some countries have their own design organizations, are connected to IIDA, or are part of a European organization. To locate an internship in the United Kingdom, the **British Institute of Interior Designers (BIID)** provides portfolios and websites for each interior designer (BIID-2, n.d.). BIID was formed through the combination of IIDA-UK Chapter and Interior Decorators & Designers Association. Its membership consists of many highly respected British interior designers (BIID-1, n.d.).

As an international organization, IIDA has membership in various countries. For example, interior designers in Portugal may be members of IIDA-Portugal. However, a European design organization provides a connection to designers in various European countries. The European Council of Interior Architects (ECIA) represents the European professional organizations in interior architecture and design and a link to 14 national organizations (ECIA). Its website (www.ecia.net) is an important connection for anyone interested in an internship in Europe; however, knowledge of the local vernacular is very important.

Australia and New Zealand

Design Institute of Australia (DIA) serves design professionals from various disciplines (DIAc, 2009). The DIA website (www.dia.org.au/) provides links to interior architecture, interior design, interior decoration, textile design, furniture design, and more (DIAb, 2009). From these links (such as interior design), members are listed with web links to a firm's website. Contact information is located on each of these sites. Additionally, this website also provides links to other Asia-Pacific Design organizations in China, Hong Kong, India, Korea, Japan, Malaysia, Thailand, South Africa, Philippines, and more (DIAa, 2009).

The Designers Institute of New Zealand (DINZ) is an organization for various design disciplines. The website (www.dinz.org.nz) provides links to professional designers from interior design to industrial design.

Asia

As an international organization, IIDA has members in Japan; however, to read its website, you must be able to read Japanese (IIDA, 2009). The Japanese Interior Designers' Association (JID) is a national organization that represents interests of interior designers in Japan (JID, n.d.) and is a contact source to interior designers.

The Beijing Hutong School combines Chinese studies with an internship. To participate in this program, you must have an architecture and/or interior design background. Information on this program is found on its website (http://internship.hutong-school.com/internship-detail.php?id=185) (Hutong School, 2006).

Lists of Firms

Appendix F provides a list of American firms with international offices; Appendix G provides a shortened list of international firms in various countries. (You can also access Appendices F and G on the CD-ROM.)

preparation

Preparing for an international internship takes a great deal of preparation in advance. The following is a list of important documents and travel needs for international travel (see details on each of the following):

1. Identification
   a. Passport
   b. Visa
   c. International student exchange ID card
2. Financial aid
3. Health insurance
4. Travel services
5. Calling card
6. Travel essentials

A Study Abroad website (www.study-abroad.com/marketplace/) provides information on travel essentials and links to sources for insurance, financial aid, and more.

Identification

The two basic types of identification for international interns are passports and visas.

Passports

Current **passports** are required for all travel outside the United States. If you do not have a passport and plan to travel internationally for an internship, the U.S. government requires that you have a valid passport for a minimum of six months. Thus, you must plan ahead—not just to have one in your possession for six months, but for the processing period, which takes between four to six weeks before planning to leave. An acceptance facility such as your local post office or a passport agency such as the clerk of court in a courthouse has information about applications and processing information. Information about the process and the locations where you can apply is found on http://travel.state.gov. It is also important to make photocopies of your passport—one left with family and one or two copies to use when traveling where an original is not needed. Your original passport is used to cash traveler's checks and, if needed, for a visit to the American Embassy (Denslow, 2006).

Visas

Visas are required to visit countries for an extended period of time. Tourists who visit less than three months are not required to have a visa. If an internship lasts less than three months, you would be considered a tourist and a visa would not be required—at least to stay in another country. But if the internship considers you an employee within a firm, a visa is required. "Most countries will require the employer to verify that you possess qualifications the firm cannot find in its current applicant pool" (Kim, 2006, p. 212). So, for even a less-than-three-month stay, a visa may still be required. Visa requirements may be different for each country. Embassies for each country can provide this information.

International firms or schools may have specific requirements. For international firms, you will be required to complete an agreement with your school. Also, when traveling abroad, a longer internship is wise, and some firms may require four months or longer.

---

field experience

BOX 3.2

travel documents

FIELD EXPERIENCE
Takeaway

The underlying theme from J.H. is that an international internship will be a different but a worthwhile experience. Additionally, being flexible in your expectations and open to learning more about another culture will take you a long way.

Refer to Box 3.1 for background on the interns who also responded to the following question.

What documents did you need to travel abroad?

A.H.: "Only a passport."

J.H.: "The documents I brought with me were:

- My passport.
- A visa (required only if you are going to be in the country more than 90 days). I didn't need one, but just be aware that this changes all the time. All South American countries are the same (90 day rule) except Brazil, which requires a visa., I do believe.
- A yellow card that states that I have had the yellow fever shot and typhoid shot that I knew Brazil required in order to enter the country and Venezuela, too, so I always carry it with me just in case I travel and in case someone asks me. I don't think it is required for Argentina.

"As it turned out, all I really needed was my passport. The others were just useful information."

Financial Aid

Financial aid can come in the form of scholarships, loans, and other sources. Scholarships are available at individual institutions, and you may obtain loans through financial institutions or individuals. CCSA provides program costs to the institution's financial aid office. CCSA also assists students from institutions outside the association to obtain a consortium agreement between their institution's financial aid offices. It is essential that students who apply for financial aid meet the deadline in order to facilitate the financial aid process (CCSA, n.d.).

Health Insurance

Whether provided by your school or your parents, having health insurance is essential. If you are registered for an internship course and have the minimum number of credits, your institution generally provides health insurance. However, don't make an assumption; rather, check with your institution to be assured that you are covered at home as well as abroad.

Travel Services: Accommodations and Transportation

After an internship has been confirmed, you will need to find a place to live. If you have contacts in your chosen city, enlist their help. The firm may also suggest places that are convenient either via transportation or within close proximity to the firm and should also suggest accommodations in a safe area.

Many cities in Europe have public transportation; however, some cities may not. Thus, researching the means of transportation is very important. After you have determined your living arrangements, locate the best and safest means of transportation. When there, observe your surroundings, note the details, and beware of any scheduling changes.

Travel Essentials

When you travel far away from home for a longer period of time, you may have special items that are important to you and provide comfort. These may include a pillow, photographs, or a memento to personalize your living arrangements. Essentials that will make traveling easier include:

- Personal items for comfort (pillow, photographs, or other items)
- Passport, visa, insurance cards
- Copies of passport and extra passport photo
- Currency of the country (allow time prior to travel to obtain the country's currency; it will make your first few days easier)
- Credit card, ATM card, and record the emergency number if cards are lost
- List of important phone numbers or other contact information
- Medical kit and medications along with copies of prescriptions
- Umbrella
- Laptop, cell phone, charger, and adapter (outlets may be different in another country) (Denslow, 2006)

You should also know how to access the U.S. embassy and keep emergency numbers close by, as well as addresses and phone numbers of family and friends at home. To contact a U.S. embassy, prior to leaving, check the website www.state.gov/countries/ for the country in which you will travel. Links will take you to information on hours of operation and phone numbers (USDS-DA, 2009). Take this information with you and also leave it with family or friends as well. Also, leave information with family or friends such as copies of your passport, credit cards, and contact information in the foreign country. Despite the temptation to take along special jewelry, leaving it behind would be wiser (especially if it would be upsetting if lost). Though there are many precautions, it is also important to enjoy the travel, and be curious and flexible in your schedule.

Concerns

Traveling alone can be difficult. Being alone is challenging in the United States but more so in places outside this country. Being alone at night or walking into an elevator with strangers are a couple concerns. Consider the following safety precautions:

- Know the areas of a city or other locations that are safe and those that are risky.
- Ask for information before you go for a walk.
- Believe the bus driver if he or she says an area isn't safe.
- Have a hotel or restaurant call a cab for you, especially in the evening.
- No matter how much you love to run outside in the morning, don't do it if your colleagues tell you there are snakes (or other hazards) in the area.
- Don't use the room service door hanger menus to order breakfast; you have to indicate how many people are in the room.
- Select small hotels where the staff know who is a guest and who isn't.
- If you travel to the same city frequently, stay at the same place.
- Schedule a time to call home. Be sure someone expects to hear from you and will be aware if you don't check in.
- Leave your cell phone number so people can call you. Remember to charge the phone and leave it on.
- Remember that women as well as men can be dangerous. Be cautious about new friends (Denslow, 2006, p. 300).

Behavior

An opportunity to intern in a foreign country is a privilege, and for this reason, it is important to remember that you are a guest in this country. Also, showing respect to the people and cultures will make you a goodwill ambassador from the United States. Therefore, the following behaviors are recommended:

- Be on time (or be sure you understand the culture's expectations related to time).
- Blend into the crowd, which means no talking or talking softly.
- Be considerate of others.
- Use words and body language that are respectful.
- Show respect to fellow workers, clerks, waitresses, and others.
- Learn the language to communicate and show courtesies.
- Dress in clothing that is appropriate to the culture.
- Sample foods provided at meals and state only your likes.
- Express appreciation for food, snacks, or other courtesies.
- Practice good table manners.

Clearly, it is important to show respect to the people and country you are visiting. These are only a few ways in which you can be respectful. It is especially important to remember that you are a guest.

transfer of credits

If student interns obtain their internship through the program of another school, the transfer of credits is generally acceptable. Most universities accept credits from other universities within the United States as well as from international institutions. Each student who considers applying for credit at a different institution should visit with the advisor at the home institution before making an application.

summary

An international internship is an opportunity of a lifetime. The experience can be mediocre to great. However, for it to become a great experience, you must be prepared. Planning ahead is crucial so that passports, visas, or other documents are completed with plenty of time to spare. Also, during the preparation process, you must consider and understand the problems that may occur and know how to handle them. Additionally, you must thoroughly research the firm, the country, and its culture to be successful.

To help you research opportunities for an international internship, Appendix F provides a list of American firms with international offices; Appendix G provides a shortened list of international firms in various countries. (You can also access Appendices F and G on the CD-ROM.)

achieving chapter objectives

Review the Chapter Objectives at the beginning of this chapter. You are now ready to put them into practice:

prepare for your international internship

First, research each aspect of the internship as follows.

1. Research possible internship destinations.

2. Select a country or countries to research.

3. Research and develop greater background knowledge of select countries.

4. Research various interior design business or organizations that include international firms.

Then create an appropriate timeline that shows how long it will take to complete each of the following aspects for an international internship:

1. Paperwork needed for international travel and internship

2. Steps to take in obtaining an international internship

3. Lead times needed for all aspects of the process

4. Costs of travel to the country, travel during internship, lodging, meals, daily living, entertainment, and other incidentals

time management

Complete the following:

1. Apply for a passport (minimum of 8 to 10 months in advance).

2. Locate and research firms (go through a similar process noted in the previous chapter).

3. Research all aspects of the country—the government, money, language, culture, business process, and more.

4. Review health insurance coverage.

5. Apply for the internship.

6. After you're accepted, determine if you need to apply for a visa.

7. Complete all documents required by the university and/or international study abroad program.

8. Locate housing.

9. Determine transportation to and from the internship as well as to other areas.

10. Study the area by mapping locations of the firm, housing, shopping, and entertainment.

11. Determine the appropriate behavior for a visitor from another country.

12. List items, documents, and appropriate clothing needed.

REFERENCES

* BIID. (n.d.a). About the BIID. Retrieved on December 22, 2008, from http://www.biid.org
* BIID. (n.d.b). Designers' portfolios. Retrieved on December 22, 2008, from http://www.biid.org
* Cooperative Center for Study Abroad (CCSA). (n/d). Program Details Retrieved on December 23, 2008, from http://www.ccsa.cc/PROGRAM_DETAILS.html
* Crown. (2009). *Euro information: The official treasury resources.* Retrieved on January 8, 2009, from http://www.euro.gov.uk/countrymenu.asp
* Denslow, L. (2006). *World wise: What to know before you go.* New York: Fairchild Books.
* Design Institute of Australia (DIAa). Asia-Pacific design organisations. Retrieved on February 1, 2009, from http://www.dia.org.au/content.cfm?id=259#New%20Zealand
* Design Institute of Australia (DIAb). Members weblinks. Retrieved on January 31, 2009, from http://www.dia.org.au/content.cfm?id=131
* Design Institute of Australia (DIAc). Role of the DIA. Retrieved on January 31, 2009, from http://www.dia.org.au/content.cfm?id=180
* Encyclopædia Britannica. (2009). "Canada." Retrieved January 24, 2009, from Encyclopædia Britannica Online: http://www.britannica.com/EBchecked/topic/91513/Canada
* Encyclopædia Britannica. (2009). "China." Retrieved January 24, 2009, from Encyclopædia Britannica Online: http://www.britannica.com/EBchecked/topic/111803/China
* Encyclopædia Britannica. (2009). "Hinduism." Retrieved January 25, 2009, from Encyclopædia Britannica Online: http://www.britannica.com/EBchecked/topic/266312/Hinduism
* Encyclopædia Britannica. (2009). "History of Latin America." Retrieved January 08, 2009, from Encyclopædia Britannica Online: http://www.britannica.com/EBchecked/topic/331694/Latin-America
* Encyclopædia Britannica. (2009). "India." Retrieved January 25, 2009, from Encyclopædia Britannica Online: http://www.britannica.com/EBchecked/topic/285248/India
* Encyclopædia Britannica. (2009). "Japan." Retrieved January 24, 2009, from Encyclopædia Britannica Online: http://www.britannica.com/EBchecked/topic/300531/Japan
* Encyclopædia Britannica. (2009). "New Zealand." Retrieved January 24, 2009, from Encyclopædia Britannica Online: http://www.britannica.com/EBchecked/topic/412636/New-Zealand
* Encyclopædia Britannica. (2009). "North Korea." Retrieved January 24, 2009, from Encyclopædia Britannica Online: http://www.britannica.com/EBchecked/topic/322222/North-Korea
* Encyclopædia Britannica. (2009). "Peso." Retrieved January 28, 2009, from Encyclopædia Britannica Online: http://www.britannica.com/EBchecked/topic/453401/peso
* Encyclopædia Britannica. (2009). "South Korea." Retrieved January 24, 2009, from Encyclopædia Britannica Online: http://www.britannica.com/EBchecked/topic/322280/South-Korea
* Environment Business Australia (EBA). (n/d). About EBA. Retrieved on January 28, 2009, from http://www.environmentbusiness.com.au/m-benefits.asp
* Europa. (2008). *Europa: European countries.* Retrieved on January 8, 2009, from http://europa.eu/abc/european_countries/index_en.htm
* European Council of Interior Architects (ECIA). (n/d). ECIA. Retrieved on February 1, 2009, from http://www.ecia.net/index.php?page=2
* Hutong School, Ltd. (2006). Beijing Hutong School: Combine internship with Chinese studies. Retrieved on January 31, 2009, from http://internship.hutong-school.com/internship-detail.php?id=185

- Interior Designers of Canada (IDC). (2007). Directory and links. Retrieved on February 1, 2009, from http://www.interiordesigncanada.org/link_assoc.html

- International Federation of Interior Architects/Designers (IFI). (2006). Retrieved on February 1, 2009, from http://www.ifiworld.org/index.cfm?GPID=16

- International Interior Design Association (IIDA). (2009). IIDA Chapters. Retrieved on January 31, 2009, from http://www.iida.org/i4a/pages/index.cfm?pageid=176

- Japan Interior Designers' Association (JID). (2009). JID is . . .. Retrieved January 31, 2009, from http://www.jid.or.jp/index_en.shtml

- Kim, G. H. (2006). *The survival guide to architectural internship and career development.* New York: Wiley.

- Kwintessential (n/d). New Zealand: Culture, etiquette and customs. Retrieved on January 27, 2009, from http://www.kwintessential.co.uk/resources/global-etiquette/new-zealand.html

- Mideastweb Middle East. (2009). Middle East countries at a glance. Retrieved on January 25, 2009, from http://www.mideastweb.org/countries.htm

- Starovoitova, G. (1999). The state of religious freedom in Russia and the CIS. *International Religious Freedom Report.* January 25, 2009, from http://www.religiousfreedom.com/nwslttr/starovoytova.htm

- Stratfor. (2008, November 17). Russia: Pushing the Ruble. *Time, Inc.* Retrieved on January 25, 2009, from http://www.stratfor.com/analysis/20081117_russia_pushing_ruble

- Transparency International. (2009). Corruption perceptions index 2009. Retrieved on January 26, 2010, from http://www.transparency.org/policy_research/surveys_indices/cpi/2009/cpi_2009_table

- UNESCO. (2008). Latin America and the Caribbean. *Education: Cultural and Linguistic diversity in education.* Retrieved on January 8, 2009, from http://portal.unesco.org/education/en/ev.php-URL_ID=20798&URL_DO=DO_TOPIC&URL_SECTION=201.html

- U.S. Department of State: Diplomacy in Action (USDS-DA). (2009). *Countries and regions.* Retrieved on January 26, 2010, from http://www.state.gov/countries/

KEY TERMS

- chronological résumé
- combination, or hybrid, résumé
- cover letter
- electronic résumé
- functional résumé
- portfolio
- résumé

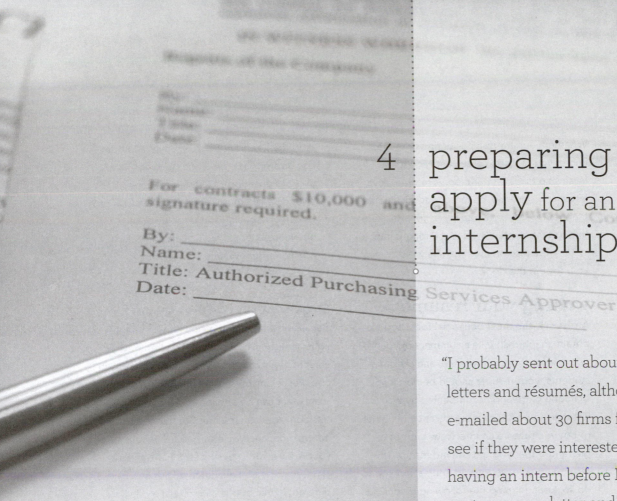

4 preparing to apply for an internship

"I probably sent out about 10 cover letters and résumés, although I e-mailed about 30 firms first to see if they were interested in having an intern before I actually sent my cover letter and résumé."

—K.F., who completed a three-month paid internship at a residential design firm

OBJECTIVES

- Write cover letters and résumés that clearly and concisely express your intent toward obtaining specific internships.

- Demonstrate innovation and creativity in the preparation of a portfolio.

- Develop a time management schedule for internship application.

Whether your internship is during or at the end of your college career, applying for an internship takes preparation. A résumé, cover letter, and portfolio are important documents that demonstrate your ability to communicate through the written word and through graphics.

They are also an essential first step to get your foot in the door.

writing your résumé

A **résumé**, the most beneficial tool used to obtain an internship, is a summary of your goals, education, experience, and skills. As students, your résumé should be no more than one page and accompanied by a cover letter. Its importance is significant in whether or not you receive an interview, but not a guarantee that you get the internship. The résumé must leave a good impression and to do so, keep in mind the following guidelines.

General Guidelines

Consider the following general guidelines as you write your résumé:

- Use light-colored paper as the background with black or dark ink. Pastel backgrounds and light-colored fonts make the résumé difficult to read and appear weaker because there is no dominant element.
- Be sure that your résumé fits into an 8-1/2-×-11-inch manila envelope. Unusual sizes may end up in the trash.
- Be creative, but the creative aspects must not detract from or cover up the content, i.e., your qualifications.
- Carefully proofread your résumé to be sure there are no spelling or grammatical errors.
- Be sure that your contact information appears in an easy-to-read font and is easily found.
- Use an easy-to-read and legible font throughout your résumé.

- Bold the headings so that they stand out.
- Use appropriate headings, such as "Objective," "Education," "Work Experience," "Honors/Activities," and "Additional Skills."
- Use single spacing but double space between sections, e.g., goals and education (Granger, 2010).

Organization of Your Résumé

Because the résumé is a summary that highlights your qualifications within a firm or your career field, it must be well organized and concise. Focus on your qualifications and achievements that can be applied to an internship position. Your résumé must contain current information, and you may need to reconstruct your résumé for a specific firm. For example, an internship at an architectural firm will have different expectations than one at a retail establishment, and, therefore, you will need to restate your objectives to fit the type of firm.

Basic Résumé Formats

The basic résumé formats are **chronological, functional, combination,** or **hybrid, résumés.**

CHRONOLOGICAL RÉSUMÉ: lists the education and experience in reverse order, from most recent to earliest.

FUNCTIONAL RÉSUMÉ: groups education and experience into sections categorized by skills or abilities, which are listed in order of importance rather than by date.

COMBINATION OR HYBRID RÉSUMÉ: combines features of the chronological and functional résumés. This type of résumé is used where more emphasis is placed on skills and abilities and less on education. The first portion is organized by skills with education listed last and in reverse chronological order.

Of these three types, the chronological résumé is the most common and preferred method for interns, and for this reason, this method will be used in this text.

Sections of Your Résumé

Sections in a chronological résumé include personal data, an objective, education, work experience, skills, honors and activities, and references. The following are guidelines for these sections of the résumé.

Personal Data

Personal data includes your name, street address, e-mail address, and phone numbers. As a student, you may need to include both permanent and local information. Do not include information about gender, age, marital status, race, or other personal data that is irrelevant to job performance, and remember that an employer cannot legally ask for this information. Including a photograph is not expected, and it is illegal for the employer to request one.

Objective

An objective is not required for an internship. However, if you choose to include one, it should be a concise and positive statement. It can be a short-term goal (e.g, "to obtain an internship") or possibly a long-term goal (e.g., "to gain experience for a career as an interior designer") that is specific to each position or firm type.

Education

The education section of your résumé should list your educational experience, beginning with your present institution, followed by your major, your minor (if relevant), and the degree you intend to earn. You may also include special courses related to your job objective. Your grade point average is not required. After

you have stated your current academic situation, follow this up by listing any previous academic institutions chronologically in reverse. Because you are a college student and working toward a degree, do not include high school information.

Work Experience

Information about your work experience is cited in this section and should relate to the internship you are seeking. For each work experience, state the business name, position title, and employment dates, followed by a brief description of duties or responsibilities.

Skills

For an internship, this is an important section that can inform the firm of your specific skills and abilities. Specific hand or computer skills are important to list here.

Honors and Activities

As a student, related professional information will most likely pertain honors (e.g., dean's list) and activities (i.e., organization and volunteer work) in college. In most cases, high school honors and activities are not included unless they are special or unusual, such as having volunteered for Habitat for Humanity. Membership in American Society of Interior Designers (ASID), International Interior Design Organization (IIDA), or others student organizations should be included. If you have held an office (president, secretary, or others), provide the title of your office and date you held the office.

References

References are managed by various methods. One method is to list references' names, street address, phone numbers, and e-mail addresses on a separate page. Another approach is to ask each reference to provide a general letter; in this case, simply state on the résumé, "References available upon request." Then prepare a list of references and their contact information, and be ready to provide it at the prospective employer's request. Regardless of the method used, be sure to ask for your references' permission before you add them onto your résumé. You may ask permission in person, on a phone call, or through an e-mail.

References must be current but should not include personal contacts such as family members or friends. Rather, references should include professors, academic advisors, organizational advisors, employers, or those who would provide positive information and are knowledgeable about your various abilities and character, such as a coach or a clergyman. Professors will know your design skills and abilities. Professors, academic advisors, and employers will also know your work ethic, ability to perform tasks and work with others, and other work-related abilities. Organizational advisors know your abilities to interact with others in a variety of situations.

A résumé worksheet and checklist will guide the development of your résumé (see Tables 4.1 and 4.2; downloadable from the CD-ROM as Appendices H and I). For an example of a successful internship résumé, see Figure 4.1. The order of the résumé by Lara Holt (Figure 4.1) is Objective, Education, Work Experience, Activities (extracurricular involvement), Skills (e.g., computer software proficiency), and Design Classes (a list a major courses relevant to the sought-after job). Amanda Williamson's résumé (see Student Portfolios on the CD-ROM) begins in a similar manner but lists work experience with the most recent first. This résumé also includes images that create a mini-portfolio and résumé in one. When developing her portfolio as a senior, Williamson began with her original internship résumé but expanded this idea of combining images with the written word (see Student Portfolios on the CD-ROM).

Electronic Résumé

An **electronic résumé** is developed using the same format and provides the same information. However, the difference is that it will be transmitted by fax or as an e-mail attachment. As with the standard résumé, it is prepared using the computer and may or may not include graphic electronic images. You can scan or save the résumé as a PDF file. You can then e-mail it directly to prospective employers upon request. The advantages of converting the résumé into a PDF file are that it is more difficult to alter, can be transmitted as an e-mail attachment, and can be opened on any computer. If placing your résumé on a website, use only your e-mail address and no physical address to ensure your personal safety and security.

TABLE 4.1 (ALSO APPENDIX H)

Preparing Your First Résumé Worksheet

RÉSUMÉ WORKSHEET

After reviewing this chapter's discussion of résumé writing, complete this worksheet using your own information. You will then be able to complete a résumé using each of the formats described in this chapter.

1. CONTACT INFORMATION:

....

Name

....

Address: Current

....

Address: Permanent

....

Phone, e-mail, and other

2. OBJECTIVE/PROFESSIONAL SUMMARY:

....

Type of position, firm, and a possible brief description

3. EDUCATION:

....

Reverse order

....

Course highlights or related courses

4. WORK EXPERIENCE:

....

Experience: full-time, part-time, summer, and design-related work experience

5. SKILLS:

....

Computer/software knowledge, language fluency, technical skills

6. HONORS AND ACTIVITIES:

....

When applying for an internship, the list of honors and activities will most likely be related to college or academics:

....

Dean's list, honor societies, certification, publication, professional/honorary organization membership, offices held, volunteer work

7. REFERENCES
References available upon request

Source: Kendall, G. T. (2005).

Designing your business: Strategies

for interior design professionals.

New York: Fairchild Books.

LARA

HOLT

Lara Holt
[E-mail]
[Address]
[City, State ZIP]
[Phone Number]

OBJECTIVE

To participate in a summer internship to gain experience in my field of interest of interior design.

EDUCATION

South Dakota State University
Student B.S. Major: Interior Design
Expected Graduation Date: Unknown
Other B.S. Major: Buisness
GPA: 2.721

WORK EXPERIENCE

May 2004 - April 2005
K-Mart - Cashier

December 2004 - August 2005
Prostrollo Motor Sales - Secretary

June 2007 - Present
Walmart - Cashier and Customer Service

ACTIVITIES

ASID Student Member 2007-2008 School Year
ASID Historian 2008-2009 School Year

SKILLS

Macintosh and PC   Learning:
Vectorworks   Revit
Microsoft Word   SketchUp
Microsoft Powerpoint
Microsoft Excel

DESIGN CLASSES

ID-150 Intro to Interior Design I   ID-319 Building Systems I
ID-151 Intro to Interior Design II   ID-320 Lighting and Acoustics
ID-215 Materials   ID-322 Interior Design Studio III
ID-222 Interior Design Studio I   ID-490 Sustainable Issues
ID-223 Interior Design Studio II   Art-121 Design I 2D
ID-224 History of Interiors   Arth-100 Art Appreciation
ID-231 Computer Aided Design   AM-242 Textiles I

References Upon Request

COVER LETTER

Lara Holt
[Address]
[City, State ZIP]
[Phone Number]

February 22, 2009

Sharon Burt
Crestwood
601 East Water Well Road
Salina, KS 67401

Dear Sharon Burt,

For the last three years, I have been a student at South Dakota State University, in Brookings, SD in the Interior Design program. At this point in my education I seek the chance to apply for an Internship for this coming us summer.

During my education experience, I have participated in many school activities. Such as being a member of ASID for two years and out of those two years, I have obtained the position of Historian on the executive board. I have also attended International Market Square (IMS) in Minneapolis Minnesota for the last two years.

As stated in my Resume, I have worked mostly in retail over the past five years. I have worked as a cashier at both K-mart and Wal-Mart in Huron. I also worked as a secretary for a car dealership. There I was responsible for answering the phones filing invoices for any car work a customer had done. I have experience in using Microsoft Word, PowerPoint and Excel. The computer programs I have worked with are Vectorworks and after the semester is finished in May, I will have experience with Revit.

I want to thank you for your time and I hope to meet with you personally or by phone for an interview. I may be in Kansas over my spring break March 10 through the 14 if schedule allows or phone interview would be desired if not able to make it. Attached are my resume and parts of my portfolio. I thank you for your consideration and I hope to hear from you soon.

Sincerely yours,

Lara Holt

Lara Holt

FIGURE 4.1 This student's résumé and cover letter were designed to gain an internship. Note how she placed the headings vertically on her résumé to display creativity.

LARA HOLT

TABLE 4.2 (ALSO APPENDIX I)

Résumé Checklist

Résumé of ....

Rate the résumé on the following points, scoring from a low of 1 to a high of 3 in each of the categories listed. Then score and compare your rating against the highest possible total score of 30. Write comments for each category receiving a score of fewer than 3.

	ITEM	SCORE 1	2	3	HOW IT COULD BE IMPROVED
1	**Overall appearance:** Do you want to read it: Is the typeface easily readable?				
2	**Layout:** Does the résumé look professional, well typed and printed, with adequate margins, and so on. Do key sales points stand out? Is it chronological?				
3	**Length:** If it were shortened, could the résumé tell the same story?				
4	**Relevance:** Has extraneous material been eliminated?				
5	**Writing Style:** Is it easy to get a picture of the applicant's qualifications?				
6	**Action Orientation:** Do sentences and paragraphs begin with action verbs?				
7	**Specificity:** Does the résumé avoid generalities and focus on specific information about experience, project, products, and so on?				
8	**Accomplishments:** Has the applicant quantified accomplishments and problem-solving skills?				
9	**Completeness:** Is all important information included?				
10	**Bottom Line:** How well does the résumé accomplish its ultimate purpose of getting the employer to invite the applicant in for an interview?				

Rating Point Total   **(maximum of 30)**

Source: Granger, M. (2004). *The fashion intern.* New York: Fairchild Books.

If peer-reviewed, this question may be asked:
"What are some other ways that you would suggest to improve this résumé?"

Pitfalls in Résumé Writing

It is easy to get caught up in writing the résumé and forget the problems that may occur. The top ten pitfalls in résumé writing include:

1. Obviously generic: the employer should feel that you are interested in their firm by stating the objective appropriate to the particular internship position and firm.
2. Too long: if possible, a one-page résumé is best.
3. Typographical, grammatical, or spelling errors: have someone proofread your résumé.
4. Hard to read: use a font style that is easy to read; the font size should be no smaller than 10 point. Bullets, underlining, asterisks, and bold highlighting should be limited.
5. Too verbose: be concise and to the point.
6. Too sparse: provide enough information: describe your skills, accomplishments, activities, awards, honors, and other relevant information.
7. Irrelevant information: do not include personal information (ages, weight, height, and so on) or dated information such as high-school activities.
8. Too snazzy: do not use unusual fonts, outlandish paper, unnecessary graphics, or personal photos.
9. Boring: use action verbs and terminology that demonstrates good communication skills. (See Box 4.1.)
10. Too modest: this is the time to brag about your abilities and sell yourself (Granger, 2010).

BOX 4.1
résumé power words

Abstracted	Appointed	Budgeted	Completed
Accomplished	Appraised	Built	Composed
Achieved	Approved	Calculated	Computed
Acquired	Arbitrated	Cared	Conceived
Acted	Arranged	Catalogued	Condensed
Adapted	Ascertained	Chaired	Conducted
Addressed	Assembled	Charged	Conserved
Administered	Assessed	Chartered	Consolidated
Advanced to*	Assisted	Checked	Constructed
Advised	Assumed	Clarified	Consulted
Advertised	Attained	Classified	Contracted
Advocated	Audited	Coached	Contributed
Aided	Augmented	Collaborated	Contrived
Allocated	Authored	Collected	Controlled
Amplified	Awarded	Comforted	Converted
Analyzed	Bargained	Commended	Cooperated
Answered	Began	Communicated	Coordinated
Anticipated	Broadened	Compared	Copied
Applied	Brought	Compiled	Correlated

* "Advanced to" rather than "promoted to"

BOX 4.1 (CONTINUED)
résumé power words

Counseled	Evaluated	Improved	Merged
Created	Examined	Improvised	Met
Crisis-solving	Exceeded	Increased	Minimized
Critiqued	Excelled	Indicated	Modeled
Dealt	Executed	Influenced	Moderated
Decided	Exhibited	Initiated	Modified
Defined	Expanded	Inspected	Monitored
Delegated	Expedited	Inspired	Motivated
Delivered	Experienced	Installed	Narrated
Demonstrated	Experimented	Instituted	Negotiated
Designed	Explained	Instructed	Nominated
Detailed	Explored	Integrated	Observed
Detected	Expressed	Interpreted	Obtained
Determined	Extended	Interviewed	Offered
Developed	Extracted	Introduced	Operated
Devised	Fabricated	Invented	Ordered
Devoted	Facilitated	Inventoried	Organized
Diagnosed	Fashioned	Investigated	Oriented
Directed	Financed	Judged	Originated
Discovered	Fixed	Justified	Overcame
Discriminated	Focused	Kept	Overhauled
Dispatched	Followed	Launched	Oversaw
Dispensed	Formed	Learned	Participated
Displayed	Formulated	Lectured	Perceived
Dissected	Fortified	Led	Perfected
Distributed	Fostered	Licensed	Performed
Documented	Founded	Lifted	Persuaded
Doubled	Gained	Listed	Pioneered
Drafted	Gathered	Listened	Planned
Drove	Gave	Located	Predicted
Earned**	Generated	Logged	Prepared
Edited	Governed	Made	Presented
Effected	Graduated	Maintained	Preserved
Eliminated	Guided	Managed	Presided
Emerged	Handled	Manipulated	Previewed
Employed	Harmonized	Mapped	Prioritized
Enabled	Headed	Mastered	Processed
Encouraged	Helped	Maximized	Produced
Enforced	Identified	Mediated	Programmed
Ensured	Illustrated	Medicated	Proposed
Established	Imagined	Meditated	Protected
Estimated	Implemented	Mentored	Proved

** "Earned" rather than "was given" indicates a person who does things rather than receives them (Granger, 2004)

Résumé Checklist

A résumé checklist can help you write your résumé. Table 4.2 has been designed specifically to evaluate résumés. By following the guidelines provided in this chapter and covered in the checklist—including eliminating the pitfalls, using power words, and reviewing your résumé—you will create a dynamic résumé of your own.

writing your cover letter

A **cover letter** is a method of marketing yourself to your prospective internship supervisor. It allows you to "introduce yourself in such a way that the employer, hopefully, will have no alternative but to read your résumé and call you for an interview immediately" (Piotrowski, 2003 * 2008, p. 595).

BOX 4.1 (CONTINUED)
résumé power words

Provided	Related	Sold	Tasted
Publicized	Relied	Solicited	Taught
Published	Remodeled	Solved	Revised and tested
Purchased	Reorganized	Specialized	Theorized
Queried	Reported	Stimulated	Timed
Questioned	Represented	Strategized	Trained
Raised	Researched	Streamlined	Transferred
Ran	Reshaped	Strengthened	Translated
Ranked	Responded	Stressed	Troubleshooting
Rationalized	Responsible for	Studied	Tutored
Read	Restored	Substantiated	Unified
Reasoned	Revamped	Substituted	Unison
Received	Reviewed	Succeeded	Updated
Recommended	Revised	Suggested	Upgraded
Reconciled	Scanned	Summarized	Used
Recorded	Scheduled	Supervised	Utilized
Recruited	Screened	Supervisor	Validated
Rectified	Selected	Supported	Verified
Rendered	Served	Surveyed	Volunteered
Reduced	Set goals	Sustained	Widened
Reestablished	Set up	Symbolized	Won
Referred	Shaped	Synthesized	Worked
Rehearsed	Simplified	Tabulated	Wrote
Reinforced	Sketched	Talked	

It is in the cover letter where you point out specific skills that the firm is seeking as well as express your personal interest in the firm. Therefore, the cover letter must be written to the specific firm and, even though some portions are the same within each cover letter, it must sound as though it were written expressly to that firm (Piotrowski, 2003 & 2008).

Organization of Your Cover Letter

Because the cover letter weighs heavily on whether it is read or not, it must not only be well written but also well organized. The cover letter is generally only one page in length. Your letter must capture the reader's attention and encourage him or her to read your résumé and call you for an interview. There are several ways to make this happen.

- Use good business writing techniques and include contact information, appropriate headings, and contents (discussed in the following section).
- Write in a formal manner (Dear Mr. or Ms.).
- Use correct spelling and excellent grammar.
- Create your own professional-looking letterhead.

Sections of Your Cover Letter

Sections of a cover letter include a return address, date, inside address, and salutation; body of letter, including the introductory request, specific information, and closing paragraph with contact information and action statement; and signature.

Return Address

Your return address may be included in your creative letterhead, or it may be written on the top left side of the cover letter. If creating your own letterhead, remember it is a formal document and must appear as such.

Date, Inside Address, and Salutation

This section must begin with the current date. If you are using an existing format, be sure to change the date each time you revise the letter. The inside address is the prospective employer's name and address and must be correct to reach the individual. Then, the salutation must have the name of the person to whom the letter is addressed and written in a formal manner, such as Dear Mr./Mrs./Ms. If you do not know who should receive the letter, your research of the firm should provide that information. Never address it to "whom it may concern" or "Personnel Office."

Body of Letter

The cover letter contains three to four paragraphs. Begin with an introductory request in the first paragraph, followed by the body of the letter (one or two paragraphs), and a closing paragraph with contact information and an action statement.

INTRODUCTORY REQUEST The first paragraph should attract the reader's attention and concisely state the letter's purpose. It must express enthusiasm and interest in the position and firm. Here are a few tips for the introductory paragraph:

1. State the purpose of the letter (internship).
2. Give the employer information about the position for which you are applying. (This may or may not be applicable with an internship.)
3. State where you learned of the position (advertisement, employee of firm, professional organization, or another source). If you know someone in the firm or know a connection to the firm, mention who you know (their name, position, and firm).

SPECIFIC INFORMATION The body of the letter may be one or two paragraphs and should contain specific information about your skills, abilities, and interests in the position. Here are a few tips for the body of the letter:

1. State why you are interested in the position.
2. State why you are interested in this particular firm.
3. State the date you will be available to begin the internship.
4. Highlight your skills and abilities as selling points.

Remember that other interior design students will be seeking internships; therefore, you need to distinguish yourself from the others by pointing out your special skills, activities, experiences, courses, and other specialties. Think about what you have done (coursework, travel, special abilities, or something unique) that sets you apart from other interior design students. In other words, most can state that they are qualified, so consider your uniqueness as an interior designer. Clearly, this is the most important paragraph or paragraphs of the entire letter.

CLOSING PARAGRAPH The closing statement is a thank you and wrap-up statement that must be concise. Here are a few tips for the closing paragraph.

1. Thank them for their time.
2. Indicate a desire for a personal interview.
3. If you are going to be in their city at a specific date and time, state that you will call to set up an interview during that time.
4. State if you will be calling back to learn the decision on a specific date or if you will wait for their phone.

5. Indicate if a résumé is enclosed and express a willingness to provide further information, if desired, such as credentials, portfolio, or references.
6. End with a statement similar to: "Thank you for your consideration" or similar wording.

Signature

Add a closing greeting such as "Sincerely" and, after four spaces, type your full name. Include "Enclosure" (or "Enc.") at the end of the letter to indicate that you are sending something with the letter such as a résumé.

Cover Letter Worksheet

A cover letter worksheet will guide you through the development of your cover letter (see Table 4.3; downloadable as Appendix J). See Figure 4.1 for an example of a successful cover letter. A cover letter checklist can be used to evaluate cover letters and, therefore, can help you in creating a cover letter that meets important criteria (see Table 4.4; downloadable as Appendix K on the CD-ROM). In Box 4.2, successful former interns share their experiences sending résumés and cover letters.

preparing a portfolio

Many interior design programs are now dedicating an entire course to portfolio development, which underscores the importance of the portfolio. Compiling a portfolio is a time-consuming but necessary and crucial part of obtaining employment—whether an entry-level position or an internship. A **portfolio** is not only a set of images, but also a visual synopsis of work completed that demonstrates your creative and technical skills and capabilities as an interior designer. When a portfolio has been created, it becomes an ongoing, progressive work completed in college to be continually updated throughout your career.

TABLE 4.3 (ALSO APPENDIX J)

Cover Letter Worksheet

Use this template to draft a résumé cover letter

Your name:

Your address:

Area code and phone number:

E-mail address:

Other contact information as appropriate:

Date:

Title and name of person to whom you are applying:

Name/title of company to which you are applying:

Company/office address:

City, state ZIP code:

Dear Mr./Ms.:

The first paragraph should tell the reader:

1. Why you are writing ("In response to your [advertisement, website posting, etc.], this letter is . . .).

2. What you are seeking (". . . to show my interest in and application for . . .").

3. The specific position you are interested in
   ("the position of [use the specific position title used by employer] . . .").

4. Your ability to practice interior design relevant to the state in which your registration/license will be held.

5. How you heard about the position ("I read of this opportunity . . .").

The body of the letter (two to three paragraphs, unless you have extensive experience to note) should spell out for the reader not only your education and experience, but also how they directly relate to the available position. One way to approach this may be to:

1. Explain how your formal education is appropriate for the position
   ("I have earned a bachelor of arts degree in interior design, as required in the posting").

   Explain further details about your education, such as honors or awards.

2. Explain how your previous internship experiences are appropriate for the position
   ("As an intern with Co. X, I gained experience relevant to this position by doing . . .").

3. Explain how your early formal work experience is appropriate for the position
   ("While working as a [name position], I performed the following tasks
   that enable me to perform this position's tasks of . . .").

4. Explain how your recent work experience is appropriate for the position
   ("As manager of projects similar to those referenced in the position, I . . .").

5. Address any concerns that might be provoked by your résumé or that you otherwise need to address.
   (This may be necessary if there are considerable gaps in your work history, for example.)

The final paragraph should include the following:

1. Thank the readers for their time and interest.

2. Express your availability for an interview, either in person or on the telephone.

3. Add a conclusion, such as "Sincerely" or "Thanking you for your consideration."

4. Leave space for your signature.

5. Write your signature.

6. Type your full name.

Add the following notation when sending a résumé.

   Enclosure: résumé

Source: Kendall, G. T. (2005). *Designing your business: Strategies for interior design professionals.* New York: Fairchild Books.

TABLE 4.4 (ALSO APPENDIX K)

Cover Letter Checklist

Cover Letter of ....

Rate the cover letter on the following points, scoring from a low of 1 to a high of 3 in each of the categories listed. Then score and compare your rating against the highest possible total score of 30. Write comments for each category receiving a score of fewer than 3.

ITEM	SCORE 1	2	3	HOW IT COULD BE IMPROVED
1 **Organization of cover letter:** Is it in a businesslike format?				
2 **Relevance to the design firm:** Can you determine if the firm was researched?				
3 **Source of information regarding the position:** Was the source stated?				
4 **Use key words or phrases to catch the review's attention:** Are key words found that relate to being a valuable part of the team?				
5 **Clarity of employment history:** Is there reference to being part of an important project or position that qualifies s/he for the position?				
6 **Good communication skills:** Does the letter demonstrate good written skills with no spelling and grammar errors?				
7 **Creative writing:** If too creative and wordy, is s/he covering up the truth?				
8 **Achievement:** Does s/he show a proven level of accomplishments?				
9 **Care and thought:** Did s/he state when they are available? Was s/he appreciative of the reader's time? Is there attention to detail?				
10 **Neatness:** Was the cover letter neat and professionally presented when received?				

Rating Point Total **(maximum of 30)**

If peer-reviewed, this question may be asked:

"What are some other ways that you would suggest to improve this cover letter?"

Ideas from sources:

Granger, M. (2004). *The fashion intern.* New York: Fairchild Books.

Piotrowski, C. M. (2003). *Professional practices for interior designers* (3rd ed.). Hoboken, New Jersey: Wiley.

BOX 4.2

sending résumés and cover letters

The following interns responded to all Field Experience questions in this chapter:

C.S. completed an unpaid ten-week internship in an interior design, remodeling, and building firm. She graduated from a large public university in a Southwestern city.

E.C. completed a paid three-month internship with an architectural firm. She graduated from a large public university in a Southwestern city.

E.J. completed an eight-week internship at an interior architectural firm. She graduated from a private university in a large Southern city.

J.E. interned at an interior design firm specializing in high-end residential interiors and hospitality design. She graduated from a private college in a large Midwestern city.

J.H. *(international internship)* completed her 12-week unpaid internship at a residential design firm in Buenos Aries, Argentina. She graduated with a double major of interior design and Spanish from a large public university in the Midwest.

J.L. completed a two-and-a-half-month, full-time internship at a commercial design firm in Illinois. She graduated from a private college in a large Midwestern city.

K.B. completed a paid eight-week internship at a commercial design firm that focused on healthcare interiors. She graduated from a private university in a large Southern city.

L.O. completed an unpaid four-day-per-week summer internship at a high-end residential firm. She graduated from a private university in a large Southern city.

M.A. completed a paid two-month internship at a high-end kitchen cabinetry manufacturer. She graduated from a large public university in a Southwestern city.

M.R. completed her seven-week paid internship at an architectural firm between her junior and senior years. She graduated from a large university in a Midwestern city.

M.S. completed an unpaid two-and-a-half-month part-time (20-30 hours per week) internship at furniture dealership. She graduated from a private university in a large Southern city.

S.C. completed a 200-hour unpaid internship in a high-end residential interior design firm. She graduated from a large public university in a Southern city.

S.M. completed an unpaid five-month internship at a high-end residential firm. She graduated from a private college in a large Midwestern city.

T.H. completed two paid internships—one in an architectural firm and the other for a furniture dealership. She graduated from a large public university in a Southwestern city.

Traditional Portfolios

The traditional portfolio contains original presentation boards, material boards, construction documents, and more. Because projects are loose, all must be carried in a presentation or portfolio case. Frequently, the size of boards often requires a large portfolio case, which is also difficult to transport, particularly on an airplane.

Digital Portfolios

The digital portfolio is less cumbersome with no loose pieces and can be much smaller, making it easier to transport. Digital portfolios are created by scanning hard copies of drawing or perspectives or converting CAD drawing into jpegs. Then, jpegs are used to create documents that are saved into PDF files. PowerPoint presentations can also be used, but there may be e-mailing challenges due to the size of files; typically, this in not recommended. Linking and directing the viewer through PowerPoint presentations does not interact as well as the PDF files.

Your digital portfolio files can be burned onto CD-ROMs and uploaded onto personal websites. These files can also be e-mailed to employers; however, be sure that they can access and navigate files easily (Kendall, 2004).

Web-Based Portfolios

You may also choose to create a web-based electronic portfolio. Compared to other electronic portfolios, the web-based portfolio is easy to access for anyone, anywhere and allows the viewer (prospective employer or human resource personnel) to access your work instantly. It also eliminates the need to e-mail large PDF files or send a CD that may contain incompatible documents.

BOX 4.2 (CONTINUED)
sending résumés and cover letters

How many résumés and cover letters did you send?

E.C.: "I sent out ten hard copies and then I started calling firms asking if they would be interested in hiring an intern before sending résumés and cover letters. I must have called over 50 firms and sent out about 20 more résumés and cover letters."

J.H. *(international intern):* "I sent one résumé and two cover letters. One basic, normal, cover letter and another that just explained my experience with interior design. I had to send the second one because the companies in Argentina were afraid because I had not had that much experience. So they wanted to know what skills I had learned in school, on other jobs, and with extracurricular activities."

M.A.: "I sent out around 80 résumés, cover letters, and work samples via e-mail to the HR departments of firms I was interested in interning for (most were not advertising an open position). I also sent about ten via e-mail to direct contacts at firms I had visited when on a study tour earlier that year."

In your résumé and cover letter, you should place your URL, or website address, with your other contact information unless it better fits somewhere else in the design of these documents.

Why the Web?

Web-based portfolios have several advantages. In addition to easy and immediate viewer access as noted previously, electronic access lets your viewer simply point and click to select what they want to see rather than scrolling through an entire portfolio on a CD or flipping through a printed copy. You can also link other forms of electronic media by sending your viewer to an electronic walk-through, video clips, article rotation, and more.

Websites allow you to customize how the viewer navigates your site and add links to other websites, such as your university or department website where the viewer can see curriculum details and other relevant information.

Building Your Site

The greatest challenge is the learning curve. Most colleges and universities have technology services available to assist you, but you will want to locate a model/ template or format you find appealing and easy to use. Some website domains are available for free through some resources whereas others are available at a small cost. Web engines such as sites.google.com or wix.com can be self-selected. The web host you choose will depend on how much you are able to invest in time and money and how much material and features you want to include on your site.

Before you begin creating your website, review several existing websites—especially local, regional, national, and international interior design firm websites and individual websites—and note what makes them successful and not so successful. Prior to venturing out on the web to create personal websites, you will need to create a template (word processing or presentation document) to develop a home page. But first, you must determine how you would like your home page to look and how you would like to link and organize the pages. This helps you begin to organize and look at the portfolio through a different way.

To help you organize a web-based portfolio, you can ask professionals to review your work and offer suggestions. Before sharing your site with potential firms, it's also a good idea to send its link to friends, fellow students, and family (especially grandparents or other stereotypically technology-challenged individuals) to see how easy or difficult it is to navigate.

On the CD-ROM that accompanies this book, you will find an excellent example of a web-based portfolio by Maddie Mcfarland, who developed it as a student at North Dakota State University.

Putting the Portfolio to Practice

More examples of portfolios are included on the CD-ROM that accompanies this book. Refer to them as you read over their descriptions as follows and be sure to read through the notes included on the last page of each example on the CD-ROM.

Running Concepts through the Portfolio

The portfolios of Katie Logan and Alex Rae Hosner were created in a class that was dedicated to internship preparation. Both present a concept that runs throughout their portfolios.

Single Page Portfolios

Michelle Ralston portfolios are single-page examples—one for commercial projects and one for residential projects.

The "Teaser" Portfolio

Often one or more pages of an electronic portfolio are sent as a "teaser" along with the cover letter and résumé. The interview then becomes the time to show your complete portfolio. The portfolios of Emily Broekmeier and Amber Gustafson are examples of teaser pages.

Post-Senior-Year-Internship Portfolios

Some students apply for internships after the senior year. In that case, the portfolio should be more extensive. It must show a variety of work such as hand sketching, hand and computer rendering, process drawings, detailing, commercial and residential projects, and more. Kayleigh Boucher's portfolio represents this type of portfolio.

The Full-Time-Employment Résumé/Portfolio Page

An internship résumé can also be the starting point for a full-time-employment résumé/portfolio page. Shown in the Student Portfolios on the CD-ROM, Amanda Williamson's 8-½-×-11-inch internship résumé was expanded into an 11-×-17-inch résumé/portfolio page. This résumé is printed front and back and folded into the 8-½- ×-11-inch size. The image, which was taken on a travel study to New York, was used on the cover of both the résumé and portfolio and became a good conversation piece for employers.

Portfolio Checklist

A checklist for portfolio content is included in Table 4.5 (Appendix L on the CD-ROM). This checklist may be adapted to meet your individual presentation needs. In Box 4.3, interns share their experiences with portfolios geared towards the internship.

TABLE 4.5 (ALSO APPENDIX L)

Portfolio Checklist

Does your portfolio contain items similar to the following?

An entire project from early sketches to completed renderings, including programming and schematic development references

Freehand sketches showing how you reached specific design conclusions

CAD renderings

Perspective and elevation drawings; isometrics

Furniture-placement floor plans; space-planning drawings

Color boards

Evidence of lettering abilities

A copy of your résumé

portfolios

Refer to Box 4.7 for
background on the
interns who responded
to the questions below.

Did you need a portfolio? If you brought one with you to the interview, what type did you bring—traditional or digital?

C.S.: "I brought my traditional to the interview but sent out my digital."

E.C.: "I sent a work sample page with my résumé and brought the portfolio in upon request."

K.B.: "I brought a traditional portfolio to my interview and had to e-mail my résumé to them afterwards."

J.E.: "I did not need a portfolio until the interview portion. I did not bring a portfolio. The original copies of my work seemed to impress the interviewers enough. (I did organize my work before the interview.)"

J.L.: "I provided both full traditional and digital portfolio samples."

S.M.: "I brought a traditional portfolio to my interview, but they did not ask to see it."

T.H.: "I needed an electronic portfolio for the architecture firm. I brought my work examples to the interview to show to them."

Did you send your portfolio with a résumé, or did you send it only when asked to do so?

J.E: "I sent a work sample with my résumé without being asked to do so—a single-page Word doc/PDF with two renderings and respective floor plans."

E.J.: "I sent a digital example, like a teaser, of my work but never my actual résumé. I also gave the link to my website that showed my work."

J.H. (international intern): "I sent a digital portfolio only when asked to do so. Reason being, I submitted all my documents (applications) online, and there was not a spot to submit a portfolio or extra documents. I wish I had submitted it to them via e-mail right away. I think it would have helped move the process along more quickly, but I didn't and everything worked out."

J.L.: "Digital provided upon request. Traditional presented at each interview."

M.A.: "I sent my portfolio only when asked to do so, but I did send a work sample to most places with the initial cover letter and résumé."

S.M.: "I brought a traditional portfolio to my interview, but they did not ask to see it."

M.S.: "I created a website and included my link in my cover letter that I mailed out to the firms."

L.O.: "I sent little teasers the size of a postcard. No one asked for me to send it before the interview."

S.C.: "I sent in my résumé and e-mailed a PowerPoint presentation as a preview of my portfolio. Then, at the interview, I presented my portfolio."

summary

A cover letter, résumé, and portfolio are necessary documents to obtain an internship. These three items will highlight your best abilities in a concise and professional manner. The cover letter will capture your prospective employer's attention and entice them to grant you an interview. Along with a well-versed cover letter, you will need a neat, creative, and easy-to read résumé that covers all applicable information that pertains to the internship position. This résumé should also be modified and placed in a portfolio to take with you to an interview. Be selective of the projects placed in a portfolio because they will lend an employer an insight into your true abilities. These projects should reflect many aspects of design (from programming to schematic design to final presentation and construction documents) with an emphasis on that company's niche. You can download each of these documents from the CD-ROM (Appendices H through L).

Preparation of these documents will take time, and advance preparation is necessary. Start at least six months in advance in preparation to apply for any domestic internship and at least twelve months in advance for any international inquiries. Create a schedule that includes personal deadlines for when your résumé, cover letter, portfolio, and electronic copies should be complete; this will greatly aid in a smooth process. All of these documents must be modified to fit the firm at the time of application; however, a generalized version will be beneficial when beginning to research companies.

achieving chapter objectives

Review the Chapter Objectives at the beginning of this chapter.
You are now ready to put them into practice:

preparing to apply for your internship

Prepare the appropriate documents needed to apply for an internship:

1. Write a résumé.

2. Write a generic cover letter.

3. Prepare an electronic portfolio.

time management

Preparing for the internship takes careful thought and time. Here is a list of steps as well as a timeline suggestion for a timely completion.

1. Develop a résumé a minimum of six months prior to a domestic internship.

2. Develop a résumé a minimum of 12 months prior to an international internship.

3. As you complete your résumé, develop a cover letter (generic), but prepare to make adjustments to coincide with each firm.

4. Select work for your portfolio. Develop a method of organizing the projects by skill, project type, or another type of category. Create a PDF file of work and burn CDs for mailing. While you are developing the résumé, begin organizing your work and developing the portfolio; however, plan for additional pieces of work as needed.

REFERENCES

- Granger, M. (2010). *The fashion intern* (2nd ed.). New York: Fairchild Books.

- Kendall, G. T. (2005). *Designing your business: Strategies for interior design professionals.* New York: Fairchild Books.

- Kim, G. H. (2006). *The survival guide to architectural internship and career development.* Hoboken, New Jersey: Wiley.

- Piotrowski, C. M. (2003). *Professional practice for interior designers* (3rd ed.). Hoboken, New Jersey: Wiley.

- Piotrowski, C. M. (2008). *Professional practice for interior designers* (4th ed.). Hoboken, New Jersey: Wiley.

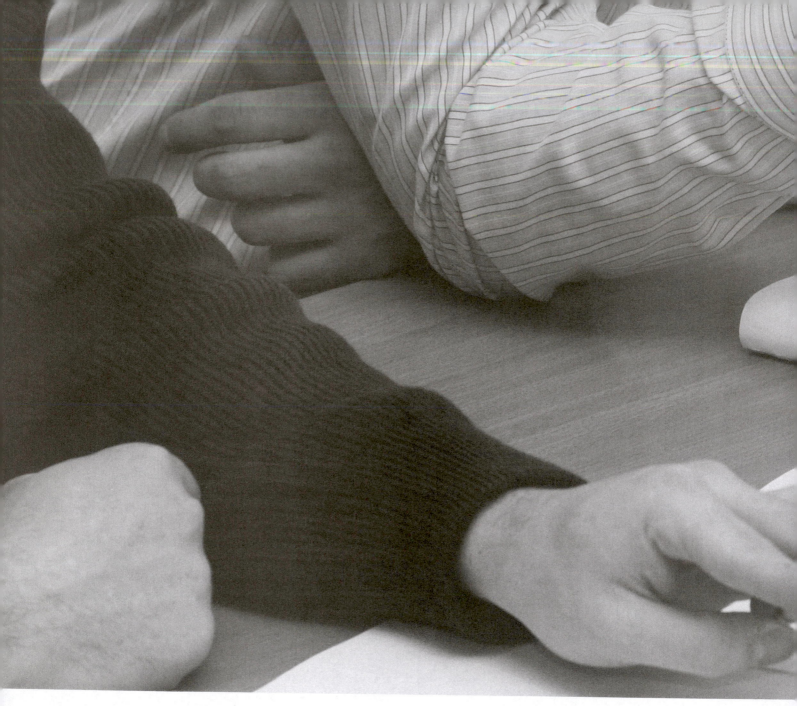

KEY TERMS

- conversational-style interview
- interview
- interviewee
- interviewer
- job application
- situational interview or case study interviews
- stress interview
- team interview

5 preparing for the interview

"I believe I was in the interview for 45 minutes before she offered me the internship on the spot. We had great chemistry—and after all the other interviews I had—I knew this was the right internship for me."

—A.W., who completed a seven-week internship at a residential design firm.

OBJECTIVES

- Thoroughly research the firm where the interview will take place.

- Develop questions concerning the firm and your position to better understand a possible employer.

- Review possible interview questions.

- Develop important listening skills through mock interviews.

- Understand the dos and don'ts of the interview.

- Research, analyze, and select appropriate business attire for an interview.

- Evaluate an interview afterwards.

- Be able to constructively handle rejection.

- Evaluate an internship offer.

- Determine how to negotiate an offer.

- Determine possible ways to accept an offer.

- Develop an interview-preparation time management schedule.

After completing your résumé and cover letter, the next step is to secure an **interview** and an internship. Before the interview, you must be well prepared. You might be caught off guard if you don't know what to expect or don't anticipate possible questions.

research

Prior to preparing for the interview, you will have researched the firm where the interview will take place. However, because you will probably research a number of firms, review the research and update any information needed. Some good ways to review and update your information include:

- If you know someone who is at or familiar with the firm, talk with them about the organization.
- Obtain and read company literature.
- Visit the firm's website and view its online portfolio.
- Know the services the firm offers and the type of projects it has completed or is currently working on.
- Know where the firm's offices are located. If there are regional offices, know their locations.
- Think of questions to ask about the firm during the interview (Granger, 2004).

the **job application form**

Though a résumé has been completed, some employers also require applicants to complete a **job application;** this is often completed before the interview. Most job applications have similar information required such as personal data, education, past work experience, and references; however, the order may vary and further details may be required. Most often these applications cannot be taken home; therefore, you will need to bring along an information sheet to accurately complete the form. Additionally, job applications vary, so read the directions thoroughly (Granger, 2006).

An **interview** is the next step in the application process. The interview is an opportunity for the **interviewer** (representative from the firm) to question and evaluate the **interviewee** (the person applying for the position). This can be most stressful; therefore, to have a low-stress and successful interview, preparation is essential (Granger, 2006). It may help to remember that the interviewer's intent is not to create a stressful situation, but to find the best possible intern for their firm (Piotrowski, 2003), and that you are also interviewing the firm as much as they are interviewing you (Kim, 2006). Both approaches reveal the importance of preparing for the interview.

interview guidelines

Preparing for the interview is as important as the interview itself. A successful interview includes practice, self-assessment, research (found earlier in this chapter), and planning ahead.

Practice

The adage "practice makes perfect" will create the perfect interview. The best interview occurs with practice—practice meeting the interviewer, practice with different interviewing styles, practice answering interview questions, practice asking questions of the interviewer, practice responding to illegal questions (discussed later in this chapter), practice your dress and your behavior (also discussed later in this chapter), and practice the conclusion of the interview.

In other words, "Practice, practice, practice!"

Meeting the Interviewer

The interviewer will most likely greet you with a handshake (Piotrowski, 2003). Thus, be prepared to shake his or her hand by carrying your portfolio in your left and having your right hand free. The interviewer will probably say, "Hello, I'm ___," and you should respond with a smile, say hello, and introduce yourself.

Frequently, you will be escorted to a conference room or the interviewer's office. Wait for the interviewer to indicate where to sit. If not, select "a chair that is either directly across from the interview or at a 90-degree angle" (p. 604). These positions are best for viewing your portfolio and maintaining eye contact.

Interviewing Styles

There are several interviewing styles. In some cases, you will be interviewed by one individual but will meet others in the firm. Remember that everyone will observe your behavior and will most likely also be involved in your review after you leave.

CONVERSATIONAL INTERVIEW Some interviewers choose to use the **conversational-style interview.** This style may not seem like an interview, but it most certainly is. The interviewer may talk about a variety of topics, which may or may not relate to the position; however, this style allows the interviewer to see if the applicant is able to organize and control a random situation. Questions are generally open-ended. If this occurs during your interview, you may consider asking the interviewer about job responsibilities, about whom you will report to during your internship, or other questions that will move the dialogue into a discussion about the position. This will allow you to discuss your background, education, and skills to qualify you as a suitable if not the best candidate for the internship (Kendall, 2005).

STRESS INVERVIEW Some interviewers choose a **stress interview** approach. They ask questions that can put you under pressure or make you feel stressed. The intent is to see your reaction in the worst conditions. Though this is not typical in interior design firms, it is wise to be prepared for this type of interview. Although some questions may make you feel uncomfortable, it is best to stay calm and realize that it is not a personal attack. Rather, your response demonstrates the ways you handle yourself under pressure (Piotrowski, 2003, 2008). Don't feel you must answer the question immediately. Often, firms find it beneficial when an interviewee takes time to think through the questions before responding. This may show that you will not jump at the first option but, rather, take time to consider a problem, weigh the options, and act wisely. However, as a word of caution, don't take to long to respond; this may be interpreted as a lack of knowledge.

SITUATIONAL, OR CASE STUDY, INTERVIEW Some interviewers will provide a scenario and ask what you would do in that particular situation. This is called a **situational** or **case study interview.** It gives the interviewer a chance to see how you think on your feet. These situational interviews are most common when applying for managerial position and less common for an internship position (Kendall, 2005; Piotrowski, 2003, 2008).

TEAM INTERVIEW Some interviews are one-on-one whereas others are in teams. The **team interview** approach brings together several individuals from the firm to ask questions and to evaluate the interviewee. In some cases, you will move from office to office as well as be interviewed by a multiple people at once. Each individual will probably have a specific question or questions to ask—each having a different part to play in the process.

It is important to be respectful of each individual and to answer questions in the same manner regardless of position within the firm. Again, the team approach will be less common when interviewing for an internship position (Piotrowski, 2003 & 2008).

Interview Questions

The interviewer will ask a variety of questions. To prepare, develop questions you believe the interviewer may ask and how you will answer them. The interview may begin with questions that relate to the firm, and this is where your research of the firm will pay off.

So, beginning with questions relating to the firm, the following are example questions or statements that an interviewer may ask. Some answers should be based on your research of the firm.

1. Why do you want to intern with this firm?
2. What do you know about our firm?
3. How did you hear about this firm?
4. Have you applied to other firms?

With the following questions, the interviewer(s) will learn more about you and your fit within the firm:

1. Tell me about yourself.
2. Why did you choose to study interior design?
3. What excites you about the interior design profession?
4. What courses have you enjoyed the most and why?
5. What types of projects did you work on? Which was your favorite? Why? What was your most challenging project? Why? (Research the firm and know their projects.)
6. What skills or talents can you bring to this firm? (Research the firm and know the skills they may expect.)
7. Describe a mistake you made in a project or assignment. What did you learn, and how has it impacted you?
8. How do you feel when your work is critiqued?
9. Describe a situation in which you felt stressed in your work or school. How did you cope?
10. Describe a team project in which you participated. What did you learn from this experience?
11. Describe a situation in which you taught other students a skill or new information. What did you learn from this experience?
12. Do you feel your scholastic work in college demonstrates your capabilities? Why or why not?
13. In what school activities have you been involved? If none, state your reason.
14. Describe the leadership positions that you have held. What have you learned from this experience?
15. What are your greatest strengths? Weaknesses? (Identify several strengths and one weakness; then, consider how each weakness could become a strength.)
16. What personal characteristics do you feel are necessary for an interior designer?
17. What qualifications do you feel will make you successful as an interior designer?
18. Who do you most admire? Why?
19. What do you hope to learn from this internship?
20. What will you add to our firm?
21. Are you willing to travel out of town and/or work weekends and evenings if necessary?
22. Do you expect compensation? If so, what or how much?
23. Where do you see yourself in five years (Granger, 2004; Kendall, 2005; Kim, 2006; Piotrowski, 2003 & 2008)?

This is a sizable list of questions, but they are not all-inclusive. You may learn of other questions by practicing an interview with career staff at your university or by visiting with interior design professionals or even professors at your university.

Questions to Ask

Develop a list of questions to ask about the firm, position, project, and other related questions. This will express your interest in the firm.

1. How many people are employed with your firm?
2. How many interior designers are on staff?
3. What are the company's plans for growth or expansion?
4. What characteristics are important to successfully secure an internship in this firm?
5. What are your expectations for and responsibilities of an intern?
6. Will I be working with one interior designer or several?
7. Who will be the internship supervisor?
8. How many interns will you be interviewing?
9. What other information do you need from me to help you make a decision?
10. When will you make a decision?

If you received an offer during the interview, you may ask about compensation. The interviewer may have previously asked this question; however, this is the best time for the discussion (Granger, 2004; Kendall, 2005; Kim, 2006; Piotrowski, 2003 & 2008).

This list will help you ask appropriate questions as well as stimulate ideas for further questions.

Illegal Questions

There are a plethora of questions that are no longer acceptable to ask during an interview or on an application. Because of the Equal Employment Opportunity Commission (EEOC), interview questions that relate to age, sex, religion, marital status, plans for children, and ethnic origin are illegal and can become discriminatory. For example, questions may be appropriately asked about future career plans; however, questions regarding future plans for children are not appropriate and must not influence the interview. In case illegal questions are asked, be sure you plan responses without being defensive or negative (Kendall, 2005; Piotrowski, 2003 & 2008) (see Table 5.1).

Conclusion of the Interview

As the interview is concluded, the interviewer may state that he or she will call you with an answer. At this time, you may ask if you can call them to inquire about their decision. As in the beginning, shake hands and thank the interviewer for his or her time, and you may also ask for a time frame when they will make a decision. The next step is to send a note or e-mail of thanks to show your appreciate for their time and consideration. This note doesn't need to be fancy—just simple and to the point. This simple follow-up is always appreciated and may even bring your name forefront once again.

TABLE 5.1

Illegal or Inappropriate Interview Questions

Illegal question may be an attempt to determine your race, skin color, age, or disability. Depending on how they are worded, the questions may be illegal or not and, in a way, are sneaky ways to learn the same information. The following are examples of these questions.

ILLEGAL	LEGAL
NATIONALITY	
Are you a U.S. citizen?	Are you authorized to work in the U.S.?
What is your native tongue?	What languages do you read, speak, or write fluently?
RELIGION	
Which religious holidays do you observe?	Are you able to work with our required schedule that includes weekends and holidays?
AGE	
How old are you?	Are you over the age of 18?
	Are you over 50?
MARITAL AND FAMILY STATUS	
Do you have or plan to have children?	Are you able to work overtime on occasion? Can you travel?
Can you get a babysitter on short notice for overtime or travel?	Travel or work overtime on short notice will be required. Is this a problem for you?
GENDER	
As a man/woman, can you handle this job?	What do you have to offer our company?
HEALTH AND PHYSICAL ABILITIES	
How much do you weigh?	Are you able to lift boxes weighing up to 50 pounds?
Do you have any health issues?	How many days of work did you miss last year? How many days of school did you miss in the last year?
Do you have any disabilities?	Are you able to perform the specific duties of this position without special accommodations?
MISCELLANEOUS	
Do you live nearby?	Are you willing to relocate, or can you be start work at 8 a.m.?
Have you ever been arrested?	Have you ever been convicted of any crime?
Were you honorably discharged from the military?	Tell me about your military experience and how it can benefit the company.

Tippit, Inc. (2010). *HR world: 30 interview questions you can't ask and 30 sneaky, legal alternatives to get the same info.*

Retrieved on February 1, 2010, from http://www.hrworld.com/features/30-interview-questions-111507/

The following interns responded to the following question:

A.W. completed a seven-week unpaid internship between her junior and senior years at a residential design firm. She graduated from a large public university in the Midwest.

E.J. interned at an interior architectural firm. She graduated from a private university in a large Southern city.

J.E. interned at an interior design firm specializing in high-end residential interiors and hospitality design. She graduated from a private college in a large Midwestern city.

J.H. *(international intern)* completed her twelve-week unpaid internship in a residential design firm in Buenos Aires, Argentina. She graduated with a double major of interior design and Spanish from a large public university in the Midwest.

J.L. completed a two-and-a-half-month, full-time internship at a commercial design firm. She graduated from a private college in a large Midwestern city.

K.B. completed a paid eight-week internship at a commercial design firm that focused on healthcare interiors. She graduated from a private university in a large Southern city.

K.F. completed a paid three-month internship in a residential design firm. She graduated from a large public university in a Southwestern city.

K.S. completed an eight-week unpaid internship for a retail establishment that provides design services. She graduated from a large public university in the Midwest.

L.O. completed an unpaid four-day-per-week summer internship at a high-end residential firm. She graduated from a private university in a large Southern city.

M.A. completed a paid two-month internship at a high-end kitchen cabinetry manufacturer. She graduated from a large public university in a Southwestern city.

M.R. completed her seven-week paid internship at an architectural firm between her junior and senior years. She graduated from a large university in a Midwestern city.

M.S. completed an unpaid two-and-a-half-month part-time (20-30 hours per week) internship at furniture dealership. She graduated from a private university in a large Southern city.

S.M. completed an unpaid five-month internship at a high-end residential firm. She graduated from a private college in a large Midwestern city.

T.H. completed two paid internships—one in an architectural firm and the other for a furniture dealership. She graduated from a large public university in a Southwestern city.

BOX 5.1 (CONTINUED)
interviews

Tell us about your interview process.

A.H. *(international intern):* "I fell in love with the culture after reading and learning about it. The goal of the organization [where I interned] and their efforts in Guatemala really inspired me. The sustainable construction was something I had learned about but hadn't seen firsthand. Now to be able to say that I have helped build a house with earth bag and tire construction, along with a school, is pretty amazing."

A.W.: "I completed a few different interviews, but the job that I was offered followed by far the most comfortable and thorough interview. Cindy (the owner) was very warm and welcoming, and her main objective was to get to know me. I think personality is just as important as portfolio. She looked through my portfolio and was very impressed. I believe I was in the interview for 45 minutes before she offered me the internship on the spot. We had great chemistry and, after all the other interviews I had, I knew this was the right internship for me."

E.J.: "All of the interviews I had consisted of my showing my portfolio and answering questions concerning my résumé and portfolio."

J.L.: "Traditional interviews as if for a permanent placement."

J.E.: "It took about a week to receive my first phone call; we set up an interview for the following week. I dressed up in accordance to how I perceived his firm (a step up from business casual) with hopes to "fit in" as best as I could. I arrived about five minutes early and was greeted by my site supervisor. He immediately handed me two simple quizzes: one of which required me to name the different types of furniture pieces and one that was a list of vendors to put into alphabetical order. After he looked over the quiz, he asked a me about 20 different questions, some about my experience with interior design, some about my personal past, and a few about what I would like to accomplish. We seemed to get along very well—after the interview questions were through, he asked if I had brought any work to show. I pulled out my hard copies and briefly described each project. He was thrilled and immediately asked if I would like the job."

J.F.: "There was e-mail correspondence and then an initial interview followed by a visit to the office for a final interview to decide between the two final candidates by the owner. Finally, I received a phone call saying I received the internship."

J.H. *(international intern):* "I had a phone interview with CDS International in English and in Spanish. Then when I got to Argentina I had an interview with my site supervisor before I started working, but it was really relaxed. She just wanted to make sure that I could learn the program and that things would be okay."

BOX 5.1 (CONTINUED)
interviews

K.B.: "I met with the principal and the two VPs of healthcare interiors and showed them my résumé. I went through the processes behind the images produced in my résumé. They had also asked me to bring in any Sketchup and Revit designs I had done in the past semester as well. They asked me questions about why I wanted to work there and what I wanted to accomplish during my internship."

K.F.: "They asked me to bring my portfolio, some original hand rendering and sketching, and a materials board. I first talked a little bit about why I chose interior design and then went through my portfolio. After that I showed them my materials board and talked about why I chose which materials and how they related to the concept of the project."

K.S.: "I had to do a phone interview because I was six hours away from the location. I sent the site supervisor my résumé and she said she would give me a call back to set up a time to interview. She also asked for a picture of myself! The call interview included simple questions to find out about me, why I was interested in this field, what I thought would be expected of me during a design internship, and what skills I had on a CAD program."

L.O.: "I was asked a variety of questions about my interest, experiences, and what I expected and would be expected to do. The portfolio coverage was brief."

M.A.: "I did not do an interview, the only pre-job offer contact I had with the company was the initial meeting with the CEO, which was during a tour of the showroom. We exchanged about five e-mails. I received the job offer after sending my portfolio at the CEO's request."

M.R.: "It depended on the firm. I had personal interviews with an individual and a panel, I had two phone interviews, and I received one offer by phone and e-mail communications."

M.S.: "I was studying in Italy at the time so I called them and had an interview over Skype."

S.M.: "I had two interviews in the same firm—first with the office manager, and then with the head designers."

T.H.: "My first interview (at an architectural firm) was pretty laid back but I was still very nervous. I had not had any classes yet on how to do an interview or how to rev up your résumé/portfolio so it was really informal. I simply showed up for the appointment and met the senior designer, we talked about schedule, school, and then, I showed her my work. After this discussion she gave me a tour of the firm and told me that the owner would call me when he's out of a meeting. The second internship that I had (at a furniture dealership) didn't really involve an interview other than through e-mail and a first meeting, which was more of an informational session than an interview."

Self-Assessment

If you have never been interviewed, taking time to evaluate yourself through role-playing or videotaping is crucial. You can accomplish this in more than one way:

1. You can videotape yourself and critique the behavior you observe.
2. You can videotape yourself and ask a professional to critique the behavior.
3. You can ask a friend or family member to interview you and provide feedback.
4. You can make an appointment with your university's career services office and have them conduct a mock interview.
5. Career service staff are trained for this purpose and would be a great source of assistance (Granger, 2004).

Analyzing Your Mock Interview

If you review your own videotape, note your first impression. The first five minutes of an interview can be the most crucial and make a lasting impression. How did you meet the interviewer? What did you say? Was your attitude positive?

Next, notice your body language. Consider the signals given through your dress, manners, and facial expressions.

Then, how did you end the interview? Did you shake hands? Did you remember their names? Did you thank them for their time? Did you leave on a positive note? Did you ask if you could contact them on a specific date? Did they say they would contact you?

All of these questions are important in making a good impression during the interview.

Planning Ahead

Plan ahead for the day of the interview. This means considering not only the questions and preparing for the interview itself but also considering your interview attire. Also, consider how you will travel to the interview site, how long it will take to get there, and how you will behave during the interview.

Dressing for the Interview

Dressing for an interview takes time and preparation. Dressing professionally will make a good first impression. You may want to research the firm's policy on dress so that you dress in an appropriate manner. Then, select the attire to wear to the interview. If alterations are needed or the garment needs pressing, make sure these are handled in plenty of time. Women should also consider the make-up and hairstyle; and make sure it is appropriate for daytime.

Traveling to the Interview

The interview site may be in the place of employment or could be offsite. When the exact location and time of the interview are set, you will need directions. Whether you are familiar with the firm's locations or not, be sure you have good directions. You will also need to arrive at the interview site a little early so you do not feel rushed and worried about being on time. A rule of thumb is to arrive with at least 10 to 15 minutes to spare. If you arrive late, interviewers will quickly assume this is standard behavior, and you may not be offered the position. Also, know your interviewer's name and how to pronounce it if it looks difficult (Granger, 2004).

Behavior during the Interview

After you arrive at the firm's front door or parking lot, employees or even the interviewer may view you; therefore, your evaluation may begin before you realize it. Although it may seem that some individuals are not interviewing you, be on your guard because they probably are observing your behavior. Pay very close attention to your body language and manners and keep a positive demeanor.

common reasons for rejection

Rejection does not mean you didn't qualify; however, it may mean someone else was better qualified, or you made some errors that put you out of the running. Possible reasons for rejection include the interviewee:

- Had a "know-it-all" attitude.
- Knew little or nothing about the firm.
- Did not ask questions about the position.
- Was late for the appointment.
- Lacked skills in various areas required by the firm.
- Presented a portfolio that did not demonstrate a variety of projects or lacked in a specific, required area.
- Dressed casually because it was a "casual day."
- Expressed him- or herself poorly.
- Used inappropriate language or profanity.
- Appeared tired.

- Looked overwhelmed.
- Demonstrated a lack of planning for the future—showed no goals or purpose.
- Had an indifferent attitude.
- Appeared more interested in money than in the position.
- Demonstrated no participation in student activities (Granger, 2006).

There are other possible reasons for rejection, but most importantly, if you are rejected, evaluate the interview process and determine the areas needing improvement. Then, the next interview will have a positive outcome.

internship offer: evaluation, negotiation, and acceptance

After you receive the internship offer, your employer must discuss:

1. How much you will be paid (or if you will be paid).
2. The dates that your internship will start and end.
3. The dates that you will not be expected to work, such as holidays.
4. How many hours you will work each week.

You can evaluate, negotiate, and accept or not. After the offer is accepted, an acceptance or thank-you letter should confirm this information—and then there will be no surprises during the internship.

BOX 5.2
preparing for the internship

The following site supervisors offered advice on the following questions.

A.G. is an interior designer at Gensler in Chicago. Gensler is an interdisciplinary design firm with offices in the United States, Europe, the Middle East, and Africa. It specializes in architecture, interior design, branding and strategy, product design, and sustainability. Its market area is broad based and includes aviation and transportation, civic and community, office building, education, entertainment, hospitality, and retail facilities.

K.C. is interior design director for Interstate Office Products (IOP) in Sioux Falls, South Dakota. IOP is an office furniture dealership and interior design firm that offers a full range of design services. Its clients include corporate offices, financial institutions, law firms, and education and healthcare facilities. It also designs and specifies products for architectural firms' projects.

K.W. and R.K. are, respectively, interior design director and senior human resources representative for AECOM in Minneapolis. AECOM is a multidiscipline architectural and engineering firm with offices in the United States, Europe, Africa, the Middle East, Australia, and New Zealand. AECOM recently joined with Ellerbe Becket (the century-old firm specializing in architecture, interiors, and engineering) to blend their global reach and local knowledge. The firm is committed to enhancing and sustaining the built, natural, and social environment. It works on a wide range of projects including corporate offices, healthcare facilities, law firms, hospitality, education, and cultural and event facilities. Its interior services include interior design, facility programming, and feasibility studies, furniture, fixtures, and equipment (FF&E), renovation and preservation, adaptive reuse, and workplace consulting.

BOX 5.2 (CONTINUED)
preparing for the internship

What advice would you be willing to share that would help students prepare and interview for an internship?

TAKEAWAY FROM
site supervisors

A theme that resonates through these comments is "eager" or "a willingness to learn." Thus, as you set goals for your internship experience, remember that being open and willing to learn will take you far.

A.G. *(interior designer, Gensler):* "Students should have a strong digital portfolio. Their work should clearly express their thought process and creativity."

K.C. *(interior design director, Interstate Office Products):* "Follow up on what you say you are going to do. If I request a résumé e-mailed, please send it and follow up with a phone call to confirm (or read receipt on their e-mail software) so they know I have received it. Many times the phone call is made (which can be the hardest), but no information follows.

Although we have not taken an intern for years, you just never know when things might change. So contact us anyway. I also keep those résumés on file for when we are looking to fill a design position."

K.W. and R.K. *(interior design director and senior human resources representative, AECOM):* "Plan to present your portfolio and all graphic materials as a consistent whole. We evaluate how students present themselves as well as what they present."

summary

Preparing for an interview takes time. Preparation includes practicing for the interview, conducting self-assessment, dressing professionally, and planning ahead. Use the Interview Preparation Checklists, downloadable as Appendix M on the CD-ROM. Good preparation will boost your confidence as you head for the interview and can pay off with an internship offer.

achieving chapter objectives

Review the Chapter Objectives at the beginning of this chapter. You are now ready to put them into practice.

prepare for your interview

1. Write an in-depth research on one firm and prepare possible appropriate questions to ask the interviewer.

2. Work in pairs and role-play the interviewer and interviewee; then, reverse roles.

   a. Videotape interviews.

   b. Evaluate yourself with the assistance of your partner.

3. Work the following scenario: a student has been offered an internship. Explain how he or she should evaluate, negotiate, and accept the offer.

time management

After you receive the call that you are to be interviewed, you must begin to prepare immediately. Much may need to take place within a few days; for this reason, you will have needed to have completed several aspects of preparation as soon as you sent out your résumé.

before the call

Prior to receiving the call for an interview, you should have completed:

1. The selection, purchase (if necessary), alteration (if needed), and preparation of appropriate articles of clothing.

2. A list of interview questions.

3. Several practice interviews.

4. A review of your résumé to determine if it needs an update, making sure that you have extra copies.

upon receiving the call

With each firm, the following should be conducted after the call has been received. Remember that there may be only a few days between the call and the interview. It may even be scheduled for the next morning. Here is what you need to do:

1. Review the firm.

2. Research the firm's dress policy.

3. Locate the interview site.

4. Determine your mode of transportation.

5. Determine how long it will take to arrive.

6. Make sure you have enough money for parking or transportation.

7. Confirm your appointment with the appropriate contact person.

8. Leave contact information with the interviewer in case there are delays or changes in the interview date or time.

9. Make a list of questions to ask for the specific firm.

10. Review a list of interview questions and illegal questions.

11. Review your portfolio and know the background and skills needed with each project (see Table 5.2).

As you plan for the interview, refer to Table 5.2, the "Interview Preparation Checklist," to help you make your final preparations. This checklist notes the information on the previous list. It also encourages you to review your résumé and reevaluate your portfolio.

REFERENCES

- Granger, M. (2004). *The fashion intern.* New York: Fairchild Books.
- Kendall, G. T. (2005). *Designing your business: Strategies for interior design professionals.* New York: Fairchild Books.
- Kim, G. H. (2006). *The survival guide to architectural internship and career development.* New York: Wiley.
- Piotrowski, C. M. (2003). *Professional practice for interior designers,* (3rd ed.). New York: Wiley.
- Piotrowski, C. M. (2008). *Professional practice for interior designers,* (4th ed.). New York: Wiley.

TABLE 5.2 (ALSO APPENDIX M)

Interview Preparation Checklist

INTERVIEW PREPARATION: ASK YOURSELF THE FOLLOWING QUESTIONS.

Have you reviewed the firm?

What is the firm's dress policy?

Where is the interview site? Do you know where the appointment is to take place and how to get there?

What the mode of transportation? Have you arranged for transportation, if needed?

How long it will take to arrive?

Do you have enough money for parking or transportation?

Have you confirmed your appointment with the appropriate contact person?

Have you left your contact information with the individual who will interview you in case there is a change or delay?

Did you make a list of questions to ask for the specific firm?

What are possible interview questions?

What are some illegal questions to be aware of?

PERSONAL PREPARATION

Your Portfolio

Does your portfolio contain your name and contact information in case you have to leave it with the interviewer for later review? (Include a copy of your résumé as well.)

Is your portfolio clean in appearance and neatly organized when opened?

Have you repaired or replaced any damaged exhibits in your portfolio?

Can you explain how each and every portfolio entry has prepared you for future work or how it relates to the position for which you are interviewing?

Can you anticipate a discussion in which you describe your portfolio?

What kinds of questions do you think will be asked about your portfolio, and can you answer them?

Does your portfolio show you to be a problem solver?

Your Résumé

Have you prepared your most recent résumé to take with you?

Are you planning to take additional copies of your résumé?

Can you explain how your résumé items (for example, education and work experience) have prepared you for future work or for the position for which you are interviewing?

Can you explain any problems that may be presented by your résumé?

Your Appearance

Do you have a suit that is appropriate for interviewing and that is comfortable, clean, and well-pressed? (Ask a trusted friend or sales associate for direction; if possible, see what others at the prospective place of employment are wearing.)

Do you have shoes, purse, briefcase (as applicable) that are clean and comfortable? (Both your suit and accessories should be fairly conservative in appearance.)

For men: Do you have a clean, pressed necktie that you can tie so that its tip touches your belt buckle?

Most of the ideas are from this source: Kendall, G. T. (2005). *Designing your business: Strategies for interior design professionals.* New York: Fairchild Books.

KEY TERMS

- adhocracy
- clan
- flat organizational structure
- hierarchical organizational structure
- hierarchy
- market
- Form W-2 (Employer's Wage and Tax Statement)
- Form W-4 (Employee's Withholding Allowance Certificate)
- professional development

6 preparing for the internship

"I learned about the people, the company, the clients, the industry, vendors, materials, the design process, construction documents, a commercial library, systems, and the overall culture within a commercial design firm. [My internship] far exceeded my expectations."

—J.L., who completed a two-and-a-half-month, full-time internship at a commercial design firm.

OBJECTIVES

- Employ various methods of professional development in preparation for the internship.

- Identify and understand the firm's organizational type: hierarchical, market, clan, or ad-hoc.

- Select the appropriate wardrobe for the internship.

- Consider ways that courses connect to the internship experience.

- Develop a time management schedule for internship preparation.

Having accepted an internship, you will need to make a few preparations. First, you must complete hiring and tax forms if you are to receive a wage for the internship, and you will need to register for internship credits if your school offers them. Then, to gain a better understanding of the firm—specifically, how the firm operates—you should determine its organizational profile or cultural type. Next, to help you more easily fit into the firm, plan your wardrobe and dress the part. Also, you will need housing if you are relocating to another area. And you will want to learn as much as you can about your new community.

As you take that first step into the design field, look for ways to develop professionally and make connections between course work and the tasks involved in the internship. Professional development, transitioning from academic theory into real-world practice, is, after all, the essential purpose of the internship.

hiring and tax forms

If you receive a paid internship, your employer will have you complete the **Form W-4, the Employee's Withholding Allowance Certificate,** which allows the employer to deduct Federal Income Tax from your wages. The amount of this tax deduction depends upon the number of exemptions claimed. Generally, as a single person, a maximum of one exemption is claimed. The employer is required to keep one copy and send the other to the IRS.

The employer must prepare and send the **Form W-2, the Employer's Wage and Tax Statement** to you by January 31 of the calendar year following employment. This form shows the amount of wages paid to you, as well as the federal, state, city, and social security (FICA) taxes that were withheld.

register for internship credits

Each interior design program will have different credit requirements. For example, some universities require three credits where others may require as many as seven. Also, some universities require internships after the completion of specific courses, such as a junior-level studio or junior standing. Such prerequisites need to be fulfilled prior to registering for internship credits. This information should be found on a program guide, in your university's catalog, or from your academic advisor. Thus, you need to review and follow your program requirements.

cultural types of organizations

There are four different organizational cultural types: **hierarchy, market, clan,** and **adhocracy.** Each of the cultural types affect the way people in the firm work together. As an intern, recognizing a firm's cultural type will help you determine where and how you will fit in the organization. This is important because a proper fit within a firm will make you feel comfortable and improve your learning experience.

Hierarchy

The chain of command in the hierarchical type of organization begins at the top and progresses down. It is highly structured and formal in a setting that has an inward orientation; in other words, the firm focuses on their own concerns rather than those dictated from the outside. Executive offices are most likely placed around the perimeter with owner or principal located in a corner office or a separate suite of rooms. Within this type of firm, the dress will be very professional—suits and ties for men, and professionally styled dresses or suits with pants or skirts for women.

Market Type of Organization

The market type is similar to a hierarchical type. In this firm, people are competitive and goal-oriented with leaders who are demanding, hard-driven, and productive. They have an external orientation; in other words, they are concerned about job completion and satisfaction of the client. They are also concerned about opinions from the outside. Their reputation is highly valued, and, therefore, the dress may be similar to the hierarchical type.

Clan Type of Organization

The clan type has similar values to the hierarchical type with an inward focus. However, the atmosphere is an open, friendly workplace with an extended-family atmosphere. The leaders are mentors—like parental figures—with group loyalty and a sense of tradition. A cohesive group is highly respected where teamwork, participation, and consensus are valued. With an emphasis on cohesion and teamwork, the clan organization may be considered a flat or level organization. In such firms, a manager works closely with their team, which may include the principal. Dress may also be more relaxed and casual.

Adhocracy

The adhocracy type is similar to the clan type in its flexibility and discretion, but it has an external focus. It is a dynamic, creative workplace where the development of innovative ideas is encouraged (Tharp, 2005). This firm conducts business in teams, and casual dress is highly recommended.

dressing the part

Planning your wardrobe prior to beginning the internship is important. A whole new wardrobe is not necessary, but you will not be wearing jeans, sweats, or shorts with flip-flops as you might when attending university classes. When you interview with the firm, observe the type of firm and the dress; this will help you plan your wardrobe.

In planning your wardrobe, begin by looking in your closet for appropriate clothing. Consider how you can mix and match the pieces you have. Then, begin making a list of clothing types you need. If money is an issue, go to a second-hand store, or in some cases, organizations have developed professional closets where students can locate appropriate clothing for their internships.

Additional factors to consider are the need for off-duty clothing and outfits for other situations that might call for variations in dress, such as more formal wear for client meetings or more durable wear if going to work sites under construction. For the latter, a variety of clothing may be needed during the day. For example, you may spend a few hours in the studio, visit with a client in the boardroom, and visit a construction site all in one day. Going to visit a job site that is under construction will require different clothing; in this case, you will probably know the day before. Then, you can bring casual slacks and tennis shoes or hard-tipped shoes (an OSHA standard for new construction sites) and change before going to the job site. Off-duty clothing should be comfortable and geared for various activities that you enjoy.

organizational cultures

The following interns responded to all Field Experience questions in this chapter:

E.J. interned at an interior architectural firm. She graduated from a private university in a large Southern city.

J.E. interned at an interior design firm specializing in high-end residential interiors and hospitality design. She graduated from a private college in a large Midwestern city.

J.F. completed a paid four-month internship at development company that specialized in both residential and commercial interior design by constructing high-end, single-family homes, condos, and commercial spaces. She graduated from a private college in a large Midwestern city.

J.L. completed a two-and-a-half-month, full-time internship at a commercial design firm. She graduated from a private college in a large Midwestern city.

K.B. interned at a commercial firm that focused on healthcare interiors. She graduated from a private university in a large Southern city.

K.C. completed a semester-long unpaid internship for a hospitality design firm. She graduated from a private college in a large Midwestern city.

K.S. completed an eight-week unpaid internship for a retail establishment that provides design services. She graduated from a large public university in the Midwest.

L.O. completed an unpaid four-day-per-week summer internship at a high-end residential firm. She graduated from a private university in a large Southern city.

M.R. completed her seven-week paid internship at an architectural firm between her junior and senior years. She graduated from a large university in a Midwestern city.

M.S. completed an unpaid two-and-a-half-month part-time (20-30 hours per week) internship at furniture dealership. She graduated from a private university in a large Southern city.

T.H. completed two paid internships—one in an architectural firm and the other for a furniture dealership—in Alaska. She graduated from a large public university in a Southwestern city.

BOX 6.1 (CONTINUED)
organizational cultures

What type of organizational culture was your firm—top-down (hierarchical) or team-effort (level organization)? What was it like to work in this type of organization?

E.J.: "The partnership was a combination of hierarchical and level organization. The partners made the final decisions, whereas the designers were on teams that made the more minor decisions."

J.E.: "A sole proprietorship. There was only one paid employee of the company until I was hired on part time. It is a hierarchical firm. I certainly had the best and worst at this particular job. The best was the experience; it simply could not be matched because I was already given design work the week I started there. I was learning every aspect of the design process as well as learning how to run a business. It was a very business-oriented workday . . . every day (absolutely no time for personal conversation), which could be considered good and bad. The most difficult was trying to learn all of these different processes (plus time management) all at once. Questions were more common than either my site supervisor or I would prefer, especially considering the amount of work we had to do. This made me feel very hesitant when asking questions because he always seemed to have something way more important going on. [The owner] does not know some of the most important programs necessary for our field, making this learning process even more difficult."

J.F.: "Single ownership with a hierarchical organization. Because it was a smaller firm, I had the opportunity to wear many hats. From helping assess floor plans and drawing elevations to choosing furnishing details and budget constraints, there was a wide array of tasks every morning."

J.L.: "The firm was a corporation. Its decision-making was a team effort. As an intern with the Chicago office, my responsibilities included providing project assistance as identified by the principals in their Monday morning workload meetings. I was considered a regular design staff member with junior design skills available to whichever team required assistance. Over the summer, I worked significantly with two of the three teams, assisting on projects for four major clients."

K.B.: "It was a corporation where decisions were made in top-down (hierarchical) and in team effort (level organization). Both, the "top" people had the final say, but the majority of the decisions were left up to the team that was assigned the project. Many of the projects were collaborations with teams across the country. I enjoyed the teamwork and the experience of being a part of a team."

K.C.: "It was team oriented in the branch where I interned. However, when the principals were in the office (they worked at a different office) they made the decisions. It was difficult sometimes to know what I should be doing and for whom. I think for an actual job it would be great. The bosses seem to trust their employees, and there is a level of respect for every employee."

BOX 6.1 (CONTINUED)
organizational cultures

K.S.: "A very small firm (a sole proprietorship or single owner). There was only a secretary, one designer, and a CADworks professional. It was tedious working in a single-owner firm. I did a lot of secretarial work answering phone calls, talking to clients, greeting guests that came in the store; the experience was not what I thought it would be. It was a busy, fast-paced business, a lot of running around."

L.O.: "It was a sole proprietorship. I liked it and understand why the owner had final say—it is her company and her name is on the final product."

M.R.: "A hierarchical business with project teams containing all levels (partner to intern) and areas. Some teams would change during the design process based on skill level and workload. I enjoyed working in this structure (hierarchical with project teams). Some project teams I was placed on allow me freedom to design as I saw fit for the client and was generally accepted for the client. Other teams I was placed on allowed little input. In other words, if the partner or design leader did not like an ideas, it was redesigned to fit their criteria."

M.S.: "A corporation where decisions were made through a team effort. I liked it because I was introduced to a wide variety of people and how they work."

T.H.: "This architecture firm was definitely level organized. The owners were both architects and although they were the bosses, they did a lot of the grunt work as well. The setting was fairly informal; although everyone was very professional, it was relaxed and you could tell that everyone got along well."

FIELD EXPERIENCE
Takeaway

Organizational cultures vary widely among different firms. It is important to research the organizational structure of the firm and consider how you might fit into that culture before you apply for an internship there.

BOX 6.2
finding the right kind
of organizational structure for you

Would you have preferred to work in a different type of organization?

K.S.: "I would like to have worked in a different firm just because I feel as though my site supervisor just wanted me for a free worker to answer her phones. I feel like I could have learned a lot more from someone else."

M.R.: "Personally, I liked working on the teams that put their trust in my knowledge and let me design for the client. I think this was a much more efficient way to do things because progress was continually made as these teams had more informal design meetings and tended to have a clearer image for the project."

Did you feel the organizational structure enhanced or inhibited your internship experience?

E.J.: "It probably enhanced the experience because I worked with the same core group of people; so I got to know them and understand how they worked better."

J.E.: "I think it enhanced my internship experience for even more reasons than stated earlier. I think after I started getting paid for my services, the expectation bar was raised drastically and brought on a completely different experience."

J.F.: "The structure is what I'm used to because I've only worked for hierarchical organizations, so I was comfortable with it."

K.B.: "It enhanced the experience because we, as interns, were included in every meeting and walk-through of the projects that we were involved in."

K.S.: "I did learn the in and outs of the paperwork and how she kept things a certain way and why that worked for her."

L.O.: "Everyone had to kind of follow certain limits about design because of the owner's personal preference."

BOX 6.2

finding the right kind of organizational structure for you

M.R.: "I think working in a firm with an overall hierarchical structure allowed for a more structured business, yet I appreciated the informal structure within some teams. Reviewing this on the business side, this is the way needed to create a successful company. I think the creativity, designs, and progress were better under the leadership of a partner who trusted the design team they placed on the project. Projects under this form of leadership were more detailed and made better progress; every team member knew what they needed to accomplish to keep the project moving forward so no two people were working on the same thing. There were not as many redesigns in these teams because they were all focused on the client and not achieving approval from the partner in charge."

In general, how did you feel about interning in that type of organization?

J.E.: "I think I've stated just that in previous paragraphs . . . but to reiterate, I certainly don't mind working for this type of organization. It was always made obvious who the boss was, and the expectations were usually very clear. I think I would prefer to work in a more level organization."

J.L.: "The firm provided a diverse and rich intern experience, which was educational, interesting, and fun. The individuals I worked with were intelligent, treated me as a team member, and were enjoyable to work with. Given diverse responsibilities, I learned about the people, the company, the clients, the industry, vendors, materials, the design process, construction documents, a commercial library, systems, and the overall culture within a commercial design firm. The experience far exceeded my expectations of experiencing a commercial design firm, its culture, and its design process, as well as my desire to understand how my diverse background might fit within an interior design firm environment."

K.B.: "I loved it and would definitely apply to work in a similar job environment, if not that same firm."

K.S.: "I made the best of the situation and did everything that I did to the best of my ability to give a good name for myself. I would prefer not working with that firm again in the future."

M.R.: "I liked interning in this type of organization. It was good experience on many levels, and I learned a lot about the company, the design industry, and various design techniques."

M.S.: "Even though it wasn't my top choice to work in a dealership, I felt it was important for me to experience that area of design."

FIELD EXPERIENCE
Takeaway

Even after researching a firm's organizational structure before applying for and embarking upon your internship, you are still bound to face many challenges. Treat each challenge as a learning experience, and remember that because you did your research and prepared yourself for what's to come, you will have what it takes to handle each new situation like a pro.

Refer to Box 6.1 for background on the interns who also responded to the following questions.

Last but not least, it is always wise to have clothing for various weather conditions, which will depend on season and the location of the internship.

relocating for the internship

If you accept an internship in a location near your school or home, this step is unnecessary. However, for those relocating for their internship, there is even more planning that goes beyond completing paperwork, knowing the firm, and planning your wardrobe. Relocating means finding housing and learning about the new location, which includes transportation, shopping, and safety concerns. You may also need to locate a second job, especially when extra income is needed to pay for daily living expenses, such as housing, food, and transportation.

Locate Housing and Transportation

If you are fortunate enough to have relatives or friends with whom you can stay, locating housing may not be necessary. Otherwise, you can search for housing by:

- Asking your internship supervisor for recommendations.
- Inquiring at rental agencies for temporary housing.
- Renting in an inexpensive hotel.
- If a college town, visiting with the school's residential housing for possible dorm room rental.
- Placing an advertisement in the local paper for a room to rent.

Learn the City, Town, or Other Internship Location

You will need to learn the city, town, or other area where you've moved in order to locate transportation routes, shopping areas, grocery stores, places of entertainment, and more. Use mapquest.com or Google Maps to locate the firm as well as where you will stay (if known) and create your transportation route. Then, use this route to locate shopping areas and grocery stores.

Safety Concerns

Just as with an international internship, traveling alone in an unfamiliar place can be difficult. Even in this country, being along at night or walking into an elevator with strangers are concerns. The following are additional safety precautions to be taken:

- Know the areas of a city or other locations that are safe and those that are risky.
- Ask for information before you go for a walk.
- Believe the bus driver if he or she says an area isn't safe.
- Have a hotel or restaurant call a cab for you, especially in the evening.
- No matter how much you love to run outside in the morning, don't do it if your colleagues tell you there are snakes (or other hazards) in the area.
- Don't use the room-service door-hanger menus to order breakfast. You have to indicate how many people are in the room.
- Select small hotels where the staff know who is a guest and who isn't.
- If you travel to the same city frequently, stay at the same place.
- Schedule a time to call home. Be sure someone expects to hear from you and will be aware if you don't check in.
- Leave your cell phone number so people can call you. Remember to charge the phone and leave it on.
- Remember that women as well as men can be dangerous. Be cautious about new friends (Denslow, 2006, p. 300).

Locate a Second Job

Be sure to inform your internship supervisor if you need a second job. Soliciting the supervisor's help will provide great insight into part-time work as well as inform them of your need for money to cover living expenses. The following are ways to locate a second job:

- Ask the supervisor for ideas in locating part-time work.
- Check classified advertisements in the local newspaper.
- Look for signage in retail store windows.
- Ask coworkers at your internship.
- Ask family or friends living in the area for ideas in locating part-time work
- Check employment agencies.
- Apply online at large department stores such as JCPenney or Walmart.

professional development

Professional development means attaining skills and knowledge for both personal development and career advancement. Professional development is a learning experience that occurs in a variety of ways, such as attending college courses; participating in workshops, seminars, and conferences; and reading trade magazines and other publications. It may also occur in informal situations through discussions, mentorships, supervision, and practice at school and workplace. Clearly, as a college student, you have begun the process of professional development.

Professional Development on the Job

When employed, you may be expected to engage in professional development, especially if you hold a certification such as the National Council for Interior Design Qualification (NCIDQ) or professional membership in the American Society of Interior Designers (ASID) or in the International Interior Design Association (IIDA). These certifications are maintained by gaining continuing education units (CEUs). CEUs are offered through organizations such as ASID, IIDA, or others.

For interns, professional development has begun in your college courses and, optimally, by attending meetings of such student organizations as those associated with ASID, IIDA, leadership organizations, an honor society, or other group that may contribute to your professional development. Other methods of continued development are reading trade publications; attending seminars, workshops, and conferences when available in your area; working as a college student toward certifications such as Leadership in Energy and Environmental Design-Accredited Professional (LEED AP), and researching new information on the InformeDesign website (http://informedesign.umn.edu) or journals such as the *Journal of Interior Design*. When in the field, you can continue your education when the opportunity arises and, in this way, you can eventually build an area of expertise.

connection between courses and internship

During your internship, consider ways that your knowledge from coursework connects to duties and tasks during your internship. It is easy to become wrapped up in the new surroundings, but it is very important to recognize these connections. Some examples may be in application of design theory, spatial relationships and organization, material selections, CAD programs, and sketching. When thinking about your education and future career, ask yourself:

- Where are the connections?
- How do they connect?
- What are the similarities between a career and coursework?
- What are differences between a career and coursework?
- What new knowledge do I still expect to gain?

This topic will be further discussed in Chapter 10.

summary

In this chapter you learned about making the first steps into the internship. This began by completing the hiring and tax forms when wages are earned and registering for internship credits. Then, because there are different organizational and cultural types that affect the manner in which the firm operates, it is important to learn the firm's type. Reviewing your interview experience and the firm's website will help make this determination.

Next, planning the appropriate wardrobe will give you confidence and professionalism. Prepare your professional wardrobe by reviewing existing pieces after which new or slightly used pieces may be purchased. Then, to feel comfortable in your new location, begin by locating appropriate housing; at the same time learn the city—transportation, shopping areas, and safety concerns—so you will feel comfortable upon arrival. If you will need a second job, begin the job hunt as quickly as possible. Finally, during your internship, look for ways to develop professionally and connect your coursework to the internship. This will provide a better learning experience.

After you have completed these tasks, you will be prepared for your internship. The next chapter will take you inside the internship.

achieving chapter objectives

Review the Chapter Objectives at the beginning of this chapter.
You are now ready to put them into practice:

preparing for the internship

The following projects will help you make connections between yourself as the intern and your internship:

1. Evaluate the firm's organization type to understand how employers and employees work.

2. Evaluate and prepare a wardrobe for an internship:

   a. Develop a list of clothing types you will need.

   b. Examine your wardrobe for professional pieces.

   c. Consider ways to mix and match outfits.

   d. List what needs to be replaced or added.

3. Choose a topic (e.g., green design in the workplace) and research information from various sources.

4. Write a reflective paper related to what you want to gain professionally from this internship.

   a. List and describe your goals for the internship.

   b. How you will fulfill these goals?

   c. What do you want to take from the internship for your future?

time management

Spending time preparing for an internship will facilitate an easier transition into your internship. Some tasks should be completed before accepting an internship whereas others will take place after you have accepted it. Of course the amount of time you need to devote to each task will vary depending on your individual situation. However, the following are ways to consider how best to allocate you time in preparation for your internship:

- Organization's cultural type. When preparing for the internship, this is a good time to begin the research of the organization's cultural types.

- Wardrobe planning. After you have narrowed your search to a few and have researched the firms, you can begin planning your wardrobe. This may be a couple months before your internship begins.

- Completion of hiring and tax forms. After accepting the internship, the firm will supply you with forms and provide a date for their completion.

- Registration of internship credits at your university. After accepting the internship, register for internship credits.

- Location of housing. After accepting the internship, begin looking for housing.

- Transportation to and from the firm. As you look for housing, look at the options for easy and safe transportation.

- Getting to know the area: grocery stores, shopping, safety issues, and more. As you look for housing, also search for information about shopping and safety.

- Possibilities for a second job. After you have accepted an offer and have started looking for housing, begin inquiring about part-time work, if needed.

- Required internship assignments. One month before leaving for your internship, review the assignment to determine what you must take with you and what your academic supervisor will expect of you.

REFERENCES

- Granger, M. (2004). *The fashion intern*. New York: Fairchild Books.

- Kendall, G. T. (2005). *Designing your business: Strategies for interior design professionals.* New York: Fairchild Books.

- Kim, G. H. (2006). *The survival guide to architectural internship and career development*. New York: Wiley.

- Piotrowski, C. M. (2003). *Professional practice for interior designers*, (3rd ed.). New York: Wiley.

- Piotrowski, C. M. (2008). *Professional practice for interior designers*, (4th ed.). New York: Wiley.

- Tharp, B. M. (2005). Four organizational culture types. In Knowledge+Research, Haworth, Inc. Retrieved on September 30, 2007, from http://haworth.com/Brix?pageID=413

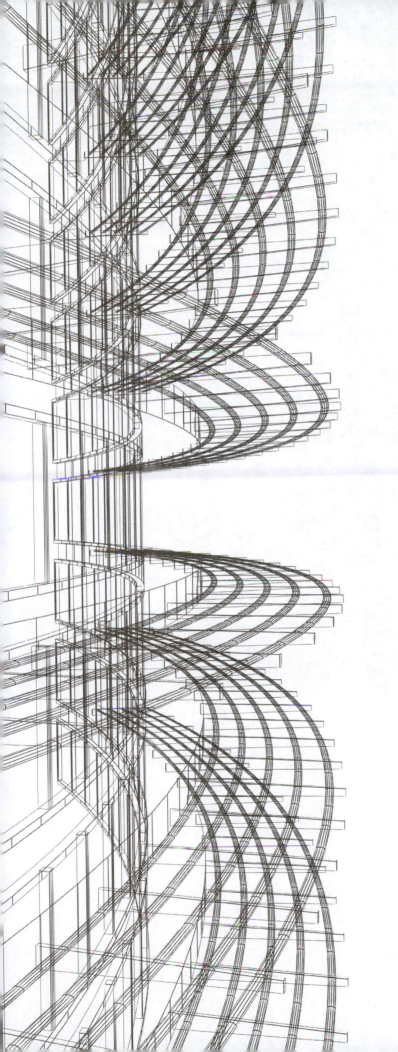

7 during the internship

> "Be professional, get your work done, ask questions, and always have open communication [with your site supervisor, coworkers, and academic advisor]."
>
> —M.R., who completed a seven-week internship at an architectural firm.

OBJECTIVES

- Practice appropriate conduct in the work place.
- Understand and keep up to date on professional ethics for interior designers.
- Practice (and stay current on) etiquette and netiquette.
- Perform internship duties in a professional and ethical manner.
- Work as a team member within the structure of the firm.
- Develop good listening skills.

- Handle conflict situations in a positive manner.
- Observe the teamwork structure and dynamics.
- Look for connections between coursework and internship experience.
- Learn about the organization in which you work and show proper respect.
- Participate in professional meetings such as ASID, IIDA, seminars, and CEUs.
- Develop a time-management schedule for your internship.

BOX 7.1

professional conduct

The following interns responded to Field Experience questions throughout this chapter:

C.S. completed an unpaid ten-week internship in an interior design, remodeling, and build firm. She graduated from a large public university in a Southwestern city.

J.E. interned at an interior design firm specializing in high-end residential interiors and hospitality design. She graduated from a private college in a large Midwestern city.

J.F. interned at an interior architectural firm. She graduated from a private college in a large Midwestern city.

J.L. completed a two-and-a-half-month, full-time internship at a commercial design firm. She graduated from a private college in a large Midwestern city.

K.B. completed a paid, eight-week internship at a commercial design firm that focused on healthcare interiors. She graduated from a private university in a large Southern city.

K.F. completed a three-month paid internship in a residential design firm. She graduated from a large public university in a Southwestern city.

M.R. completed her seven-week paid internship at an architectural firm between her junior and senior years. She graduated from a large university in a Midwestern city.

S.M. completed a five-month internship at a high-end residential firm. She graduated from a private college in a large Midwestern city.

As an intern, you are representing yourself and your future placement. But just as important, you are also acting as a representative or ambassador of your academic institution. In this role, you can "influence future internship placements for better or worse" (Granger, 2004). Therefore, you must conduct yourself in a professional manner, be ethical, know proper **etiquette** and **netiquette,** learn how to handle conflicts, and remember your position.

professional conduct

Professional conduct is the idea that professionals are expected to perform duties in a competent manner. It also means that when you enter an internship (and later an entry-level position) there are certain standards acceptable in the design discipline. With membership in the American Society of Interior Designers (ASID) and International Interior Design Association (IIDA), professionals agree to follow the profession's code of **ethics** (Piotrowski, 2008), and if not followed, financial and professional failure can be the result. Consequences of unethical behavior affects those directly involved as well as repercussions through the profession (Kendall, 2005).

Ethics

To fully grasp the understanding of ethics, let's examine the terms *ethics* and *code*; then, we will apply to their definitions to the phrase, **code of ethics.** *Ethics* is concerned with moral values—good and bad, right and wrong (Ethics, 2009). *Code* is an unvarying rule or regulation (Code, 2009). Thus, the code of ethics is a rule or regulation related to moral values of good and bad, right and wrong.

BOX 7.1 (CONTINUED)
professional conduct

What did you learn about professional conduct during your internship?

K.B.: "Personal business is supposed to stay personal and left to time when you are not at work. The people, however, were extremely personable and would work to help one another. The VPs supervised us and made sure that everyone got their work done, but they were also there for emotional support."

K.F.: "One of the designers who had interviewed me had expressed how important professionalism was to them. They said that appearance was one of the most important decisions in selecting me for the job because some of their clients are very traditional."

J.E.: "I learned how to handle both clientele and vendors; talking with either on the phone or in person are two completely different approaches."

J.L.: "The firm practiced the highest level of ethics and professional conduct one might expect from any respected and significant corporation."

M.R.: "Be professional, get your work done, ask questions, and always have open communication [with your site-supervisor, coworkers, and academic advisor]."

Did any issues come up concerning professionalism or ethics during your internship?

K.B.: "Only once. The day they had a round of layoffs, it was awkward. Everyone was upset. No one really spoke to the interns unless they were apologizing, and we were not sure exactly how to conduct ourselves."

J.E.: "My school certainly did not teach enough about professionalism. We never even touched on how to properly approach different types of situations. Luckily, I have a background in the restaurant industry as well as amazing parents who taught me a lot growing up. Had I not had this background, this experience would have been much more different—my fellow intern seemed to have a major issue with this."

J.F.: "A normal amount of both professionalism and ethics was lacking from certain members of the staff, and although it didn't inhibit the quality of their work, it did impact the way I thought about them."

Professional Codes of Ethics: ASID and IIDA

The code of ethics for both ASID and IIDA focuses on responsibility to the public, the client, other interior designers and colleagues, and the profession (ASID, 2009; IIDA, 2009). ASID also includes responsibility to the employer (ASID, 2009); IIDA includes the responsibility of the Association or IIDA (IIDA, 2009). Boxes 7.1 and 7.2 are the ASID Code of Ethics and Professional Conduct and IIDA Code of Ethics, respectively. Members of ASID or IIDA must adhere to their code of ethics and conduct themselves in a manner that is respectful (ASID, 2009; IIDA, 2009). If not followed, charges can be made against the offending interior designer.

Interior designers who do not have membership in ASID or IIDA are not required to follow the organization's codes. However, as members of the profession, being respectful of each other and conducting themselves in a professional and an ethical manner is both good behavior and good business (Piotrowski, 2008).

BOX 7.1 (CONTINUED)

professional conduct

How did you handle situations that could have compromised your ethical standards?

C.S.: "I stayed out of the office drama and tried not to take part in any situation because I was just a temporary employee."

K.B.: "On the day there were layoffs, we interns kept to ourselves and did not approach anyone unless they asked us to."

J.E.: "The owner told me that he would like to hire me on after my 300 hours were up. He told me this when I still had about 50 hours to go. The other intern, however, would not be getting hired on. He did not expect me to keep my mouth shut, but I was not the type to "rub it in anyone's face." I'm not sure whether or not the other intern knows, even three months later, that I still work there."

J.F.: "I confronted them and documented any incidents so that there was a record and paper trail to follow up with, as needed."

S.M.: "There was only one time that I felt like I had to compromise my ethics. I am against fur and a fur representative came in to show the designers their line. It really reinforced the fact that I am completely against the use of fur in the industry. I met with the representative, but I couldn't bring myself to touch the product."

BOX 7.2

ASID code of ethics and professional conduct

1.0 PREAMBLE

Members of the American Society of Interior Designers are required to conduct their professional practice in a manner that will inspire the respect of clients, suppliers of goods and services to the profession and fellow professional designers, as well as the general public. It is the individual responsibility of every member of ASID to uphold this code and bylaws of the Society.

2.0 RESPONSIBILITY TO THE PUBLIC

2.1 Members shall comply with all existing laws, regulations, and codes governing business procedures and the practice of interior design as established by the state or other jurisdiction in which they practice.

2.2 Members shall not seal or sign drawings, specifications, or other interior design documents except where the member or the member's firm has prepared, supervised, or professionally reviewed and approved such documents, as allowed by applicable laws, rules, and regulations.

2.3 Members shall at all times consider the health, safety, and welfare of the public in spaces they design. Members agree, whenever possible, to notify property managers, landlords, and/or public officials of conditions within a built environment that endanger the health, safety, and/or welfare of occupants. If, during the course of a project, a Member becomes aware of an action to be taken by, or on behalf of the Member's client, which in the Member's reasonable opinion is likely to result in a material adverse effect on the health, safety, and welfare of persons occupying or using the space, the Member shall refuse to consent to, or participate in, that action, and if required by law and/or under circumstances the Member deems reasonably prudent to do so, the Member shall report such action to the governmental agency having jurisdiction over the project.

2.4 Members shall not engage in any form of false or misleading advertising or promotional activities.

2.5 Members shall neither offer, nor make any payments or gifts to any public official, nor take any other action, with the intent of unduly influencing the official's judgment in connection with an existing or prospective project in which the members are interested.

2.6 Members shall not assist or abet improper or illegal conduct of anyone in connection with any project.

3.0 RESPONSIBILITY TO THE CLIENT

3.1 Members' contracts with clients shall clearly set forth the scope and nature of the projects involved, the services to be performed, and the methods of compensation for those services.

3.2 Members shall not undertake any professional responsibility unless they are, by training and experience, competent to adequately perform the work required.

BOX 7.2 (CONTINUED)

ASID code of ethics and professional conduct

3.3 Members shall fully disclose to a client all compensation that the member shall receive in connection with the project and shall not accept any form of undisclosed compensation from any person or firm with whom the member deals in connection with the project.

3.4 Members shall not divulge any confidential information about the client or the client's project, or utilize photographs of the client's project, without the permission of the client.

3.5 Members shall be candid and truthful in all their professional communications.

3.6 Members shall act with fiscal responsibility in the best interest of their clients and shall maintain sound business relationships with suppliers, industry, and trades.

4.0 RESPONSIBILITY TO OTHER INTERIOR DESIGNERS AND COLLEAGUES

4.1 Members shall not interfere with the performance of another interior designer's contractual or professional relationship with a client.

4.2 Members shall not initiate, or participate in, any discussion or activity which might result in an unjust injury to another interior designer's reputation or business relationships.

4.3 Members may, when requested and it does not present a conflict of interest, render a second opinion to a client or serve as an expert witness in a judicial or arbitration proceeding.

4.4 Members shall not endorse the application for ASID membership and/or certification, registration or licensing of an individual known to be unqualified with respect to education, training, experience, or character, nor shall a member knowingly misrepresent the experience, professional expertise of that individual.

4.5 Members shall only take credit for work that has actually been created by that member or the member's firm, and under the member's supervision.

4.6 Members should respect the confidentiality of sensitive information obtained in the course of their professional activities.

5.0 RESPONSIBILITY TO THE PROFESSION

5.1 Members agree to maintain standards of professional and personal conduct that will reflect in a responsible manner on the Society and the profession.

5.2 Members shall seek to continually upgrade their professional knowledge and competency with respect to the interior design profession.

BOX 7.2 (CONTINUED)

ASID code of ethics and professional conduct

5.3 Members agree, whenever possible, to encourage and contribute to the sharing of knowledge and information between interior designers and other allied professional disciplines, industry, and the public.

6.0 RESPONSIBILITY TO THE EMPLOYER

6.1 Members leaving an employer's service shall not take drawings, designs, data, reports, notes, client lists, or other materials relating to work performed in the employer's service except with permission of the employer.

6.2 A member shall not unreasonably withhold permission from departing employees to take copies of material relating to their work while employed at the member's firm, which are not proprietary and confidential in nature.

6.3 Members shall not divulge any confidential information obtained during the course of their employment about the client or the client's project or utilize photographs of the project, without the permission of both client and employer.

7.0 ENFORCEMENT

7.1 The Society shall follow standard procedures for the enforcement of this code as approved by the ASID Board of Directors.

7.2 Members having a reasonable belief, based upon substantial information, that another member has acted in violation of this code, shall report such information in accordance with accepted procedures.

7.3 Any violation of this code, or any action taken by a member which is detrimental to the Society and the profession as a whole, shall be deemed unprofessional conduct subject to discipline by the ASID Board of Directors.

7.4 If the Disciplinary Committee decides the concerned Member did not violate the Society's Code of Ethics and Professional Conduct, it shall dismiss the complaint and at the concerned Member's request, a notice of exoneration from the complaint shall be made public. If the Disciplinary Committee decides that the concerned Member violated one or more provisions of the Society's Code of Ethics and Professional Conduct, it shall discipline the concerned Member by reprimand, censure, suspension, or termination of membership. The Disciplinary Committee may, in its discretion, make public its decision and the penalty imposed. The Disciplinary Committee does not impose any other form of penalty. The Disciplinary Committee cannot require payment of any monies or mandate certain action to be taken by the concerned Member.

Source: American Society of Interior Designers (ASID). (2009). ASID code of ethics & professional conduct. Retrieved on April 18, 2009, from http://asid.org/about/ethics/default.htm

BOX 7.3
IIDA code of ethics

Preamble

Professional and Associate Members of the International Interior Design Association shall conduct their interior design practice in a manner that will encourage the respect of clients, fellow interior designers, the interior design industry, and the general public. It is the individual responsibility of every Professional and Associate Member of IIDA to abide by the Code of Professional Ethics and Conduct, Bylaws, Policies, and Position Statements of the Association.

Definitions

The terms used in this Code shall be defined in the same manner in which they are defined in the Bylaws, Policies, and Position Statements of the Association.

Responsibility to the Public

In performing professional services, Professional and Associate Members shall exercise reasonable care and competence, and shall conform to existing laws, regulations, and codes governing the profession of interior design as established by the state or other jurisdiction in which they conduct business.

In performing professional services, Professional and Associate Members shall at all times consider the health, safety, and welfare of the public.

In performing professional services, Professional and Associate Members shall not knowingly violate the law, or counsel or assist clients in conduct they know, or reasonably should know, is illegal.

Professional and Associate Members shall not permit their name or signature to be used in conjunction with a design or project for which interior design services are not to be, or were not, performed under their immediate direction and control.

Professional and Associate Members shall not engage in any form of false or misleading advertising or promotional activities and shall not imply, through advertising or other means, that staff members or employees of their firms are Professional or Associate Member unless such is the fact.

Professional and Associate Members shall not make misleading, deceptive, or false statements or claims about their professional qualifications, experience, or performance.

Professional and Associate Members shall not, by affirmative act or failure to act, engage in any conduct involving fraud, deceit, misrepresentation, or dishonesty in professional or business activity.

In performing professional services, Professional and Associate Members shall refuse to consent to any decision by their clients or employers which violates any applicable law or regulation, and which, in the Professional and Associates Members' judgment, will create a significant risk to public health and safety.

BOX 7.3 (CONTINUED)
IIDA code of ethics

Professional and Associate Members shall not attempt to obtain a contract to provide interior design services through any unlawful means.

Professional and Associate Members shall not assist any person seeking to obtain a contract to provide interior design services through any unlawful means.

Responsibility to the Client

Professional and Associate Members shall undertake to perform professional services only when they, together with their consultants, are qualified by education, training, or experience to perform the services required.

Before accepting an assignment, Professional and Associate Members shall reasonably inform the client of the scope and nature of the project involved, the interior design services to be performed, and the method of remuneration for those services. Professional and Associate Members shall not materially change the scope of a project without the client's consent.

Prior to an engagement, Professional and Associate Members shall disclose, in writing, to an employer or client, any direct or indirect financial interest that they may have that could affect their impartiality in specifying project-related goods or services, and shall not knowingly assume or accept any position in which their personal interests conflict with their professional duty. If the employer or client objects to such financial or other interest, Professional and Associate Members shall either terminate such interest, or withdraw from such engagement.

Professional and Associate Members shall not reveal any information about a client, a client's intention (s), or a client's production method(s) which they have been asked to maintain in confidence, or which they should reasonably recognize as likely, if disclosed, to affect the interests of their client adversely. Notwithstanding the above, however, Professional and Associate Members may reveal such information to the extent they reasonably believe is necessary (1) to stop any act which creates a significant risk to public health and safety and which the Professional or Associate Member is unable to prevent in any other manner; or (2) to prevent any violation of applicable law.

Responsibility to Other Interior Designers and Colleagues

Professional and Associate Members shall pursue their professional activities with honesty, integrity, and fairness, and with respect for other designers' or colleagues' contractual and professional relationships.

Professional and Associate Members shall not accept instruction from their clients which knowingly involves plagiarism, nor shall they consciously plagiarize another's work.

Professional and Associate Members shall not endorse the application for membership in the Association of an individual known to be unqualified with respect to education, training, or experience; nor shall they knowingly misrepresent the experience, professional expertise, or moral character of that individual.

BOX 7.3 (CONTINUED)
IIDA code of ethics

Professional and Associate Members shall only take credit for work that has actually been created by the Member or the Member's firm or under the Member's immediate direction and control.

Responsibility to the Association and Interior Design Profession

Professional and Associate Members agree to maintain standards of professional and personal conduct that will reflect in a responsible manner on the profession.

Professional and Associate Members shall seek to continually upgrade their professional knowledge and competency with respect to the interior design profession.

Professional and Associate Members shall, wherever possible, encourage and contribute to the sharing of knowledge and information among interior designers, the interior design industry, and the general public.

Professional and Associate Members shall offer support, encouragement, and information to students of interior design.

Professional and Associate Members shall, when representing the interior design profession, act in a manner that is in the best interest of the profession.

Professional and Associate Members may only use the IIDA appellation in accordance with current Association policy.

Professional and Associate Members shall not knowingly make false statements or fail to disclose any material fact requested in connection with their applications for membership in the Association.

Source: IIDA (2009). IIDA Code of Ethics. Retrieved on April 18, 2009, from http://www.iida.org/i4a/pages/index.cfm?pageid=304

As an intern, you need to read and understand these codes of ethics. It will be ethical for you as well as your supervisor to follow these codes whether or not you are a member of one of the professional organizations.

Etiquette and Netiquette

Etiquette is another system of rules that regulates social and professional behavior. **Netiquette**, or Internet etiquette, is a set of guidelines for e-mail communication (Van Rospach, Spafford, & Moraes, 1995).

Etiquette

In social situations, there are norms of behavior that are customary and enforced by societal pressures. Although no formal trial or sentence for misconduct occurs for breach of etiquette, societal pressures shun people or individuals with poor etiquette (Etiquette, 2009). For example, poor table manners are offensive and affect one's image and personal image as well.

Business etiquette skills in the workplace can directly affect productivity, profits, and retention (Emily Post Institute, 2008c). Success is often based on being considerate, respectful, and honest within the business world. Workplace etiquette also involves behavior such as how you dress, punctuality, and manners. This means that you must pay attention to the details such as polished shoes, pressed and stain-free clothing, limited jewelry, punctuality, and other such concerns (Emily Post Institute, 2008b).

Netiquette

Much of our communication today (social and business) is through electronic means. Electronic communications can be easily misunderstood; the reason is that it is impossible to see facial expressions and body language or be aware of environmental conditions. Therefore, electronic communication must be very carefully written. Landsberger (1996) and Emily Post Institute (2008a) provide guidance for social electronic interaction and communications.

NETIQUETTE TIPS Here are tips gleaned from Landsberger and Emily Post Institute:

- When writing an e-mail, provide a subject line to reflect the content.
- Carefully choose your language.
  a. The mood or facial expressions cannot be viewed through e-mail.
  b. All capital letters represent shouting.
  c. Check your grammar and vocabulary.
  d. Make a good impression through your choice of words.
  e. Keep your e-mails concise so that they will be read.
- Carefully select information for e-mail correspondence. E-mails are not anonymous; they can be traced back to you, and can be forwarded to anyone.
- Forward e-mail messages only when you have permission from the original sender.
- Keep it professional at work, and keep out the personal information.
- Do not use other's images and content without permission.
- Use distribution lists only with permission.
- Do not send or forward spam, junk mail, or chain letters.
- Do not respond to personal attacks.
- If leaving a position, let others know your new e-mail address.
- Always respond to e-mail messages unless they are junk mail or forwards.
- Respond to e-mails in a timely fashion (Emily Post, 2006; Landsberger, 2008).

From this list, you can see that writing e-mails must take serious thought and should never be used in a way that may be misunderstood. Keep in mind that e-mails are always retrievable.

differences among organizations' cultural types

In Chapter 6, we looked at four different organizational cultural types: hierarchy, market, clan, and adhocracy. Firms identify with one of these types. Regardless of the type, some firms support internships and others do not; some employees of a firm may consider having interns beneficial whereas others feel they are bothersome. As you research and contact various firms, and even as you begin to work within a firm, you are likely to run into some stumbling blocks. Some problems may be difficult to understand or even recognize within the culture of a particular organization.

Problems within an organization's cultural type often stem from one of the following situations:

1. Cultural mismatch—Your culture does not align with the organization's cultural type. For example, you enjoy creative endeavors but during the internship you realized that the employees were engaged in their own creative endeavors and had little time to mentor you.

2. Cultural misunderstanding—You are unable to determine the organization's cultural type. The firm seemed to work as a team at times and yet was very formal and rigid in structural approach to design projects.

3. Cultural ignorance—You cannot identify the organization's cultural type. This is similar to the previous scenario, but here you do not have a clear understanding of organizational cultural types and how they affect the way an organization works.

4. Cultural refusal—You or members of the organization refuse to accept the organization's culture. In this case, tension between employees and the employer was likely occurring (Kaser, Brooks, & Brooks, 2007, p. 141).

As noted in Chapter 6, developing an understanding of the four organizational types and selecting a firm that best fits you will eliminate the problems noted. To help identify the different types, look at the firm's spatial organization. Are the offices closed and separated, or are the offices open with workstations grouped in teams? You may also want to observe the interaction between people. Is there a very formal or more relaxed atmosphere? How do they welcome clients or an intern? For example, a market type will focus on clients and provide a comfortable atmosphere for them. It will also welcome interns and develop good mentoring relationships. These are a few ways to look for cues into the organizational cultural type.

handling conflicts

During the internship, you will develop relationships with other designers and staff. These working relationships are extremely important because you will spend the majority of your waking hours at work. Some relationships will be pleasant or confrontational, mentoring or ignoring, strong or weak, cordial or distant. Developing positive relationships with coworkers is an important way to learn more about the workplace and about others; moreover, it fosters more successful work outcomes, to say nothing of being personally rewarding. Nevertheless, conflicts can arise. It is important to develop strategies for handling negative coworkers (Kaser et al., 2007); see suggestions for such strategies later in this chapter.

Casual conversation of controversial topics can cause conflict. So, it is best to avoid topics such as politics or religion. Also, the use of some terms can cause conflict. For example, the use of slang or vulgar words in conversations could be offensive and should be avoided. Thinking twice before speaking is always a good policy; this applies to both professional and ethical behavior.

Conflicts Related to Organizational Culture

All conflicts have at least two sides to the story—each individual with different perceptions of the same issues. "The type of organizational culture can play a role in how your relations with coworkers develop" (Kaser et al., 2007, p. 141). Difficulties may arise in the following ways:

1. Criticism of others, participation on office gossip, or making negative comments.
2. Office arguments between coworkers.
3. **Office politics** involving rewards and promotions, competition, retribution, and punishment.
4. Social invitations that may be friendly or inappropriate, or wanted or unwanted (p. 142).

Avoid Criticism and Gossip of Others in the Workplace

Sometimes within a firm, one employee may criticize another. Because you are the intern and the outsider, you must avoid involvement in conversations that criticize others, or involve gossip or negative comments. Instead, your guideline will be to "act professionally in the work environment and respect others" (Kaser et al., 2007, p. 142).

Avoid Office Arguments

Office arguments may also occur and should also be avoided. Particularly, as an intern, you are the outsider and a guest within the firm. Your purpose of being in the firm is to learn, not to be involved in confrontations. If led into an argument, you must share with and get advice from your **internship supervisor.** Then, treat the situation as a learning experience and not as a problem (Kaser et al., 2007).

Observe Office Politics from the Sidelines

Office politics is the way a firm "rewards and punishes, promotes and demotes, encourages competition among departments and workers, and applies ethics to the office environment" (Kaser et al., 2007, p. 142). Office politics vary from one firm to another, and it takes time to fully understand the firm's politics. In most cases, interns are not involved in office politics unless they are in the firm for a longer period of time. Thus, as an intern, rather than becoming involved, it would be best to make notes in your journal to use as a learning experience. Then, you can discuss this with your internship supervisor or **academic supervisor.**

Hold to Your Professional Ethical Standards

Though professional ethical behavior in the workplace is expected, not everyone adheres to these standards. This behavior may be emotional, verbal, or even sexual abuse. Depending upon the behavior, it may be considered harassment and create a hostile environment. As an intern, you may find a coworker or even a superior who lacks professional ethics. If you find yourself in this type of situation, you have choices: (1) you can tell your supervisor who can deal with it; (2) you can ask your academic advisor for advice; (3) you can leave the internship; (4) you can ignore it; or (5) you can tell the individual that his or her behavior is inappropriate and that you will not tolerate it. The unfortunate part of simply ignoring it is that the individual may eventually inflict some real harm to someone else and/or behave poorly with someone who may bring charges. And in the meantime, the behavior may affect the firm's as well as the individual's reputation. No matter what choice you make, holding to your professional ethical standards is the best policy.

Seek Guidance before Accepting Social Invitations

Another area of concern involves accepting social invitations. Social invitations to company-sponsored gatherings are generally acceptable, but work-related invitations could be dangerous and should be avoided. An example is receiving a social invitation to a movie or dinner by an employee of the firm you know little about. In this situation, you would be alone with a near-stranger, whereas meeting and visiting with the employee during a company-sponsored event provides safety in numbers that would include employees and their guest. If you receive a work-related invitation, it would be best to visit with your internship or academic supervisor before accepting or declining it; there may even be specific rules within the firm regarding social conduct. Also, as an intern, there is no requirement to accept social invitations.

As Kaser et al. (2007) stated, "What appears to be friendly and non-threatening to one person might appear to be inappropriate to another person. Judgment and caution should guide your behavior in this area to avoid problems" (p. 143).

Relationship with Internship Supervisor

The internship supervisor is the person who will supervise, monitor, and evaluate your work within the firm. As with your college professors, this will be one of your most important relationships during your internship, and for this reason, a positive relationship is to your advantage. According to Kaser et al. (2007), a good internship supervisor will do the following:

1. Make time for you by being approachable.
2. Show interest in your learning and career.
3. Give you meaningful assignments that are related to your learning contract objectives.
4. Monitor you and provide constructive criticism and feedback.
5. Show appreciation and recognize you for the work you do.
6. Motivate you to expand your learning opportunities (p. 143).

Clearly, a good internship supervisor encourages learning and helps you connect knowledge from your education into the discipline.

Remembering Your Position

An internship is a great learning experience that helps you transition from college to the working world. During this time, you may experience situations where you feel undervalued for several reasons, such as working menial jobs, organizing the resource room, photocopying, answering phones, and generally not being allowed to make decisions. Though menial tasks are mundane, you will be expected to perform such tasks. By completing them, you may have free time to help a designer who has a bid deadline to meet and would have otherwise lost the project. Also completing these tasks shows that you are willing to do what you can to support the work of the firm—even if it means vacuuming, dusting, or other menial tasks. Keep in mind, too, that menial tasks can offer you the opportunity of learning more about the office. What is in that resource room—are there books or journals that you have not seen before? What are you feeding through the photocopier? Who will get a copy of it and why? Who is making those phone calls and what do they want? These are people you may be dealing with in your future career. As an intern, you can take advantage of every second in the internship environment to learn.

Taking a Deep Breath

If at some point you feel underappreciated, just take a deep breath and remember that your position as intern requires you to:

1. Respect those in authority.
2. Respect other designers or staff within the firm.
3. Respect others' space and time.
4. Look for tasks to help others.
5. Ask if you can assist.

Showing respect for your supervisor and others with whom you work will afford you greater respect as well.

professional organizations

Involvement in a professional organization is highly respected. If you have the opportunity, attend seminars, workshops, or general meetings for a professional organization such as ASID, IIDA, or another design-related organization. These meetings provide opportunities for networking, learning new information, and more. As you will read in Chapter 8, this is expected for professional development.

summary

In any design firm, you will be expected to perform duties appropriate to the profession. And in performance of duties, good professional behavior is essential. Professional conduct includes following codes of ethics and using ethical behavior, etiquette, and netiquette. Generally speaking, being ethical means discerning between good and bad, right and wrong, and choosing the higher ground. ASID and IIDA have codes of ethics that interior designers follow. Failure to do so for members of these groups, and, in some cases for unaffiliated professionals, may result in legal action.

Etiquette is another system of rules that regulates social and professional behavior. Today, netiquette, or Internet etiquette, has become a set of guidelines for e-mail communication. As an intern, you are expected to perform internship duties in a professional and ethical manner as well as to conduct yourself in a professional manner.

Business structure within a design firm may require you to work as a team member. Additionally, critical listening skills can help handle conflicts within the workplace. However, during the internship, it is best to develop strategies to avoid conflicts.

Especially important during the internship, you must look for connections between coursework and internship experience. This will help you better understand the application of knowledge learned, increase your internship experience, and provide greater service to the firm.

Professional organizations are important for any field. For interior designers, being involved in ASID, IIDA, or Interior Designers of Canada (IDC) helps members learn more about their profession, provides seminars and continuing education, and creates opportunities for networking among interior designers. As an intern, involvement in the organization will help you learn more about your profession.

achieving chapter objectives

Review the Chapter Objectives at the beginning of this chapter.
You are now ready to put them into practice.

study your internship experience

The following assignments are related to behavior during the internship:

1. Investigate possible conflicts that may arise and explain ways each conflict may be resolved.

2. Read the codes of ethics for ASID or IIDA and make notes of areas of particularly importance to your internship.

time management

During your internship, you will be working at the firm as well as completing assignments for college credit. Managing your time at the firm and during your free time will be important. After reading this chapter and Chapter 8, prepare a time schedule to complete the required assignments (see Table 7.1; downloadable as Appendix N on the CD-ROM). Table 7.2 is an example of a complete week during an internship.

REFERENCES

- ASID (2009). ASID code of ethics & professional conduct. Retrieved on April 15, 2009 from http://asid.org/about/ethics/default.htm

- Emily Post Institute. (2008a). Business ~ technology etiquette: Net-iquette. Retrieved on April 19, 2009, from http://www.emilypost.com/business/netiquette.htm

- Emily Post Institute. (2008b). Business ~ workplace. Retrieved on April 19, 2009, from Etiquettehttp://www.emilypost.com/business/first_impression.htm

- Emily Post Institute. (2008c). Emily Post business etiquette seminars. Retrieved on April 19, 2009, from http://www.emilypost.com/seminars/business.htm

- Encyclopædia Britannica. (2009). "Code." Retrieved on April 15, 2009, from Encyclopædia Britannica Online: http://www.britannica.com/EBchecked/topic/123881/code

- Encyclopædia Britannica. (2009). "Ethics." Retrieved on April 15, 2009, from Encyclopædia Britannica Online: http://www.britannica.com/EBchecked/topic/194023/ethics

- Encyclopædia Britannica. (2009). "Ettiquette." Retrieved on April 15, 2009, from Encyclopædia Britannica Online: http://www.britannica.com/EBchecked/topic/194521/etiquette

- Granger, M. (2004). *The fashion intern.* New York: Fairchild Books.

- IIDA (2009). IIDA code of ethics. Retrieved on April 15, 2009 from http://www.iida.org/i4a/pages/index.cfm?pageid=304

- Kaser, K., Brooks, J. R., and Brooks, K. (2007). *Making the most of your internship.* Mason, OH: Thomson South-Western.

- Kendall, G. T. (2005). *Designing your business: Strategies for interior design professionals.* New York: Fairchild Books.

- Kim, G. H. (2006). *The survival guide to architectural internship and career development.* New York: Wiley.

- Landsberger, J. (1996). Study guides and strategies: The ten commandments of e-mail "netiquette". Retrieved on April 19, 2009, from http://www.studygs.net/netiquette.htm

- Piotrowski, C. M. (2003). *Professional practice for interior designers,* (3rd ed.). New York: Wiley.

- Piotrowski, C. M. (2008). *Professional practice for interior designers,* (4th ed.). New York: Wiley.

- Van Rospach, C., Spafford, G., and Moraes, M. (1995). Netiquette (Internet etiquette). Retrieved on April 19, 2009, from http://www.livinginternet.com/i/ia_nq.htm

TABLE 7.1 (ALSO APPENDIX N)

Personal Time Schedule

Use the following symbols to organize your time during the internship: IN (Intern Hours); IA (Internship Assignments); PRE (Prepare for Work); PT (Personal Time); LNH (Lunch); DNR (Dinner); SLP (Sleep). Add other symbols appropriate to your situation.

Date:

	TIME	Monday	Tuesday	Wednesday	Thursday	Friday	Saturday	Sunday
SYMBOLS:	4 a.m.							
IN-Intern hours	5 a.m.							
IA-Intern Assignments								
PRE-Prepare for Day	6 a.m.							
PT-Personal Time	7 a.m.							
BRK-Breakfast								
LNH-Lunch	8 a.m.							
DNR-Dinner								
SLP-Sleep	9 a.m.							
ADDITIONAL	10 a.m.							
SYMBOLS:								
CM-Commute time	11 a.m.							
CLN-Clean	12 p.m.							
	1 p.m.							
	2 p.m.							
	3 p.m.							
	4 p.m.							
	5 p.m.							
	6 p.m.							
	7 p.m.							
	8 p.m.							
	9 p.m.							
	10 p.m.							
	11 p.m.							
	12 a.m.							
	1 a.m.							
	2 a.m.							
	3 a.m.							

Week #:   From: To:

TABLE 7.2

Personal Time Schedule Example

Use the following symbols to organize your time during the internship: IN (Intern Hours);
IA (Internship Assignments); PRE (Prepare for Work); PT (Personal Time); LNH (Lunch); DNR (Dinner); l
SLP (Sleep). Add other symbols appropriate to your situation.

		Date:	June 2	June 3	June 4	June 5	June 6	June 7	June 8	
		TIME	Monday	Tuesday	Wednesday	Thursday	Friday	Saturday	Sunday	
SYMBOLS:		4 a.m.	SLP	SLP	SLP	SLP	SLP	SLP	SLP	
IN-Intern hours		5 a.m.	SLP	SLP	SLP	SLP	SLP	SLP	SLP	
IA-Intern Assignments		6 a.m.	PRE/BRK	PRE/BRK	PRE/BRK	PRE/BRK	PRE/BRK	SLP	SLP	
PRE-Prepare for Day		7 a.m.	CM ½ hr	CM ½ hr	CM ½ hr	CM ½ hr	CM ½ hr	SLP	SLP	
PT-Personal Time		8 a.m.	IN	IN	IN	IN	IN	SLP	PRE/BRK	
BRK-Breakfast		9 a.m.	IN	IN	IN	IN	IN	BRK	CH	
LNH-Lunch		10 a.m.	IN	IN	IN	IN	IN	CLN	CH	
DNR-Dinner		11 a.m.	IN	IN	IN	IN	IN	CLN	PT	
SLP-Sleep		12 p.m.	LNH	LNH	LNH	LNH	LNH	CLN	PT	
		1 p.m.	IN	IN	IN	IN	IN	LNH	LNH	
ADDITIONAL SYMBOLS:		2 p.m.	IN	IN	IN	IN	IN	SHP	PT	
CM-Commute time		3 p.m.	IN	IN	IN	IN	IN	SHP	PT	
CLN-Clean		4 p.m.	IN	IN	IN	IN	IN	PT	PT	
SHP-Shopping		5 p.m.	CM ½ hr	CM ½ hr	CM ½ hr	CM ½ hr	CM ½ hr	PT	PT	
CH-Church		6 p.m.	IA 1 hr	IA 1 hr	IA 1 hr	IA 1 hr	IA 1 hr	PT	PT	
		7 p.m.	DNR	DNR	DNR	DNR	DNR	DNR	DNR	
		8 p.m.	PT	PT	PT	PT	PT	PT	IA 1 hr	
		9 p.m.	PT	PT	PT	PT	PT	PT	IA 1 hr	
		10 p.m.	PT	PT	PT	PT	PT	PT	PT	
		11 p.m.	PT	PT	PT	PT	PT	PT	PT	
		12 a.m.	SLP	SLP	SLP	SLP	SLP	SLP	SLP	
		1 a.m.	SLP	SLP	SLP	SLP	SLP	SLP	SLP	
		2 a.m.	SLP	SLP	SLP	SLP	SLP	SLP	SLP	
		3 a.m.	SLP	SLP	SLP	SLP	SLP	SLP	SLP	

Week #:   From: To:

KEY TERMS

- academic supervisor

- activity log

- daily journal

- goal reports

- learning experience goal (LE)

- professional

- development goal (PD)

- site supervisor

- topic assignments

- weekly reports

8 | reporting the internship

"The journal helped me reflect on what I was actually doing each day to further my education. That reflection helped me realize and learn more about the industry and what my day-to-day work life will be like."

—M.A., who completed a two-month internship at a high-end kitchen cabinetry manufacturer.

OBJECTIVES

- Participate in various phases of the design process during your internship.

- Participate in solving simple to complex design problems during the internship.

- Observe a client interview.

- Participate in the development of a project's program requirements.

- Maintain a record that informs the academic supervisor of daily activities and becomes a cumulative log of your internship experiences.

- Analyze learning experiences to identify personal growth and development.

- Connect coursework to internship experience in journals.

- Set or use predetermined goals for each week.

- Examine elements of business practice within the firm, such as business development, marketing, strategic planning, financial management, and others

- Observe or participate in an assessment process such as work productivity, square-footage ratios, post-occupancy evaluation, life-cycle assessment, and walk-throughs.

- Investigate specific aspects of interior design practice that relates theory to actual situations and circumstances through topic assignments.

- Express ideas clearly in written communication (e.g., journals, goals, and other assignments) in order to become a more effective communicator.

You've finally landed your internship, reviewed and prepared yourself for what to expect, and now you are there—in an office or out in the field with activity all around you. You're in the thick of it. Who has time to take notes when there's so much more you might be able to do?

why report?

The reason for reporting your internship is to make sure you capture every bit of this learning experience, take full advantage of it, study it with the assistance of those with more experience than you, and ultimately grow into a better and wiser interior designer and person.

In other words, you report to your academic supervisor to provide a connection to your education.

Reporting your internship also provides opportunities for interaction among the interior design firm, the community within which the firm is located, the student, and the university.

As an intern, you will be responsible for reporting your learning experiences to your **academic supervisor,** and to do so you will need to have an organized plan to present and evaluate these experiences. To complete some assignments, you will be required to visit with persons other than your **site supervisor,** such as other designers, support staff, sub-contractors, installers, and/or fabricators. These additional contacts help you make the connection between yourself (as an interior designer) and all parts of the design community. This approach will provide a complete understanding of your internship organization.

Gaining an Edge on Your Future Career

Every university or college will have different expectations for their interns; therefore, the ideas presented in this chapter may be adjusted to your academic requirements. Your academic advisor may ask you to use them

as your complete process for reporting your internship or may suggest you take advantage of some of the tools to enhance a process they have found tried and true in their own instruction. In any case, it is important that you read through and explore all of the ideas and reporting tools in this chapter to gain an edge on what to look for during your internship and what you take away from it in order to move on into a richer, more fulfilling career.

reporting to your site supervisor

As an intern, you will be expected to report to your site supervisor as required by the firm. Conversely, the firm or studio accepting an intern agrees to (1) provide a positive working environment and opportunities to both assist and learn from employees; (2) facilitate the intern completing courses' assignments by answering questions and providing appropriate experiences within the work setting; (3) and regard the intern as one would an employee in matters of dependability, basic responsibilities, and good work habits.

reporting to your university instructor

Some academic requirements may have interns report to the academic supervisor on a weekly basis, whereas others may expect reporting at different intervals. Weekly reports may include logging hours, daily journals, goal reporting, and/or topic assignments. Reports may be submitted as required by your academic supervisor.

weekly reports

Reporting internship activities is a combination of calculating hours, describing and reflecting on daily activities, setting and accomplishing goals, and investigating and reporting on a specific weekly topic.

Weekly **reports** include one or more of the following:

- An **activity log**
- A **daily journal**
- **Goal reports**—learning experience **(LE)** and **professional development (PD) goals**
- A **topic assignment**

You will turn in these reports as required by your academic supervisor. Evaluation is based on verification that the reports are received on time and follow the appropriate guidelines. At the end of the internship, some academic supervisors may also require a final notebook or CD. Additional materials may be included in this notebook, such as reference materials you found helpful.

Activity Log

A spreadsheet (Appendix O, also available on the CD-ROM) contains charts to record weekly hours, an activity log for one day each week, and a recap of hours by week for the internship.

Hours are recorded for each day of the week; then, activities performed for one day of the week are coded and recorded in 15-minute intervals. The purpose of this activity log is to record the tasks performed and activities experienced as a sampling of the internship that identifies and clarifies the tasks associated with the position. At the conclusion of the internship and for evaluation purposes, the activity log also serves as a record that is summarized and used to make generalizations about the experience. This is discussed in Chapter 9. Therefore, accurate recording is important because it is used to complete the last topic assignment.

One Day Per Week

To complete the activity log, one day of each week is randomly selected for the sample day. Inevitably this day will vary from week to week and show a variety of routines. A record of activities will be maintained for each 15-minute period by using the code system included in Table 8.1. (Also see Appendix P; the document is also available on the CD-ROM.) If tasks are performed that are not listed, you can create new codes as well as a "dictionary" of these new codes to be included as part of the weekly report.

A system for making notations during the activity log day should be developed that is easy to manage and efficient to use in filling out the chart. It will be easier if you keep a tally throughout the day than if you attempt to recall activities later. This is a good habit to develop, and it fits into a standard procedure used by most firms to establish a record of time spent on a project to bill the client.

Daily Journal Report

The daily journal describes and reflects upon each day of the internship and is part of the weekly report submitted to the academic supervisor. You may report each day at the firm.

Report formatting should be done in a businesslike manner, which means you must identify that it is your report. A typed narrative that is both descriptive and reflective will discuss major events, accomplishments, and occurrences of the day. See Appendix Q for the manner in which the journal may be formatted; the form is also available on the CD-ROM.

TABLE 8.1 (ALSO APPENDIX P)

Activity Log Code

C	Calculations	Calculations made to determine the amount of fabric, wallpaper, paint needed for client.
Cl	Cleaning	Cleaning up office, putting away samples, reorganization of resource room, etc.
Co	Coordinating	Coordinating fabrics, colors, furniture, etc., for the client—putting the design together.
C S	Checking Stock	Making sure supplies needed are in stock—includes business forms, drawing paper, tools, etc.
D	Discussion	Discussion with supervisor about solutions for client—work in general.
Dr	Drawing/Drafting	Drawing floor plan, elevations, sketches, perspectives.
E	Errands	Running errands.
F	Filing	Filing client information, forms, information on clients.
L B	Lunch Break	Lunchtime does not count as time worked toward internship hours required for the credit.
M	Mail	Daily sorting of mail.
Me	Measuring	Measuring rooms, furniture in client's home or business.
M S	Material Selection	Selection of fabrics, paper, etc.
O	Office	Paperwork done in firm's business office—e.g., common bookkeeping.
Op	Opening	Opening workroom, getting out necessary items for the day.
Or	Ordering	Writing up orders of merchandise to companies, manufacturers, and local workmen who assist us.
P	Pricing	Figuring prices for all materials used for client so that job can be accurately quoted to client.
P D	Professional Development	Reading recent articles, tests, and periodicals pertaining to job and assignments. Attending professional meetings.
P L	Price Lists	Updating prices, destroying discontinued samples.
Ph	Phone	Time spent on phone with clients, vendors, workrooms, and such.
R	Resources	Time spent in resource room reviewing and researching fabrics, wallpaper, etc.—becoming familiar with manufacturers.
Sh	Shopping	Shopping with supervisor and/or client in showrooms and various stores for merchandise needed for client.
Sp	Specifications	Writing up specifications for client.
T	Travel	Time spent traveling to clients' home, showrooms, etc.

Additional activities codes you have created: (write in below)

Note: The word materials in explanations of the code includes all items used in interior design, such as wallpaper, fabric, blinds, installation costs, etc. Source: Nussbaumer, L. L., & Isham, D. D. (2009). Professional practicum student manual: Interior design. Unpublished manuscript.

Ideas for Reporting

The following questions will provide examples of what to include in your report.

1. What activities did you perform?
2. For what reason did you engage in those activities? What will be the end result? Can you see the relationship of the activities you performed to the total operation? How did you contribute to the profitability of the organization?
3. With whom did you work? What was his or her role? What did you learn from this experience?
4. What events or responsibilities allowed you to apply knowledge and theory from college classes?
5. How closely does theory describe reality?
6. In what ways did you practice your human relationship skills? Were they effective? Why or why not?
7. How has your knowledge and understanding of the organization increased?
8. How have your professional skills been enhanced through an experience or encounter of the day?
9. Did you meet new people? How did you react to them, or they to you?
10. What conversations did you have with anyone related to the firm or your educational goals?
11. Were you able to use your knowledge to assist someone to better understand interior design?
12. What changes are taking place in your attitude toward:
    a. Yourself?
    b. The practice of interior design?
    c. Your career choice or your classes?
    d. The firm, people you are with at the firm, and/or other people?
13. Why have these changes taken place?
14. Are there things you don't understand about the practice of interior design? What are they? How can you find answers to these questions?

These questions are only a guide and should not be used as an outline for the daily entry (Nussbaumer & Isham, 2009).

Connection between Courses and Internship

One of the most important reflections is to make connections between the learning experiences in the internship to your college courses. For example, selecting materials for projects relates to knowledge learned from design and/or color theory, materials, specifications, and more. Managing or working with people on a project relates to knowledge learned about business practices or interpersonal skills.

Goal Reports

You may define and carry out goals that relate to both your professional and your personal growth. Keep in mind, as discussed in Chapter 1, that the two are often interconnected.

Levels of Goals

Goals vary in degrees of sophistication and complexity. Early in the internship, simple goals that involve recall or organization of basic information are appropriate and readily available as you become familiar with the internship site and colleagues. Increasingly complex goals will be possible as you gain experience and knowledge of the organization and operation of the firm (Nussbaumer & Isham, 2009). To help you format your goals, refer to Appendix R, also available on the CD-ROM.

journal writing

The following interns responded to Field Experience questions throughout this chapter:

A.W. completed a seven-week unpaid internship at a residential design firm between her junior and senior years. She graduated from a large public university in the Midwest.

E.J. interned at an interior architectural firm. She graduated from a private university in a large Southern city.

J.E. interned at an interior design firm specializing in high-end residential interiors and hospitality design. She graduated from a private college in a large Midwestern city.

J.F. interned at an interior architectural firm. She graduated from a private college in a large Midwestern city.

J.H. interned at a residential design firm in Buenos Aires, Argentina. She graduated with a double major in interior design and Spanish from a large public university in the Midwest.

K.F. completed a paid three-month internship in a residential design firm. She graduated from a large public university in a Southwestern city.

K.P. completed a one-year, paid internship in a small residential and commercial design firm. She graduated from a large public university in a Southwestern city.

L.O. interned at a high-end residential firm. She graduated from a private university in a large Southern city.

M.A. completed a paid two-month internship at a high-end kitchen cabinetry manufacturer. She graduated from a large public university in a Southwestern city.

M.J. completed her internship at a firm that designed and built model homes and provided in-house design services. She graduated from a large public university in a Southwestern city.

M.R. completed her seven-week paid internship at an architectural firm between her junior and senior years. She graduated from a large university in a Midwestern city.

T.H. completed two paid internships—one in an architectural firm and the other for a furniture dealership—in Alaska. She graduated from a large public university in a Southwestern city.

The following are descriptions of the lower- and higher-level goal categories. Number one and two are lower-level goals, and numbers three through five are high-level goals.

1. Simple goals of copying, recording, and/or recall.
2. Lower-level goals of assembling and organizing information on a topic.
3. Intermediate goals of comparisons based on planned observations.
4. Complex goals requiring analysis of selected data.
5. Sophisticated goals analyzing sources of information, viewpoints, values, and objectives (Nussbaumer & Isham, 2009).

Topic Assignments

Topic assignments cover various aspects of interior design practice and can be created to teach you about the firm as well as increase knowledge of both the design and business sides of the firm. Examples of topic assignments include describing the organization of the studio or firm and your orientation to the firm and personnel; examining the resource library; learning about presentation methods used; describing ways the firm utilizes the design process; observing and discussing client meetings; and so forth.

The topic assignment format is similar to a daily journal and goal reports and must be written as a report. (See Appendix S; this form is also available on the CD-ROM.)

BOX 8.1 (CONTINUED)
journal writing

What did you learn by completing the journal during your internship?

J.H.: "I learned that I really didn't have very many duties but that the internship got better every single week and that I learned a lot."

K.P.: "I did not do the internship for school credit, so I did not journal. However, I kept a personal record of the things that I worked on each week. I found it helpful to record the things that I had accomplished."

M.A.: "The journal helped me reflect on what I was actually doing each day to further my education. That reflection helped me realize and learn more about the industry I am going into and what my day-to-day work life will be like."

M.R.: "The journals gave me an opportunity to write mini reports on a something in particular that I learned that day. I felt like they were small professional development papers and not really a 'journal' in the manner of documenting my experience because so much more happened that would never fit into one of the journal requirements."

T.H.: "The journals helped me to realize how much I was really getting every week from my internships. Laying out everything I did and my feelings about those things definitely gave me the perspective to really understand what it was that I was learning."

BOX 8.2
assignments

FIELD EXPERIENCE
Takeaway

Assignments focus your attention on specific details and help you learn more about how a business operates. Assignments also help you understand the importance of managing time and being motivated.

Refer to Box 8.1 for background on the interns who responded to the following question.

What did you learn by completing assignments during your internship?

A.W.: "Completing goals, objectives, and journals through my internship allowed me to gather my thoughts on what I had learned each and every day—and it also made me ask the right questions and get the most out of my experience."

J.F.: "Insight into the industry. The tasks made me more aware of what was required day to day."

K.F.: "The assignments we had included reading and writing about a book and creating a poster about our internship experience. The book was helpful because it brought a different perspective to my design education. We are always taught how important legislation is, and while I definitely think it is, the book we read, *The Power of Design,* brought about the perspective that limiting who can design actually decreased the ability of design to get to the entire population. The poster assignment was good because it allowed me to showcase all the different projects I was able to help out with at my internship. It also took my journaling into account because I could go back and look through what I did throughout the summer."

K.P.: "The importance of time and how to manage it."

L.O.: "Every day is different and sometimes you will have to do things you don't want; but as long as you are positive, people will notice."

M.J.: "I learned more than anything how to be self-motivated. During the summer it is hard to do "homework," but there are always going to be things in life, in the profession, that you don't want to do. But to find motivation and the positives from it is something I am glad I learned and can take with me into the future."

Recording and Billing Software

As an intern, you have various options to record hours. An Excel spreadsheet is appropriate and used as an example in Appendix O, also available from the CD-ROM. Other methods may also be used that relates to billing, project management, e-mail software, or day planners.

Quicken is an example of billing software. VIP Task Manager is an example of project management software. E-mail software such as Entourage, Outlook Express, and others include a calendar, which is an excellent method to track time for projects. This feature includes to-do lists as well as scheduling and time tracking on a daily, weekly, or monthly basis. Day planners such as Franklin Covey include the calendar as well as space for projects, prioritizing, daily planning, and weekly planning pages.

Some software is free and either included with the computer's system software or as part of the office package for word processing. Other software such as the VIP Task Manager or Franklin Covey is available for purchase. Also, some software packages are available for either Macintosh or PC systems; others are compatible for both. Careful consideration of your needs—and computer compatibility (consider what system you use at home and what system is used at the office)—is important prior to making a purchase. Keep in mind, too, that using software that is already part of the system or a program eliminates an extra expense.

field experience

BOX 8.3

time sheets

FIELD EXPERIENCE
Takeaway

Keeping time sheets gives you a detailed record that you can use in a myriad of ways to analyze and draw important conclusions from your experiences. This valuable information will save you time and prepare you for greater experiences down the road and throughout your career.

Refer to Box 8.1 for background on the interns who responded to the following question.

What did you learn by completing time sheets during your internship?

J.E.: "Completing time sheets really helped with time management—most definitely one of the hardest aspects of starting a new job."

J.F.: "It was helpful to remember the amount of time it takes to accomplish certain tasks and to track billable hours."

field experience

BOX 8.4

following through on your goals

What goals were most helpful?

M.A.: "I think my goal to work for a well-known company will be helpful because I will have that recognized name on my résumé, and the goal of furthering my skills with real world experience was definitely helpful."

M.J.: "The one goal I accomplished that will help me most in the field was my participation in the design process. I knew the process from school, but to work through it for a real client was a scary thought. This experience has made me more confident in my abilities."

M.R.: "My learning-experience goals were by far the most helpful when it came to expanding my knowledge and learning what I needed to be successful in my field."

FIELD EXPERIENCE
Takeaway

Goal setting is essential, but following through on goals provides you with an invaluable experience. Remember the words of Norman Vincent Peale, quoted in Chapter 1: "If you want to get somewhere, you have to know where you want to go and how to get there. Then never, never, never give up."

This is the key to success.

Refer to Box 8.1 for background on the interns who responded to the following question.

length of internships and reporting requirements

Required internship hours may vary from one university to another. If a 280-hour internship is required, it will take seven to eight weeks (occasionally more) to complete an on-site experience. Students should complete topic assignments in the sequence.

Total internship hours may vary from 100 to 400 depending upon the requirements at your university. With 100 hours, some goals and assignments may be eliminated to meet university requirements. With more than 280 hours (nine- and ten-week internships), some assignments may be more in-depth and reported at two-week intervals. For example, the LE goal—researching a topic such as sustainable design—may be more in-depth research that may not only involve reading but also interviewing suppliers or other designers. The topic assignment requires you to list support staff, contractors, installers, or others important for completion of a project. It also requires that you interview one of these individuals; other suppliers or support staff may be interviewed for more in-depth information. Clearly, if your internship hours are less than 20 hours per week, or if more in-depth information is requested, it may take more than one week to complete the assignment. The site supervisor and academic supervisor will work with you to determine acceptable assignments as well as the length of time needed to complete them.

documentation

For the purpose of grading and for your own use, you should print and professionally organize reports and correspondence into a three-ring binder with tabulated sections, or organize the files on a CD. You may find additional materials beyond your reports to add to this binder, such as research of materials, articles read, photographs of work, and so on. These may serve as references during your senior year and as you enter the field of interior design.

checking out with your site supervisor

At the end of your internship, your site supervisor may complete an evaluation form (Appendix U, also available on the CD-ROM) about your capabilities and performance. The form will then be mailed directly to the academic supervisor; however, the site supervisor is also encouraged to schedule a conference and review your performance before you leave the firm. This form provides two methods of evaluation: (1) multiple choice and (2) open-ended questions. The multiple-choice evaluation enables the academic supervisor to assess and compare responses regarding attitudes, abilities, initiative, appearance, and much more. The open-ended questions give the site supervisor an opportunity to share specific information regarding your performance and preparedness for the internship and future employment. It is recommended that the site supervisor discuss the evaluation and performance with you for important feedback.

summary

An internship provides an invaluable learning experience. However, reporting adds value to that experience. Thus, reflective and analytical reports, goal setting and achievement, and appropriate topic assignments allow you to go beyond just doing the job. Use the reporting tools on the CD-ROM (Appendices O through S).

Reporting the internship allows you to learn even more about yourself. In the next chapter, you will begin the process of evaluating your experience to determine your best fit in the field.

achieving chapter objectives

Review the Chapter Objectives at the beginning of this chapter.
You are now ready to put them into practice.

time management

In reporting to the academic supervisor, good time-management skills will be most helpful. For example, daily journaling should be completed each evening; allow about one-half to one hour to work on journal entries. Some interns find that they are able to use part of their lunch hour to make journal entries when the information is fresh from the morning events. LE and PD goals may be chosen early in the week and can be worked on throughout the week; this may add approximately one-half to one hour twice a week. Topic assignments should be read early in the week so that if interviews or contacts need to be made, the appointments can be set at convenient times for the site supervisor or support persons. These assignments may take one to two hours a week to write, but the research and information may be acquired during work hours. Writing portions of the report should be completed each day. In this way, good time-management skills will occur with less stress when completing the report.

REFERENCES

• Nussbaumer, L. L., & Isham, D. D. (2009). *Professional practicum student manual: Interior design.* Unpublished manuscript.

• Piotrowski, C. (2008). *Professional practice for interior designers.* Hoboken, New Jersey: Wiley.

KEY TERMS

- evaluation
- self-evaluation
- summary chart

9 | evaluating the internship

"The internship helped me determine that I will never work in another residential firm! My passion lies in much bigger projects— hotels, restaurants, and casinos."

—E.J., who completed an eight-week internship at an interior architectural firm.

OBJECTIVES

- Evaluate your internship learning experience through critical thinking.

- Determine future plans through analysis of your internship.

- Review your overall time-management skills.

After you have completed your internship, congratulations will be in order. But your real reward is so much more than a slap on the back and a "job well done." It is, of course, really all about what you have learned and how you have grown.

It may be tempting at this point to just look forward, moving into your next classes and career—both important and exciting steps.

But after you have completed your internship, it is also important to take the time to evaluate your experience. You have earned this valuable experience, and you should take full advantage of it.

An **evaluation** will help you realize what you have learned and what you still need to learn. Thus, the purpose of this chapter is to help you evaluate your internship—the learning experience as well as the best way to carry this new knowledge into your professional career. To do this, a writing assignment has been integrated into the chapter rather than appearing at the end.

analysis of activities log

To complete the final assignment (as noted in Chapter 8), complete an analysis of your activities log. This will point out the tasks you spent your time performing.

To summarize and analyze this information in the activity log, take the following steps:

1. Make a **summary chart** with categories on one axis and sequence of weeks on the other. Table 9.1 is an example summary chart. To complete the task, use the form in Appendix T, available on the CD-ROM.

2. Use the activities log to locate your selected random day from each week. Then, enter the 15-minute units in each category by week.
3. Total across and down the chart for each category and week.
4. Make note (a footnote technique works) of special events, which would be indicative of a shift in the internship experience, i.e., a new design project.
5. Review the chart to see what trends occurred (Nussbaumer & Isham, 2009).

Using the summary chart, write a brief analysis by answering the following questions:

1. Can you see any consistent increases or decreases in the units among categories? Particularly, notice tasks most often completed.
2. What are the reasons for the trends you have identified (Nussbaumer & Isham, 2009)?

accountability for the evaluation

Having answered the previous questions and noted where the majority of your time was focused, you should now have a better understanding of your site supervisor's conclusion. Before your internship is complete, your site supervisor should discuss his or her evaluations with you. This will help you understand areas of accomplishment and improvement as well as the connection to your evaluation. This is important for any type of work, but it will certainly be important for you in making a decision for your future

evaluating the learning process

During your internship, you reflected about the learning experiences in your journal. These statements helped personalize your experience. However, now that the internship is complete, a **self-evaluation** of the internship will enhance your learning experience. Using Appendix W, assess your performance during the internship. Then answer the questions related to your internship experience and your original goals. You may also factor in an evaluation of the site supervisor (Appendix V, available on the CD-ROM).

At the end of the evaluation, you have the opportunity to assign yourself a grade as an intern. By answering the questions on this evaluation that include assigning yourself a grade and considering the site supervisor's evaluation, you will have gained even further knowledge and insight into your internship, the learning process, and your future goals.

making decisions for the future based on the internship

Your completed evaluation should help determine your interests and your general preferences within a category, such as an architectural or interior design firm, kitchen and bath design, retail establishment, and so on. In each of these categories, you should consider the specialties that would best suit you.

Begin this analysis by making a list of the duties and responsibilities of each of the following categories. (To aid in this process, you may want to use a textbook from your professional practices course. This text may be Gordon T. Kendall's book *Designing Your Business: Strategies for Interior Design Professionals*. You may also choose to add categories to this list or delete those that do not interest you.)

TABLE 9.1 (SAME AS APPENDIX T)

Activity Log Recap:
An Example of a Summary Chart of the Internship's Activities

ACTIVITIES	WK 1	WK 2	WK 3	WK 4	WK 5	WK 6	WK 7	WK 8	WK 9	WK 10	TOTALS
PL-Price Lists	1	2	3	3	5	3	4	2	2	2	27
Dr-Drawing/Drafting	3	3	2	2	1	2	2	3	3	3	24
R-Resources	2	4	2	2	2	2	2	2	1	1	20
Me-Measuring	1	2	3	2	1	1	2	3	0	0	16
Op-Opening		1	1	1	1	1	1	1	1	1	9

Source: Nussbaumer, L. L., & Isham, D. D. (2009). Professional practicum student manual: Interior design. Unpublished manuscript.

BOX 9.1

evaluating the learning experience

The following interns responded to Field Experience questions throughout this chapter:

A.W. completed a seven-week unpaid internship at a residential design firm between her junior and senior years. She graduated from a large public university in the Midwest.

E.J. interned at an interior architectural firm. She graduated from a private university in a large Southern city.

J.E. interned at an interior design firm specializing in high-end residential interiors and hospitality design. She graduated from a private college in a large Midwestern city.

J.H. interned at a residential design firm in Buenos Aires, Argentina. She graduated with a double major in interior design and Spanish from a large public university in the Midwest.

K.S. completed an eight-week unpaid internship for a retail establishment that provides design services. She graduated from a large public university in the Midwest.

M.A. completed a paid two-month internship at a high-end kitchen cabinetry manufacturer. She graduated from a large public university in a Southwestern city.

M.J. completed her internship at a firm that designed and built model homes and provided in-house design services. She graduated from a large public university in a Southwestern city.

M.R. completed her seven-week paid internship at an architectural firm between her junior and senior years. She graduated from a large university in a Midwestern city.

What goals did you hope to accomplish during your internship? Did you feel your goals were met by your experience?

K.S.: "I wanted to push myself so I set goals to speak up to the designer when I wanted more responsibility; otherwise, I would have stayed in the store the whole time instead of going out and meeting clients and getting hands-on experience.

"Also, I wanted to use my sales experience to get a client started with our firm. I would say that this can be challenging because it is hard to talk to your employer about getting to learn more and go out into the field with them to see what happens, but if you don't you may get stuck in an office the whole time not learning anything. So I think I challenged the designer more than anything.

"By the end of the internship I did get a woman in with our designer to redesign her log cabin. When I called my employer back after I had left to come back to school, she said that the lady had done her kitchen with them and my employer was now designing the basement of the cabin. She thanked me for my hard work."

BOX 9.1 (CONTINUED)
evaluating the learning experience

M.A.: "My goals were to work for a large well-known company, work on a LEED project, and build relationships that could potentially get me a job in the future. I also wanted to further my skills with real world experience. I actually met every goal except for working on a LEED project because this type of company was not involved in any. I met many people within the company, and others in the industry that could be potential employers or contacts in the future. And I definitely got experience doing things that furthered my skills and real-world experience such as specifying products and materials."

M.J.: "My goals were to simply gain insight into the business side of interior design, to view and participate in the design process, and to determine if residential was really what I wanted to concentrate on. My goals were met: I got to see first hand the business side of things, how the economy affects our jobs, how to work with clients, and how to work with vendors. I also got to see their process and also work in their process hands on."

M.R.: "I wanted more experience and to be more knowledgeable in my field. My experiences surpassed anything I could have hoped for."

J.H. *(international intern):* "My goals were:

- To gain more knowledge of international business.*
- To gain a better professional Spanish vocabulary.*
- To meet with clients.*
- To be active in a design charrette.
- To go on site visits.
- To network.
- To learn new computer programs the firm might use.*
- To get to know the city a culture really well.*

"I feel that I achieved a little over half of my goals, but the other half was unreachable due to the situation. I achieved the goals with the stars by them.

"As far as design charrettes, there were none. There was one time when the site supervisor asked for other options, but we didn't all sit down and design. It was more of 'what do you think, I want an opinion.' I didn't go on any site visits. Every time that the site supervisor went somewhere she always had a million other things that she had to do and always met up with other people or had other plans after the visit. I met a lot of people, but didn't feel like networking was a total success. If I could put a half of a star on there I would, but I can't."

field
experience

BOX 9.2
learning from journaling

What did you learn by completing the journal during your internship?

J.H.: "I learned that I really didn't have a variety of duties, but that the internship got better every single week and that I learned a lot."

K.S.: "The journal helped schedule my time."

M.R.: "The journals gave me an opportunity to write mini-reports on things I learned that day and helped me document my experience."

FIELD EXPERIENCE
Takeaway

One intern noted that journaling helped her schedule her time and complete the journal, goals, and assignments on a timely basis. Another student noted that the journal helped her realize that even though her duties did not vary, she learned a lot about design in a different country. From this, it is clear that journaling allows students to look back on the day's events and write about their learning experience. It is not a list of tasks completed; rather, it is a reflection on what they learn from completing the task.

Refer to Box 9.1 for background on the interns who responded to the following question.

For example, which of the following would you prefer to be?

1. An interior designer in an architectural firm. If so, which quality would you prefer?
   a. Small firm
   b. Large firm
   c. Residential projects
   d. Commercial projects
   e. Residential and commercial projects
2. An interior designer in an interior design firm. If so, which quality would you prefer?
   a. Small firm
   b. Large firm
   c. Residential projects
   d. Residential and commercial projects
   e. Commercial projects
3. A residential designer working with two or three designers.
4. An interior designer for a contractor.
5. A space planner in an office system franchise or architectural firm.
6. A sales or manufacturer's representative for a vendor (in-store or traveling).
7. A color renderer for an interior design or architectural firm.
8. A CAD operator in an architectural firm.
9. A sales position in a retail establishment.
10. A kitchen and bath designer for a small design firm.
11. An interior design educator in higher education.

---

field experience

BOX 9.3

completing goals

What did you learn by completing the assignments during your internship?

A.W.: "Completing goals, objectives, and journals through my internship allowed me to gather my thoughts on what I had learned each and every day. It also made me ask the right questions and get the most out of my experience."

J.H. *(international intern):* "I learned a lot about the business side of interior design."

K.S.: "The assignments challenge you just like your personal goals. The assignments make you ask your employer for different experiences."

M.R.: "I grew the most from my personal goals because they were something I was able to guide myself. Discovering something I was interested in that could pertain to the direction I want to take my career after graduation will benefit me for years to come. It also helped me see personally what my interests were because they were not limited to just the office and the general requirements for my internship."

BOX 9.4

intern evaluations from site supervisors

The following site supervisors agreed to share the following evaluations of their interns.

TAKEAWAY FROM
site supervisors

The site supervisors' evaluations indicate that these students were prepared for their internships. For example, they all had a well-rounded knowledge of software and design. Having well-rounded knowledge of design provides greater opportunities for learning during the internship. The site supervisors also stated that the students were pleasant and willing to work and to learn. These qualities are important for residential firms where designers continually meet the public as well as for commercial firms where teamwork is expected. One area for improvement was that students needed to be more confident. However, as some site supervisors have noted, confidence comes with experience.

D.R. is a designer at Finishing Touch Design Studio, a residential/retail firm in Aberdeen, South Dakota.

D.T. is an architect and executive vice president at DWL Architects + Planners, an architectural firm in Phoenix, Arizona.

K.D. is manager of sales and design at Crestwood Design Center, a manufacturer of custom cabinetry in Salina, Kansas.

S.C. is an interior designer at DWL Architects + Planners, an architectural firm in Phoenix, Arizona.

D.R. (designer, Finishing Touch Design Studio): "The student intern was eager to learn, exceptional with customers, and overall a wonderful addition to the store. She caught on very quickly to product knowledge and had a good eye for design. The only improvement suggestion is to just keep on designing because with every job you gain experience and confidence."

D.T. (architect and executive vice president, DWL Architects + Planners): "The student intern has many fine qualities that are going to take her far in the design industry. She has a great eye for fabrics and design. The only thing I could think of, and it is really minor, is that she would benefit from stronger confidence in herself (not that she is not confident by any means). This is something that comes with more experience in the field, and it will definitely come to her. She will go far in the industry; she has the talent and the drive. I truly hope that I have the opportunity to work with her again in the future."

K.D. (manager of sales and design at Crestwood Design Center): "The student intern had a positive attitude, pleasant personality, willingness to do whatever was asked of her. Her tasks were completed timely and correctly. She was even-keeled, flexible, and a quick learner. She will need to be a little more assertive and outgoing, especially if she is in the residential market. She should work on taking the initiative in the workplace and/or project."

S.C. (interior designer, DWL Architects + Planners): "The student intern was consistently sincere and dedicated and has excellent listening skills. She was able to take minimal direction to a logical and thorough conclusion. She has a great breadth of experience but just needs time to develop more depth and a skill that is uniquely her own. She has to express the desire to work more in a team structure and to develop her skills in Revit (or other BIM software)."

Next, list qualities that allowed you to excel during your internship. Then, review and list your MBTI personality traits. When you have completed this task, connect the responsibilities to the qualities and personality traits. This should help you see where you best fit into the design field. With this information, you have armed yourself with knowledge to help you find the entry-level position most suited for you.

field experience

BOX 9.5
planning after the internship

How has the internship helped you determine your future plans?

A.W.: "I was offered work [at the firm where I interned] after my internship was complete. In the year that passed before graduation, the economy in Colorado Springs took a hit, and Cindy could no longer afford to employ me. I then applied for commercial ID jobs in Colorado and South Dakota, and ended up with a job at FourFront Design in Rapid City. I think it was a blessing in the end because I feel I am happier doing commercial design with an architecture firm. You never know what you love until you've done it."

E.J.: "It showed me the different tasks and responsibilities that I enjoy more than others as well as the different tasks that came more naturally to me."

J.E.: "The internship helped me determine that I will never work in another residential firm! My passion lies in much bigger projects—hotels, restaurants, and casinos."

J.H.: "It made me realize that although residential design was not that bad, I could not do it forever. I also realized that being just an AutoCAD operator would get boring after a while. As far as the future goes, I am more confused than ever. Not only do I have to decide which path to take, but I have to decide if I want to do design, or do I want to do something with international travel and with my Spanish, or do I want to do them both.

"My original plan was to get my Masters in architecture because I think someday I would love to teach interior design, but I am scared of the debt and the economy at the moment. Even though I can't say what I am going to be doing I can say that I have chosen to move to Texas after I graduate. Whether or not I get a design job, go to graduate school, or end up working for ISA (International Studies Abroad) I have my options and I am excited for them."

K.S.: "It assured me that I do want to do residential design just for the personal relationships you develop with your clients!"

summary and final evaluation

Just a few questions remain. Where do you see yourself in the future? Did the internship and the evaluation give you direction? How have you developed professionally? And what do you need to improve for future success?

A final reflective statement should answer these questions and help you look forward to a bright and successful future.

time management reviewed

You should also consider your time-management skills.

The following are questions to answer and tasks to complete based on your answers.

1. Did I complete tasks in a timely manner, or did I procrastinate?

2. Where was I successful in managing my time?

3. Where do I need improvement with time management?

4. Create a list of ways to improve.

5. Pick a date in the future (one month or more) and reexamine the list to determine how you are doing.

Good time-management skills will help you become more successful and allow you to move toward success.

REFERENCES

• Granger, M. (2004). *The fashion intern*. New York: Fairchild Books.

• Kendall, G. T. (2005). *Designing your business: Strategies for interior design professionals.* New York: Fairchild Books.

• Kim, G. H. (2006). *The survival guide to architectural internship and career development.* Hoboken, New Jersey: Wiley.

• Nussbaumer, L. L., & Isham, D. D. (2009). *Professional practicum student manual: Interior design.* Unpublished manuscript.

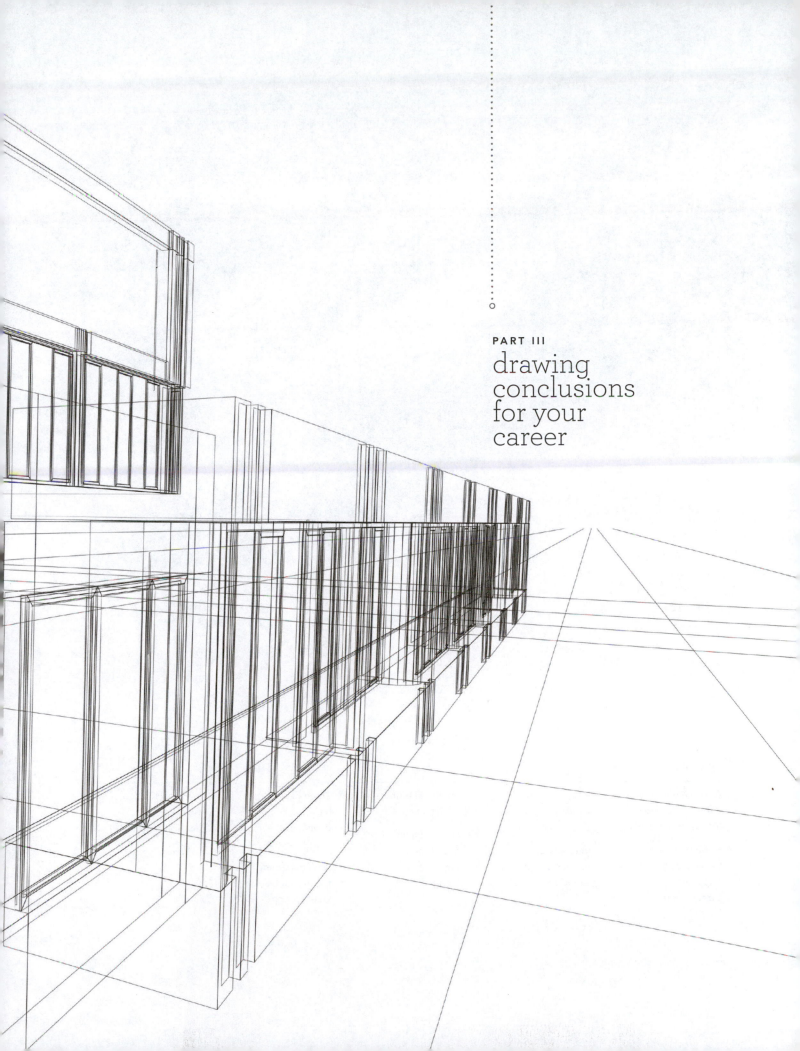

PART III
drawing
conclusions
for your
career

KEY TERMS

- American Society of
  Interior Designers
  (ASID)

- Evidence-
  Based Design
  Accreditation
  Certification
  (EDAC)

- Interior Design
  Experience
  Program (IDEP)

- International
  Interior Design
  Association (IIDA)

- Interior Designers
  of Canada (IDC)

- Leadership in
  Energy and
  Environmental
  Design (LEED)

- Three Es
  (education,
  experience, and
  employment)

- National Council
  for Interior Design
  Qualification
  (NCIDQ)

- National Kitchen
  and Bath
  Association (NKBA)

10 pathways to success: from internship to career

"I am currently a student member of ASID, but plan to continue as a professional member. Being active and involved with your industry peers is essential in today's market, and making contacts within our industry is extremely important in being successful."

—J.F., who completed a four-month paid internship at a development company that specialized in high-end residential and commercial interior design.

OBJECTIVES

- Discover the progression from education to experience to employment.

- Based on your internship and academic experience, reconsider the attributes and skills necessary for various careers; then reevaluate the type of business or firm where you would feel most comfortable and best fit in.

- Understand the Interior Design Experience Program.

- Understand what you need to do to pass the NCIDQ exam and why it could be valuable to your career.

- Appreciate the value of membership in professional organizations and certification of specializations.

Interior design programs in higher education provide the knowledge you need to begin your internship. Then, whether completed during your college career or after graduation, the internship experience exposes you to the day-to-day workings within the interior design field. The internship also introduces you to and provides experience with professionals within the firm and industry partners who supply the firm with products and/or services. In some cases, you may count your internship experience toward hours needed to take the **National Council for Interior Design Qualification (NCIDQ)** exam (discussed toward the end of the chapter). Lastly, with both an education and internship experience, you are better equipped for entry-level positions within the interior design field.

education

Your education provides a wealth of knowledge. A general list of knowledge and skills you should have learned and applied during your academic career includes:

- Understanding the global impact on design.
- Applying sustainable concepts and practices to projects.
- Understanding the impact of human behavior on the designed environment.
- Applying human factors (e.g., anthropometrics, proxemics, ergonomics, and universal design).
- Applying the design process.
- Collecting information to solve a design problem.
- Working as a team member within multidisciplines.
- Communicating effectively through visual, verbal, and written formats.

- Understanding business practices.
- Applying professional and ethical behavior.
- Understanding and applying historical precedents to design solutions.
- Applying design theory in 2D and 3D formats.
- Applying appropriate colors and lighting into projects.
- Selecting furniture, fixtures, equipment, and finish material that meet appropriate performance criteria.
- Understanding the environmental systems and controls applied to interior spaces.
- Understanding interior construction and building systems.
- Understanding and applying appropriate regulatory standards to projects.

What It Takes to Prepare You for Your Internship

These skills and knowledge are what it takes to prepare you for an internship experience and eventually for full employment. However, even with all the knowledge and skills obtained during your education, it is impossible to learn every detail of the design profession. Types of firms and positions vary greatly in the field; therefore, learning continues through experience into full employment.

experience

Each firm provides an internship experience in accordance with its type of business. To understand which type of firm or business you are best suited to enter and explore through an internship, you can evaluate yourself as discussed in Chapter 2. However, some students learn during their internship experience that a particular firm is not where they belong, and some may learn after they begin employment. (See Box 10.1.)

BOX 10.1

right internship, wrong career

The following interns responded Field Experience questions throughout this chapter

E.C. completed a paid three-month internship with an architectural firm. She graduated from a large public university in a Southwestern city.

E.J. interned at an interior architectural firm. She graduated from a private university in a large Southern city.

J.E. interned at an interior design firm specializing in high-end residential interiors and hospitality design. She graduated from a private college in a large Midwestern city.

J.F. completed a paid four-month internship at a development company that specialized in both residential and commercial interior design by constructing high-end, single-family homes, condos, and commercial spaces. She graduated from a private college in a large Midwestern city.

J.L. completed a two-and-a-half-month, full-time internship at a commercial design firm in Illinois. She graduated from a private college in a large Midwestern city.

K.B. interned at a commercial firm that focused on healthcare interiors. She graduated from a private university in a large Southern city.

K.C. completed a semester-long unpaid internship for a hospitality design firm. She graduated from a private college in a large metropolitan city in the Midwest.

K.F. completed a paid three-month internship in a residential design firm. She graduated from a large public university in a Southwestern city.

K.P. completed a one-year, paid internship in a small residential and commercial design firm. She graduated from a large public university in a Southwestern city.

L.O. completed an unpaid four-day-per-week summer internship at a high-end residential firm. She graduated from a private university in a large Southern city.

M.A. completed a paid two-month internship at a high-end kitchen cabinetry manufacturer. She graduated from a large public university in a Southwestern city.

M.J. completed her internship at a firm that designed and built model homes and provided in-house design services. She graduated from a large public university in a Southwestern city.

M.S. completed an unpaid two-and-a-half-month, part-time (20-30 hours per week) internship at furniture dealership. She graduated from a private university in a large Southern city.

S.C. completed a 200-hour unpaid internship in a high-end residential interior design firm. She graduated from a large public university in a Southern city.

BOX 10.1 (CONTINUED)
right internship, wrong career

During your internship did you discover that you chose a
business that was not right for you?

E.C.: "I decided I would like to work for a larger firm that collaborates on projects more. I
also discovered that I would love to work for an architecture firm and that I am capable of
interior architecture tasks."

J.E.: "Yes! I determined that I would never work in another residential firm! My passion lies in
much bigger projects—hotels, restaurants, casinos . . ."

K.F.: "Yes. I wasn't sure which type of design I wanted to do. Now I know that I would like to
do some sort of commercial design."

K.P.: "It helped me confirm that I want to work in healthcare design."

L.O.: "I now know that I might not want to work in a small office all day. But I also learned
that some people are really helpful and are willing to teach you anything if you ask [so the
experience wasn't a loss]."

M.A.: "Yes, before my internship I was dead set on working for a large architectural firm; but
after my internship experience I realized that there are many other parts of interior design that
I find attractive and would be willing to try. I never had the intention of working for a kitchen
manufacturer, but I did enjoy the work, clients, and projects. I still would like to work for a
large architectural firm, but I do realize the benefits and possibilities of working for a smaller
office with more focused projects. Knowing this will make my job search a little broader and
hopefully easier."

M.J.: "Yes it did. I would have loved to go back to work with the firm I interned with;
however, the economy has taken its toll and they are sufficiently staffed at the time. It
absolutely confirmed my love for residential design, as well as model home design, and I am
now in the process for looking for a career in this aspect of design."

M.S.: "Even though I liked working in a furniture dealership, I don't know if it is something I
would like to pursue in my future plans. I appreciate what they do, but it is not exactly what I
want to do."

S.C.: "Yes! I discovered the necessity of photography to the profession of interior design
and architecture. Although I am not currently working at a design firm, I am sharpening
my photography skills with my knowledge of interior design and architecture so that I may
become an interiors and architectural photographer."

Connecting Your Internship with Employment

There are many internship opportunities within the field of interior design. These include working in a retail establishment, a residential design firm, a kitchen and bath design firm, an office systems franchise, or with a facilities manager in a corporate office, an architectural firm—the list goes on farther than you can imagine. An internship in any of these situations may lead to full-time employment. Often after completing an internship, a student is offered a full-time position within the firm.

Professional Attributes

To help you focus more sharply on the connection between an internship and employment, refer to Table 10.1 to reconsider some of the attributes or skills needed in each firm listed previously and discussed in Chapter 2.

Between your education and internship, you will develop skills and a strong knowledge base that afford endless opportunities for employment.

TABLE 10.1

Professional Attributes Vital to Various Careers in Interior Design

TYPE OF FIRM OR BUSINESS	PROFESSIONAL ATTRIBUTE
Retail establishment	Ability to sell
Residential design firm	Ability to work with a variety of people
Kitchen and bath design	Ability to apply knowledge of construction, draw details, and be precise in measurements
Office systems franchise or facilities managers within a corporate office	Ability to work with office systems and furniture on a large scale
Architectural firm (large or small)	Ability to work in teams and with designers from a variety of disciplines

BOX 10.2

education and choice of internship

Based on these responses, it appears well worth the effort to take time prior to applying for an internship to consider where your studies would naturally lead you. In which areas did you excel? What did you find more challenging? And equally important, what have you most enjoyed doing?

Maybe you won't get your first choice. Some will have little or no choice. But simply asking yourself these questions and searching for the best fit will sharpen your self-awareness and knowledge of the working world around you; this will result in a better experience regardless of where you may wind up.

Refer to Box 10.1 for background on the interns who responded to the following question.

Describe how your education led you to your choice of internship.

E.J.: "It did not really lead me to my choice of internship. I needed to take what I was offered."

J.E.: "I think the studio classes and construction documents were most helpful in my future decisions. I was 'forced' to do a residential and office space my first two years. They were fun, but I did get bored before the semester was over. The next class, we were given the option to do a restaurant and I loved it. I am now doing a restaurant and hotel for my thesis project and I couldn't be more excited about it! Even after 20 weeks of doing the same project, my excitement continues to grow as my project transforms into a three-dimensional space (on paper)."

K.B.: "Our professor, at the time, spoke to us individually and helped us to choose places to apply based on what we excel in."

K.C.: "From school I knew I wanted to do commercial design."

L.O.: "I just took what was offered to me. During this time I felt we could not be picky and I was lucky to find an internship in general. If you don't love it, at least you learn what you don't enjoy doing."

M.S.: "Since I was abroad I took the first one that was offered to me."

S.M.: "This is my second career. I think since I had previous design experience, it was very important to me that I worked at a place that I could identify with."

field
experience

BOX 10.3
future goals and certifications

FIELD EXPERIENCE
Takeaway

Regardless of what stage you may find yourself in your career, it is vital to get informed and stay informed on career certifications that will help you evaluate and reach your goals.

Refer to Box 10.1 for background on the interns who responded to the following question.

Describe your goals for the future regarding NCIDQ, LEED, AP, or other certifications.

E.J.: "I want to pass the NCIDQ eventually, and I already have my LEED AP so I would like to just complete CEUS for my LEED accreditation."

K.B.: "Definitely NCIDQ. Maybe LEED, but I feel like there might be something developed in the future that might replace it."

K.C.: "I would like to become LEED certified and become an NCIDQ certified professional."

J.E.: "I will pursue the NCIDQ as well as LEED AP. I'm sure I will pursue more certifications based upon what certificates will most help my future plans."

J.F.: "I would love to pass my NCIDQ exam and also become a LEED AP."

J.L.: "After completing my bachelor's degree, I intend to pursue ID coursework; I sat for and passed LEED Green Associate. I am now searching for permanent employment. When I have the appropriate work requirements, I will sit for both NCIDQ and LEED AP. I already have a BS in accounting and an MBA; therefore, I will not be seeking further advanced degrees."

L.O.: "I would like to get LEED accredited and eventually take the NCIDQ."

M.S.: "LEED AP and a master's degree in architecture."

S.C.: "I don't plan to become NCIDQ certified; I want to use my knowledge in interior design and architecture to help photograph accomplishments and projects."

S.M.: "I would like to do all at some point in time."

Interior Design Experience Program (IDEP)

It is possible to count internship hours toward taking the NCIDQ exam. (The value of taking and passing the NCIDQ exam is discussed later in this chapter.) However, this depends on whether or not your internship hours are being used for college credits. If credits are not an academic requirement, you may participate in the **Interior Design Experience Program (IDEP)** program.

The NCIDQ exam may be taken after two to three years in an interior design position. The IDEP program provides a transition between formal education and professional practice and the exam. The advantage of IDEP is that it monitors and records entry-level work experience as well as administers the NCIDQ exam.

What IDEP Gives You

NCIDQ (2009) created the IDEP program to develop competencies for the following interior design practice:

- Promoting the acquisition of professional discipline, skills, and knowledge.
- Validating experience through consistent documentation.
- Providing an instrument for quantifying work experience for licensing and future career opportunities.
- Developing career-networking relationships among entry-level designers, work supervisors, and experienced mentors.
- Preparing participants for the NCIDQ examination.
- Enhancing the professionalism of the practice of interior design (NCIDQ, 2009).

These competencies coincide and enhance the knowledge and skills gained during your education.

What You Must Give IDEP

The IDEP program requires a completion of 3,520 hours of design work experience. Before completing your education, you may earn a maximum of 1,760 hours of qualified work experience toward the IDEP program. This means that internship hours occurring between junior and senior year may qualify as long as you have completed 96 semester hours (144 quarter hours) of education. However, as noted earlier, internships taken for college credit do not count as work experience toward the IDEP program. Although no reason is given for this, it may be considered "double dipping," and, therefore, unfair by NCIDQ. So if you want to apply for the IDEP program but need internship credits to complete your education, you will need to complete the academic requirements first. If you are able to document internship hours and work during the school year, a maximum of 1,760 hours may be used prior to graduation. The remaining 1,760 hours must be completed after graduation (NCIDQ, 2009).

Enrollment Requirements and Required Enrollment

Though enrollment in the IDEP program is voluntary, some state boards, provincial associations, and employers may require participation because it provides a verifiable, diverse interior design experience. In 2010, the program cost was $255 to be paid in three $85 installments: (1) with application, (2) at the midpoint of program, and (3) at program completion. Generally, the participant pays the fees; however, some employers pay fees as an employee benefit.

Your IDEP Team

There are three people involved in your IDEP experience: your supervisor, your mentor, and yourself. Generally, the supervisor is the participant's direct supervisor within the firm. This individual provides day-to-day training and support. The mentor is an interior designer who periodically offers support and advice to the participant. Though the mentor is generally not employed in the same firm, they must be an NCIDQ certificate holder or a licensed or registered interior designer.

Reporting Your IDEP Experience

Tracking your experience occurs on the online IDEP log and is submitted to NCIDQ for review after your supervisor verifies the log for accuracy and completeness. Your supervisor meets regularly with you to discuss and sign off on your work, whereas your mentor meets or confers with you periodically to discuss your experience and ways to complete your experience in all phases of the design process and professional practice.

Foundation for a Solid Career

Clearly, IDEP is valuable for you and your employer by assisting in training you to become a competent interior designer. Through this process you will be able to provide your firm with exemplary interior design services and work, individually or collaboratively, with a team of professionals in designing the built environment. Through this process, you will obtain quality professional experience that is structured to focus on specific skills and knowledge and that provides a seamless transition between formal education and professional practice (NCIDQ, 2009).

---

field
experience

BOX 10.4
IDEP and NCIDQ

FIELD EXPERIENCE
Takeaway

The more you know about the IDEP program, the more likely you may be to take advantage of it. To find out more about IDEP, visit the NCIDQ web page, "Getting Started with IDEP" (www.ncidq.org/IDEP/ GettingStarted.aspx).

Refer to Box 10.1 for background on the interns who responded to the following question.

Will you consider the Interior Design Experience Program (IDEP) program to help you complete National Council for Interior Design Qualification (NCIDQ)? If so, what are your plans?

J.E.: "Yes, I certainly would consider the IDEP program for assistance. Honestly, I do not know all that much about the IDEP program. But anything to help with such a difficult certification would be nice!"

J.L.: "Yes, but no plan yet established. Locating permanent employment is currently my top priority."

K.B.: "Maybe. I have not researched enough about it yet."

employment

After completing your education, an internship, and 3,520 hours with the IDEP program, you can take the next step in becoming a professional interior designer. That step is successfully completing the qualifying NCIDQ examination. After you have passed the exam, you are able to apply for licensing in participating states. Many state licensing boards and provincial associations require proof that you have the high-quality, diverse interior design experience that the IDEP program provides (NCIDQ, 2009). This means that the IDEP program is an important tool in the process.

More Benefits for Those Who Pass the NCIDQ

Other opportunities are open to those who pass the NCIDQ. These include professional membership within organizations such as the **American Society of Interior Designers (ASID), International Interior Design Association (IIDA),** and **Interior Designers of Canada (IDC).** Before taking the NCIDQ exam, members of these organizations may use the title of Allied ASID, Associate IIDA, Provisional IDC. After passing the NCIDQ exam, you can move from being an allied or associate member to a professional member of these organizations and use the title of ASID, IIDA, or IDC behind your name. This status demonstrates to clients and employers your level of competence and knowledge of the field.

Certification of Specialization

Other certifications are possible for interior designers who specialize in areas such as sustainable design practices or evidence-based design. (See Table 10.2.) For example, the **Leadership in Energy and Environmental Design (LEED)** is recognized as a green building certification system. Interior design professionals may study and take one of the LEED exams (e.g., commercial interiors). After passing the exam, you become an accredited professionals and may use the acronym (LEED AP) with your name (USGBC, 2010). Some healthcare designers are now taking the **Evidence-Based Design Accreditation Certification (EDAC)** exam. The EDAC exam is an educational and assessment program that tests your understanding of ways that healthcare building design decisions are relative to research evidence and results of project evaluation (CHD, 2009).

Interior designers who specialize in lighting design often take the National Council on Qualifications for the Lighting Professions (NCQLP) exam. The NCQLP exam tests an interior designer's knowledge on effective and efficient lighting practices. After passing the exam, you become an accredited professional and may use the acronym NCQLP (LC) with your name (NCQLP, 2010).

Interior designers who specialize in kitchen and bath design may choose to take the exam for **National Kitchen and Bath Association (NKBA)** certifications. There are seven different exams related to that test that involve understanding of design, construction, and business related to kitchens and baths. You may take one exam and later be qualified for another six. Certifications include:

- Associate Kitchen and Bath Designer (AKBD)
- Certified Kitchen Designer (CKD)
- Certified Bathroom Designer (CBD)
- Certified Kitchen Educator (CKE)
- Certified Bathroom Educator (CBE)
- Certified Master Kitchen and Bath Designer (CMKBD)
- Certified Master Kitchen and Bath Educator (CMKBE) (NKBA, 2010)

field
experience

BOX 10.5
joining ASID and IIDA

FIELD EXPERIENCE
Takeaway

Membership in ASID and IIDA will help you develop networking skills and "stay in the loop," keeping up to date with trends and important changes in the industry and professional community.

Refer to Box 10.1 for background on the interns who responded to the following question.

Do you plan to join ASID and IIDA as an Allied or Associate member when you graduate? If so, describe its value to you and your future endeavors.

E.J.: "I would like to continue being a member of IIDA. I think IIDA will continue to be a means by which I can be involved in the larger interior design community by meeting other professionals and learning more about different happenings in the industry."

J.E.: "Most definitely. I believe these groups are extremely valuable networking tools as well as a fantastic way to 'stay in the loop' of the industry. I do not think they are as valuable to belong to while I am a student. Most events are difficult to attend without having a business card and a full-time job."

J.F.: "I am currently a student member of ASID, but plan to continue as a professional member. Being active and involved with your industry peers is essential in today's market, and making contacts within our industry is extremely important in being successful."

J.L.: "Yes, done. I have always found professional organizations critical to staying current in one's field as well as for networking."

K.B.: "Yes. Just to be in an organization with other members of their profession is definitely a good idea for anyone, no matter what the profession."

K.C.: "I plan on joining IIDA; I think it is a great way to stay in the loop and continue my design education."

L.O.: "Yes, I feel it would be most valuable for contacts."

M.S.: "Yes, I feel that it is very important to network with people in your field. This is how you find out who is hiring."

S.C.: "I was Allied ASID [for a year] but plan to become an Industry Partner in the future. I also have plans to become a member of AIAP (the Association of Independent Architectural Photographers). "

S.M.: "I am a member of IIDA. It's a networking tool at this point."

TABLE 10.3

Specialty Certifications

CERTIFICATION	SPECIALTY
Leadership in Energy and Environmental Design (LEED)	Green building certification system. LEED AP credential signifies advanced knowledge in green building practices. Interior design professionals may study and take one of five LEED exams. Some exams are more appropriate for interior design and include Building Design + Construction, Homes, or Interior Design + Construction.
Evidence-Based Design Accreditation Certification (EDAC)	Educational and assessment program testing interior designer's understanding of how healthcare building design decisions are made relative to research evidence and results of project evaluations.
National Council on Qualifications for the Lighting Professions (NCQLP)	Education and testing program testing interior designer's knowledge on effective and efficient lighting practices. NCOLP (LC) credential signifies knowledge, understanding, and ability to apply lighting principles and techniques.
National Kitchen and Bath Association certifications	Education and testing an interior designer's understanding of design, construction, and business related to kitchens and baths. Interior designers may take exams related specifically to kitchen, baths, or education. You may take one exam and later be qualified another six: A few examples of certifications include: Associate Kitchen and Bath Designer (AKBD) Certified Kitchen Designer (CKD) Certified Bathroom Designer (CBD) Certified Kitchen Educator (CKE) Certified Bathroom Educator (CBE) Certified Master Kitchen and Bath Designer (CMKBD) Certified Master Kitchen and Bath Educator (CMKBE)

summary

Education, experience, and employment (the **three Es**) are each an important phase toward actualizing your career goals. Each step provides new skills and knowledge as well as strong mentorship, whether from an educator, a supervisor, or interior design mentor. Use each opportunity to learn, grow, and flourish in the interior design field.

Although sometimes they may seem unattainable, set your goals high. The higher the goal, the greater your chances of reaching the goal and achieving success

REFERENCES

- Council for Interior Design Accreditation (CIDA). (2009). *Professional standards 2009*. Council for Interior Design Accreditation.

- Center for Health Design (CHD). (2009). *EDAC*. Retrieved on January 15, 2010, from www.healthdesign.org/edac/

- United States Green Building Council (USGBC). (2010). *Intro—What LEED is*. Retrieved on January 15, 2010, from www.usgbc.org/DisplayPage.aspx?CMSPageID=1991

- National Council for Interior Design Qualification (NCIDQ). (2009). *Interior design experience program (IDEP)*. Retrieved on January 8, 2010, from www.ncidq.org/IDEP.aspx

- National Council on Qualifications for the Lighting Professions (NCQLP). (2010). *About NCQLP*. Retrieved on January 31, 2010, from www.ncqlp.org/About

- National Kitchen and Bath Association (NKBA) (2010). Kitchen & Bath Design & Sales Consultant. Retrieved on January 15, 2010, from http://nkba.org/students_careers_information_salesconsultant.aspx

- National Kitchen and Bath Association (NKBA). (2010). *Levels of cetification*. Retrieved on January 31, 2010, from https://www.nkba.org/industry_education_certification_about_levels.aspx

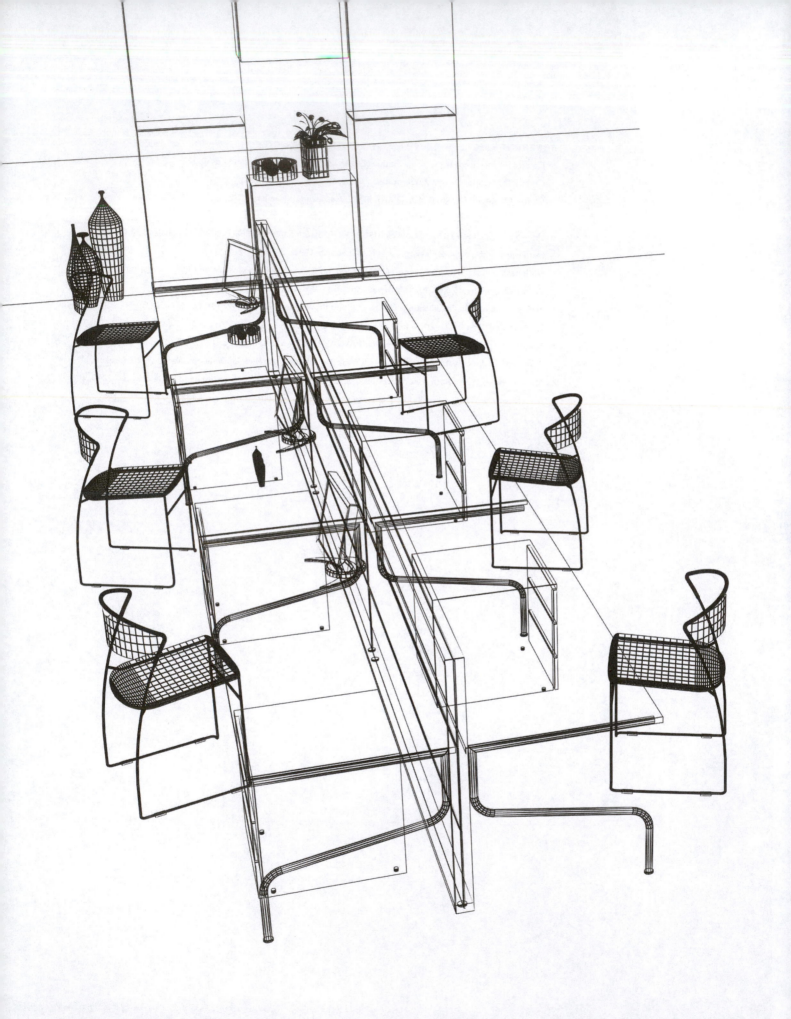

appendices

Self-Quiz: Setting Goals

If you answer *yes* to these questions, you manage your time well.
Answering *no* means you have some work to do in time management.

YES	NO	QUESTIONS
		1 During the past year, have you logged the way you spend time for at least one week?
		2 Do you write out a weekly time plan that includes objectives, activities, priorities, and the time estimated to complete them?
		3 Can you find large blocks of uninterrupted time when you need it?
		4 Do you prepare a daily activity list that identifies priorities and the time estimated to complete them?
		5 Do you control interruptions and drop-in visitors rather than allowing them to control you and your time?
		6 Do you meet all deadlines and finish all your work on schedule?
		7 Do you start projects on time without procrastinating or put them off until the last minute?
		8 Is your desk well organized and free of clutter?
		9 Do you avoid getting involved in other people's work, such as solving their problems, doing things they could—or should—be doing for themselves?

Goal Setting: Establishing My Goals—Part 1

As you establish goals, give yourself permission to have some fun!

Communicate your goals to anyone you want to be part of your support system.

By doing so, you will have just completed the first step toward reaching your goals!

MY MOST IMPORTANT **ACADEMIC** GOAL

....

....

....

MY MOST IMPORTANT **CAREER** GOAL

Upon graduation ....

In 3 years ....

In 5 years ....

MY MOST IMPORTANT **LEADERSHIP** GOAL

During College ....

During Career ....

In my Community ....

MY MOST IMPORTANT **FAMILY/HOME** GOAL

Current ....

In 3 years ....

In 5 years ....

MY MOST IMPORTANT **LEISURE** GOAL

Current ....

In 3 years ....

In 5 years ....

MY MOST IMPORTANT **SELF-TIME** GOAL

Current ....

In 3 years ....

In 5 years ....

Goal Setting: Establishing My Goals—Part 2

To complete this list in establishing goals, answer the following questions:

- Daily goals: What tasks must be completed and in what order (prioritized)?

- Weekly goals: What must be accomplished during a specific week, and on what day must it be completed?

- Monthly goals: What needs to be accomplished this month? What day must it be completed? How long will it take? (Allow for emergencies, other work, or the unforeseeable.)

- Quarterly goals: Ask yourself questions similar to those for the monthlies.

- Yearly goals: Look ahead!

DAILY GOALS:

WEEKLY GOALS:

MONTHLY GOALS:

QUARTERLY GOALS:

YEARLY GOALS:

Time Management: Personal Daily Time Record Log
Recording of Tasks, Energy Levels, and Interruptions

Name:

Day:

Date:

TIME	ACTIVITY	IMPORTANCE	ENERGY LEVEL	INTERRUPTIONS PHONE	OTHER
7:00 a.m.		1 2 3 4 5	H M L		
8:00 a.m.		1 2 3 4 5	H M L		
9:00 a.m.		1 2 3 4 5	H M L		
10:00 a.m.		1 2 3 4 5	H M L		
11:00 a.m.		1 2 3 4 5	H M L		
12:00 p.m.		1 2 3 4 5	H M L		
1:00 p.m.		1 2 3 4 5	H M L		
2:00 p.m.		1 2 3 4 5	H M L		
3:00 p.m.		1 2 3 4 5	H M L		
4:00 p.m.		1 2 3 4 5	H M L		
5:00 p.m.		1 2 3 4 5	H M L		
6:00 p.m.		1 2 3 4 5	H M L		
7:00 p.m.		1 2 3 4 5	H M L		
8:00 p.m.		1 2 3 4 5	H M L		
9:00 p.m.		1 2 3 4 5	H M L		
10:00 p.m.		1 2 3 4 5	H M L		
11:00 p.m.		1 2 3 4 5	H M L		
12:00 a.m.		1 2 3 4 5	H M L		

U.S. Architectural Design Firms
(International locations listed in italics)

ARROWSTREET
(www.arrowstreet.com)
Somerville, Mass.

ASTORINO
(www.astorino.com)
Pittsburgh (includes residential projects).
Other locations: Palm Beach Gardens, Fla.;
Pittsburgh; and Naples, Fla.

**BEYER BLINDER BELLE
ARCHITECTS & PLANNERS LLP**
(www.beyerblinderbelle.com)
New York City.
Other location: Washington, D.C.

BHDP ARCHITECTURE
(www.bhdp.com)
Cincinnati.
Other locations: Columbus, Ohio;
and Research Triangle Park, N.C.

BRPH ARCHITECTS-ENGINEERS INC.
(www.brph.com)
Melbourne, Fla.
Other locations: Atlanta; Fort Myers; Greenville,
S.C.; Orlando, and West Palm Beach.

BSA LIFESTRUCTURES
(www.bsalifestructures.com)
Indianapolis.
Other location: Chicago.

CARRIER JOHNSON
(www.carrierjohnson.com)
San Diego.
Other locations: Costa Mesa and Oakland.

CHONG PARTNERS ARCHITECTURE
(http://chongpartners.com)
San Francisco.

COOPER CARRY
(www.coopercarry.com)
Atlanta.
Other locations: New York City;
Newport Beach; and Washington, D.C.

**COSTAS KONDYLIS
AND PARTNERS LLP**
(www.kondylis.com)
New York City.

**CRABTREE ROHRBAUGH &
ASSOCIATES, ARCHITECTS**
(www.cra-architects.com)
Mechanicsburg, Pa.
Other location: Charlottesville, Va.

CTA ARCHITECTS ENGINEERS
(www.ctagroup.com)
Billings, Mont.
Other locations: Austin; Boise;
Bozeman, Mont.; Covington; La.; Denver;
Great Falls, Mont.; Helena, Mont.;
Jackson, Wyo.; Kallspell, Mont.;
McCall, Idaho; Missoula, Mont.;
Norfolk, Neb.; and Seattle.

**CUNINGHAM GROUP
ARCHITECTURE PA**
(www.cuningham.com)
Minneapolis.
Other locations: Bakersfield; Biloxi;
Los Angeles; Las Vegas; *Madrid, Spain;*
and *Seoul, Republic of Korea.*

DEKKER/PERICH/SABATINI LTD.
(www.dpsdesign.org)
Albuquerque.
Other locations: Amarillo and Las Vegas.

DES ARCHITECTS & ENGINEERS
(www.des-ae.com)
Redwood City, Calif.

DLR GROUP
(www.dlrgroup.com)
Omaha.
Other locations: Chicago, Colorado
Springs, Denver, Des Moines, Honolulu,
Kansas City, Lincoln, Minneapolis, Omaha,
Orlando, and Philadelphia.

**EINHORN YAFFEE PRESCOTT
ARCHITECTURE & ENGINEERING PC**
(www.eypaedesign.com)
Albany.
Other locations: Boston, New York,
Orlando, and Washington, D.C.

ELKUS MANFREDI ARCHITECTS
(www.elkus-manfredi.com)
Boston.

U.S. Architectural Design Firms

(International locations listed in italics)

EPPSTEIN UHEN ARCHITECTS INC.
(www.eua.com)
Milwaukee.
Other location: Madison, Wisc.

EWINGCOLE
(www.ewingcole.com)
Philadelphia.
Other locations: Cleveland, Irvine, Las Vegas, Philadelphia, and Washington, D.C.

FANNING/HOWEY ASSOCIATES INC.
(www.fhai.com)
Celina, Ohio.
Other locations: Chicago; Columbus, Ohio (Dublin); Detroit; Indianapolis; Michigan City, Ind.; Raleigh, N. C.; and Washington, D.C.

FKP ARCHITECTS INC.
(www.fkp.com)
Houston.
Other locations: Charlotte, N.C., and Dallas.

FLAD & ASSOCIATES
(www.flad.com)
Madison, Wisc.
Other locations: San Francisco; Stamford, Conn; Gainesville, Fla; Tampa; Atlanta, GA; Raleigh, N.C.; and Madison, Wisc.

FREEMANWHITE INC.
(www.freemanwhite.com)
Charlotte, N.C.

GOODWYN, MILLS & CAWOOD INC.
(www.gmcnetwork.com)
Montgomery, Ala.
Other locations: Andalusia, Ala.; Birmingham, Ala.; Eufaula, Ala.; Fort Walton Beach, Fla.; Greenville, S.D.; Huntsville, Ala.; Mobile; Nashville; Prattville, Ala.; and Vernon, Ala..

GOULD EVANS
(www.gouldevans.com)
Kansas City, Mo.
Other locations: Lawrence, Kans; Phoenix; and Tampa.

GREENBERGFARROW
(www.greenbergfarrow.com)
Atlanta.
Other locations: Atlanta, Boston, Chicago, Dallas, Los Angeles, New Jersey, New York, and St. Petersburg.

GRUZEN SAMTON LLP
(www.gruzensamton.com)
New York City.
Other location: Alexandria, Va.

H+L ARCHITECTURE
(www.hlarch.com)
Denver.
Other location: Colorado Springs.

HAMMEL GREEN AND ABRAHAMSON INC.
(www.hga.com)
Minneapolis.
Other locations: Los Angeles, Milwaukee, Rochester, Sacramento, and San Francisco.

HARLEY ELLIS DEVEREAUX
(www.harleyellis.com)
Southfield, Mich.
Other locations: Chicago; Los Angeles; Riverside, Calif.; and San Diego.

HEERY INTERNATIONAL INC.
(www.heery.com)
Atlanta.
Other locations: Albany; Baltimore; Boise; Burlington, Mass.; Chicago; Cleveland; Dallas; Denver; Folsom; Houston; Iowa City; Long Beach; Los Angeles; Miami; Nashville; Newark; Orlando; Phoenix; Philadelphia; Portland; Raleigh; Seattle; San Diego; Tacoma, Calif.; Trenton; Tucson; and Washington, D.C.

HMC ARCHITECTS
(www.hmcarchitects.com)
Ontario, Calif.
Other locations: Central Valley, Calif.; Irvine; Las Vegas; Los Angeles; Reno; Sacramento; San Diego; and San Jose.

HNEDAK BOBO GROUP
(www.hbginc.com)
Memphis.

HNTB COS. HNTB ARCHITECTURE INC.
(includes interior design)
(www.hntb.com)
Kansas City.
Other locations: Las Vegas, Los Angeles, New York City, Seattle, and Washington, D.C.

HUNTONBRADY ARCHITECTS
(www.huntonbrady.com)
Orlando.

U.S. Architectural Design Firms
(International locations listed in italics)

JOHNSON FAIN
(www.johnsonfain.com)
Los Angeles.

KAPLAN MCLAUGHLIN DIAZ
(www.kmdarchitects.com/)
San Francisco.
Other locations: Centro de Ciudad, Los Angeles,
Portland, Santa Fe, Seattle, and *Mexico.*

KARLSBERGER
(www.karlsberger.com)
Columbus, Ohio.
Other locations: Ann Arbor, Birmingham,
and New York

KKE ARCHITECTS INC.
(www.kke.com)
Minneapolis.
Other locations: Irvine, Las Vegas,
Pasadena, Phoenix, and Tucson.

KLINGSTUBBINS
(www.klingstubbins.com)
Philadelphia.
Other locations: Cambridge, Las Vegas,
Raleigh, San Francisco, and Washington, D.C.

L. ROBERT KIMBALL & ASSOCIATES INC.
(www.kimballcorp.com)
Ebensburg, Pa.

LEE BURKHART LIU INC.
(www.lblarch.com/)
Marina del Rey, Calif.

LEGAT ARCHITECTS INC.
(www.legat.com)
Waukegan, Ill.
Other locations: Chicago; Columbus,
Ohio; Crystal Lake, Ill; and Oak Brook, Ill.

SASAKI ASSOCIATES INC.
(www.sasaki.com)
Watertown, Mass. (Boston).
Other location: San Francisco.

**LITTLE DIVERSIFIED
ARCHITECTURAL CONSULTANTS**
(www.littleonline.com)
Charlotte, N.C.
Other locations: Dallas, Durham,
Los Angeles, Orlando, and Washington D.C.

**LOONEY RICKS KISS
ARCHITECTS INC.**
(ww.lrk.com/)
Memphis (includes residential projects).
Other locations: Baton Rouge; Boulder;
Celebration, Fla; Dallas; Jacksonville;
Nashville; Princeton; and Rosemary
Beach, Fla.

LPA INC.
(www.lpainc.com)
Irvine, Calif.
Other locations: Roseville, Calif.

LS3P ASSOCIATES LTD.
(www.ls3p.com)
Charleston, S.C.
Other locations: Charlotte, N. C.; Columbia,
S.C.; Raleigh, N.C.; and Wilmington, N.C.

MBH ARCHITECTS
(www.mbharch.com/)
Alameda, Calif.

MCG ARCHITECTURE
(www.mcgarchitecture.com)
Pasadena.
Other locations: Cleveland, Denver, Irvine,
Las Vegas, New York, and San Francisco.

MICHAEL GRAVES & ASSOCIATES:
(www.michaelgraves.com)
New York City.
Other location: Princeton.

MORRIS ARCHITECTS
(www.morrisarchitects.com)
Houston.
Other locations: Los Angeles
(international projects), Orlando.

MOSELEY ARCHITECTS
(www.moseleyarchitects.com)
Richmond.
Other locations: Charlotte, N.C.;
Harrisonburg, Va.; Raleigh-Durham, N.C.;
Virginia Beach; and Warenton, Va.

NILES BOLTON ASSOCIATES INC.
(www.nilesbolton.com)
Atlanta.
Other locations: Alexandria, Va., and
San Jose.

U.S. Architectural Design Firms
(International locations listed in italics)

NTDSTICHLER ARCHITECTURE
(www.ntdstichler.com)
San Diego.
Other locations: Auburn, Calif.;
Los Angeles; Phoenix; Salinas; Tucson;
and Visalia, Calif.

ODELL ASSOCIATES INC
(www.odell.com/)
Charlotte, N.C.
Other locations: Louisville, Raleigh,
Richmond, and Tulsa.

OWP/P
(www.owpp.com/)
Chicago.
Other location: Phoenix.

OZ ARCHITECTURE
(www.ozarch.com)
Denver.
Other location: Boulder.

PARKHILL SMITH & COOPER INC.
(www.team-psc.com)
Lubbock.
Other locations: Amarillo, El Paso,
and Midland.

PAYETTE
(www.payette.com)
Boston.

PGAL
(www.pgal.com)
Houston.
Other locations: Alexandria, Atlanta, Austin,
Boca Raton, Boston, Dallas, Fort Lauderdale,
Las Vegas, and Phoenix.

RBB ARCHITECTS INC.
(www.rbbinc.com)
Los Angeles.
Other location: Oakland.

RNL
(www.rnldesign.com)
Denver.
Other locations: Los Angeles, and Phoenix.

SCHENKELSHULTZ
(www.schenkelshultz.com)
Fort Wayne, Ind.
Other locations: Atlanta, Fort Myers,
Indianapolis, Jacksonville, Naples,
Orlando, Raleigh, Sarasota, Tampa,
and West Palm Beach.

**SHEPLEY BULFINCH
RICHARDSON AND ABBOTT**
(www.sbra.com)
Boston.

SHW GROUP LLP
(www.shwgroup.com)
Dallas.
Other locations: Austin, Charlottesville, Detroit,
Houston, San Antonio, and Washington, D.C.

SMITHGROUP INC.
(www.smithgroup.com)
Detroit.
Other locations: Ann Arbor, Chicago,
Los Angeles, Madison, Minneapolis,
Phoenix, Raleigh-Durham, San Francisco,
and Washington, D.C.

SOLOMON CORDWELL BUENZ
(www.scb.com/)
Chicago.
Other locations: and San Francisco.

SPECTOR GROUP
(www.spectorgroup.com/)
Woodbury, New York.
Other location: New York City.

**STEVENS & WILKINSON
STANG & NEWDOW, INC.**
(www.sw-sn.com)
Atlanta.
Other location: Columbia, S.C.

THE DURRANT GROUP INC.
(www.durrant.com)
Dubuque, Iowa.
Other locations: Atlanta; Denver; Des Moines;
Dubuque; Hilo, Hawaii; Honolulu; Madison;
Phoenix; St. Louis; and Tucson.

U.S. Architectural Design Firms

(International locations listed in italics)

THE NEENAN CO.
(www.neenan.com)
Fort Collins, Colo.
Other locations: Fort Worth, Tex.; Glenwood
Springs, Colo., and Vancouver, Wash.

THE S/L/A/M COLLABORATIVE INC.
(www.slamcoll.com)
Glastonbury, Conn.
Other locations: Atlanta, Boston, and Chicago.

TSOI/KOBUS & ASSOCIATES INC.
(www.tka-architects.com)
Cambridge, Mass.

TSP
(http://teamtsp.com)
Sioux Falls, S.D.
Other locations: Marshall, Minn; Marshalltown,
Iowa; Minneapolis; Omaha; Rapid City, S.D.;
Rochester, Minn.; Sheridan, Wyo.; Sioux Falls.

WHR ARCHITECTS, INC.
(www.whrarchitects.com)
Houston.
Other locations: Dallas; and Ocean Grove, N.J.

ZIMMER GUNSUL FRASCA PARTNERSHIP
(www.zgf.com)
Portland.
Other locations: Los Angeles, New York
City, Seattle, and Washington, D.C.

Possibilities for Firms

AREA OF FOCUS	COMMERCIAL FIRM
Design	RNL
	Perkins + Will
Contract Flooring	Lee's Carpets
	Armstrong
	Dal Tile
	Shaw
Systems	Herman Miller
	Hayworth
	AllSteel
	Knoll
Corporate	Target
	Macys
	Crate and Barrel
	Pottery Barn
	Walmart

AREA OF FOCUS	RESIDENTIAL FIRM
Furniture Designers	Garbo
	Century
Cabinet Manufacturers	Showplace
	KraftMaid
	Merillat
Designers/Showrooms	Onby Design (national)
	DOTI (national)
	DeWitt Design (Sioux Falls, SD + Tucson, AR)
	Ethan Allen (national)
Interior Architecture	Interior Architects (international)
	STUDIOS Architecture
	Mark Cavagnero Associates
	Christoff:Finio Architecture
	David Jameson Architect
	NBBJ
	Diller Scofidio + Renfro
	Lyn Rice Architects
	Lehman Smith McLeish
	Robert M. Gurney, FAIA
	designLAB architects

U.S. Architectural Design Firms with International Offices

(International locations listed in italics)

A. EPSTEIN AND SONS INTERNATIONAL INC.
(www.epstein-isi.com)
Chicago.
Other locations: *Bucharest, Romania;* Los Angeles; New York; *Warszawa, Poland;* and *Shenzhen, China.*

ARQUITECTONICA
(www.arquitectonicainteriors.com)
Miami.
Other locations: *Dubai, Hong Kong,* Los Angeles, Miami, New York, *Paris, Madrid, Manila, Sao Paulo, Shanghai,* and *Lima.*

BERMELLO AJAMIL & PARTNERS INC.
(www.bamiami.com)
Miami.
Other locations: *Dubai;* Fort Lauderdale; Long Beach, Calif.; and New York.

BURT HILL
(www.burthill.com)
Washington, D.C.
Other locations: *Abu Dhabi; Ahmadabad, India;* Boston; Butler, Penn.; Cleveland; New York; Phoenix; Philadelphia; State College, Penn.

CANNON DESIGN
(www.cannondesign.com)
Grand Island, N.Y.
Other locations: Baltimore, Boston, Buffalo, Chicago, Los Angeles, New York, Phoenix, San Francisco, St. Louis, *Toronto, Vancouver, Victoria,* Washington, D.C.

CORGAN ASSOCIATES INC.
(www.corgan.com)
Dallas.
Other locations: *Beijing, London,* Miami, New York, Phoenix.

CUBELLIS INC.
(www.cubellis.com)
Boston.
Other locations: Atlanta; Baltimore; Chicago; Dallas; *Dubai;* Englewood Cliffs; Fort Lauderdale; Freehold, N.J.; New York; Orange County; Pasadena; Philadelphia; Rocky Hill, Conn.; Tyson's Corner, Va.; Wayne, Penn.; and Weymouth, Mass.

CUH2A
(www.cuh2a.com)
Princeton.
Other locations: Bethesda, Md.; Boston, Chicago, Dallas, Denver, *Dubai, London,* New York, Omaha, Phoenix, Rochester, and San Francisco.

DAVIS BRODY BOND AEDAS
(www.davisbrody.com)
New York City.
Other locations: *Sao Paulo, Spain;* and Washington, D.C.

EDI ARCHITECTURE INC.
(www.ediarchitecture.com/)
Houston.
Other locations: *Luanda, Angola;* New York; Newport Beach, Calif.; and San Francisco.

ELLERBE BECKET
(www.ellerbebecket.com)
Minneapolis.
Other locations: Dallas; *Doha, Qatar; Dubai;* San Francisco; and Washington, D.C.

FXFOWLE ARCHITECTS, LLP
(www.fxfowle.com)
New York City.
Other location: *Dubai.*

U.S. Architectural Design Firms with International Offices

(International locations listed in italics)

GENSLER
(www.gensler.com)
San Francisco, Calif.
Other locations: Atlanta, Austin;
Baltimore; *Beijing;* Boston; Charlotte;
Chicago; Dallas; Denver; Detroit;
Dubai; Houston; La Crosse; Las Vegas;
London; Los Angeles; Morristown,
New York; New York City (Midtown and
Wall Street); Newport Beach; Phoenix;
San Diego; *San Jose, Costa Rica;* San Jose;
San Ramon; Seattle; *Shanghai;* Tampa; *Tokyo;*
and Washington D.C .

GHAFARI ASSOCIATES LLC
(www.ghafari.com)
Dearborn, Mich.
Other locations: *Baroda, India;* Chicago;
Doha, Qatar; Indianapolis; and *Paris.*

**GRESHAM, SMITH,
AND PARTNERS**
(http://www.gspnet.com)
Nashville.
Other locations: Atlanta; Birmingham;
Charlotte; Chipley, Fla.; Cincinnati;
Columbus; Dallas; Ft. Lauderdale; Jackson,
Miss.; Jacksonville, Fla., Knoxville; Louisville;
Memphis; Mobile; Richmond; *Shanghai;*
and Tampa.

HDR
(www.hdrinc.com)
Omaha.
Other locations: *Canada, United Arab Emirates,
United Kingdom,* and United States (multiple
locations).

**HELLMUTH, OBATA & KASSABAUM,
INC. HOK**
(http://www.hok.com)
St. Louis.
Other locations: Atlanta, *Beijing,
Brisbane,* Chicago, Dallas, Denver, *Dubai,
Hong Kong,* Houston, Kansas City, Knoxville,
London, Los Angeles, *Mexico City,* Miami,
Nashville, New York, *Ottawa,* San Francisco,
Shanghai, Singapore, Tampa, *Toronto,* and
Washington, D.C.

HKS INC.
(www.hksinc.com/)
Dallas.
Other locations: *Abu Dhabi,* Arlington, Atlanta,
Denver, Detroit, Fort Worth, *India,* Las Vegas,
Los Angeles, *Mexico City,* Miami, Nashville,
Oklahoma City, Orange County, Orland,
Palo Alto, Phoenix, Richmond, Salt Lake City,
San Francisco, Tampa, *United Kingdom,* and
Washington, D.C.

HLW INTERNATIONAL LLP
(www.hlw.com)
New York City.
Other locations: *London;* Los Angeles;
and *Shanghai.*

**LANGDON WILSON ARCHITECTURE
PLANNING INTERIORS**
(www.langdonwilson.com)
Los Angeles.
Other locations: *Beijing, Kuwait,* Orange
County, and Phoenix.

LEO A DALY
(www.leoadaly.com)
Omaha.
Other locations: Atlanta; Denver; Dallas; *Hong
Kong;* Honolulu; Houston; *Istanbul;* Las Vegas;
Los Angeles; Miami; Minneapolis; Phoenix;
Tianjin, China; and Washington, D.C.

MULVANNYG2 ARCHITECTURE
(www.mulvannyg2.com)
Bellevue, Wash.
Other locations: Irvine, Portland, *Shanghai,*
and Washington D.C.

NBBJ
(www.nbbj.com)
Seattle.
Other locations: *Beijing,* Columbus, *Dubai,
London,* Los Angeles, *Moscow,* New York, San
Francisco, and *Shanghai.*

PAGESOUTHERLANDPAGE
(www.pspaec.com/)
Houston.
Other locations: Austin, Dallas, Denver,
London, and Washington D.C.

U.S. Architectural Design Firms with International Offices
(International locations listed in italics)

PAUL STEELMAN DESIGN GROUP
(www.paulsteelman.com/partners)
Las Vegas.

PERKINS EASTMAN
(www.perkinseastman.com)
New York City.
Other locations: Arlington; Boston; Charlotte;
Chicago; *Guayaquil, Ecuador*; *Mumbai, India*;
Oakland; Pittsburgh; *Shanghai*; Stamford,
Conn; *Toronto*; and *Dubai*.

PERKINS+WILL
(www.perkinswill.com)
Atlanta.
Other locations: *Africa*, *Asia*, Boston, Chicago,
Dallas, *London*, Hartford, Houston, Los
Angeles, *Middle East*, New York, Philadelphia,
Seattle, *Vancouver*, and Washington, D.C.

RAFAEL VINOLY ARCHITECTS PC:
(www.rvapc.com)
New York City.
Other locations: Culver City, Calif.; and *London*.

RTKL ASSOCIATES INC.
(www.rtkl.com)
Baltimore.
Other locations: Chicago, Dallas, *London*, Los
Angeles, *Madrid*, Miami, *Shanghai*, *Tokyo*, and
Washington DC.

SKIDMORE OWINGS & MERRILL LLP
(www.som.com)
New York City.
Other locations: *Brussels*, Chicago, *Hong Kong*,
San Francisco, *London*, Los Angeles, *Shanghai*,
and Washington, D.C.

**SMALLWOOD, REYNOLDS, STEWART,
STEWART & ASSOC. INC.**
(www.srssa.com/)
Atlanta.
Other locations: *Abu Dhabi*, *Beijing*, *Dubai*,
Singapore, *Shanghai*, and Tampa.

**STEELMAN PARTNERS
WORLDWIDE**
Atlantic City.
Other locations: *Hong Kong*; Las Vegas;
Macau, China; and *Zhuhai, China*.

STEFFIAN BRADLEY ARCHITECTS
(www.steffian.com)
Boston.
Other locations: *Barcelona Spain*; *London*;
and *Guanzhou, China*.

**SWANKE HAYDEN
CONNELL ARCHITECTS**
(www.shca.com)
New York City.
Other locations: *Istanbul*; *London*; Miami;
Moscow; *Paris*; *Sheffield, England*; and
Washington, D.C.

THE LAWRENCE GROUP
(www.thelawrencegroup.com)
St. Louis.
Other locations: Austin; *Beijing*;
Davidson, N.C.; Denver; New York; and
Philadelphia.

**THOMPSON, VENTULETT,
STAINBACK & ASSOCIATES INC.**
(www.tvsa.com/)
Atlanta.
Other locations: Chicago, and *Dubai*.

TRO JUNG|BRANNEN
(www.trojungbrannen.com)
Boston.
Other locations: *Beijing*, Birmingham, *Dubai*,
Hartford, Memphis, and Sarasota.

VOA ASSOCIATES INC.
(www.voa.com)
Chicago.
Other locations: *Dubai*; Highland, Indiana;
Orlando; *Sao Paulo, Brazil*; Seattle, and
Washington, D.C.

U.S. Architectural Design Firms with International Offices

(International locations listed in italics)

WARE MALCOMB
(www.waremalcomb.com)
Irvine, Calif.
Other locations: Chicago, Denver, Inland Empire, Irvine, Los Angeles, New Jersey, Phoenix, Sacramento, San Diego, and *Toronto*.

WIMBERLY ALLISON TONG & GOO (WATG)
(www.watg.com)
Honolulu.
Other locations: Irvine, *London*, Orlando, Seattle, and *Singapore*.

International Architectural and/or Interior Design Firms

Asia

Japan

KLEIN DYTHAM ARCHITECTS
(www.klein-dytham.com)
Tokyo, Japan

China

MOHEN-DESIGN
(www.mohen-design.com)
Shanghai, Japan

Canada

CALLAND & STEEN DESIGN INC.
Steen Lin, B.I.D. Int.ARIDO, Interior Designer;
(no website; e-mail: steen@callandandsteen.com)
Toronto.

ARDES GROUP
(www.ardesgroup.com)
(Residential Design)
Vancouver.

**B+H (BREGMAN +
HAMANN ARCHITECTS)**
(www.bharchitects.com)
Toronto.
Other locations: Dubai; India;
Sarajah, UAE; Shanghai; Vancouver.

BUSBY PERKINS + WILL
(www.busby.ca)
Vancouver.

COHOS EVAMY
(www.cohos-evamy.com)
Calgary.

CORBETT BRAGG ARCHITECTS
(http://corbettbragg.ca)
Vancouver.

CIBINEL ARCHITECTS LTD.
(www.cibinel.com)
Winnipeg.

**DIMAIO DESIGN ASSOCIATES
ARCHITECT INC.**
(website under construction: http://dimaiodesign.ca)
(e-mail: info@dimaiodesign.ca)
Windsor, Ontario.

**HELLMUTH, OBATA +
KASSABAUM, INC. (HOK)**
(www.hok.com)
Calgary.
Other locations: Ottawa, Toronto, and Vancouver.

**KASIAN ARCHITECTURE INTERIOR
DESIGN AND PLANNING LTD.**
(http://www.kasian.com)
Calgary.
Other locations: Dubai, Edmonton,
Toronto, and Vancouver.

KASSNER GOODSPEED ARCHITECTS
(www.kgarch.ns.ca)
(includes Residential Design)
Halifax.

**KUWABARA PAYNE MCKENNA
BLUMBERG ARCHITECTS (KPMB)**
(www.kpmbarchitects.com)
Toronto.

**LM ARCHITECTURAL GROUP AND
ENVIRONMENTAL SPACE PLANNING**
(www.lm-architects.com)
Winnepeg.

MAGED BASILIOUS ARCHITECT
(www.mbarchitect.ca)
Windsor.

MORIYAMA & TESHIMA ARCHITECTS
(www.mtarch.com)
Toronto.
Other location: Ottawa.

NICK MILKOVICH ARCHITECTS INC.
(www.milkovicharchitects.com)
Vancouver.

RAW DESIGN
(http://www.rawdesign.ca)
Toronto.

RIJUS HOME & DESIGN LTD
(http://rijus.com)
(Residential Design)
Dunnville, Ontario.

International Architectural and/or Interior Design Firms

SWEENY STERLING FINLAYSON & CO. ARCHITECTS INC.
(www.andco.com/)
Toronto.

ZEIDLER PARTNERSHIP ARCHITECTS
(www.zeidlerpartnership.com)
Toronto.

Latin America

Mexico

BUSCANDO LA AURORA
(www.buscandolaaurora.com)
Mexico City.

HELLMUTH, OBATA + KASSABAUM, INC. (HOK)
(www.hok.com)
Mexico City.

KMD ARCHITECTS
(www.kmdarchitects.com)
Centro de Ciudad Santa Fe.

MAREST ARCHITECTS
(www.marest-architects.com)
Mexico City.

PASCAL ARQUITECTOS
(www.pascalarquitectos.com)
Mexico City.

Europe

Denmark

3XN ARCHITECTS
(www.3xn.dk).
Copenhagen.

France

ATELIERS JEAN NOUVEL
(www.jeannouvel.com)
Paris.

BLUE ARCHITECTURE
(www.blue-architecture.com)
Nice.

CARBONDALE
(www.carbondale.fr)
Paris.

CGARCHITECTES
(www.cgarchitectes.fr)
Rennes.

DOMINIQUE PERRAULT ARCHITECTURE
(www.perraultarchitecte.com)
Paris.

GUILLOT+ARCHITECTES
(www.gplusa.net)
Paris.

Germany

ARCHITECTS + PLANNERS KRAMM+STRIGL
(www.kramm-strigl.com)
Wiesbaden.

ARCHIFACTORY.DE
(www.archifactory.de)
Bochum.

ARCHITECTS - ENGINEERS UNITY
(www.aeunity.com)
Neumuenster.

BEHNISCH ARCHITEKTEN
(www.behnisch.com)
Stuttgart and Muchen.
Other locations: Boston; and Venice, Calif.

WITTFOHT ARCHITEKTEN
(www.wittfoht-architekten.com)
Stuttgart.
Other locations: Talinn; and Zurich, Switzerland.

Italy

5+1AA SRL
(www.5piu1aa.com)
Genoa.

ANDREA PACCIANI ARCHITECT
(www.andreapacciani.com)
Parma.

ANTONINO CARDILLO ARCHITECT
(www.antoninocardillo.com)
Rome.

MAP AR4CHITETTI
(www.maparchitetti.it)
Firenze.

International Architectural and/or Interior Design Firms

MARIO BELLINI ARCHITECTS
(www.bellini.it)
Milan.

MASSIMILIANO FUKSAS ARCHITETTO
(www.fuksas.it)
Rome.

MARCO FAZIO
(www.mjfstudio.it)
Arezzo.

NUMO ARCHITETTI
(www.numo.it)
Rome.

STUDIO SCALZI
(www.studioscalzi.com)
Milano.

STUDIOADD ARCHITETTURA DISEGNO D'INTERNI
(www.studioadd.it)
Rome.

STUDIODIM ASSOCIATI
(www.studiodim.it)
Florence.

UNA2
(www.una2.net)
Genoa.

WM WORKSHOP
(www.wmworkshop.com)
Treviso.

Spain

LKS STUDIO
(www.lksstudio.es)
Madrid.
Other locations: Barcelona and Malaga.

R&A ARQUITECTOS
(www.ra-arquitectos.com)
Barcelona.

ROLDÁN + BERENGUÉ ARCHITEKTS: R+B STUDIO
(www.roldanberengue.com)
Barcelona.

United Kingdom

AOK
(www.amok.co.uk)
(Residential Design)
London.

ARTILLERY ARCHITECTURE AND INTERIOR DESIGN
(www.artillery.co.uk)
London.

AUKETT TYTHERLEIGH INTERIOR ARCHITECTS
(www.think-at.com)
London.

B3 ARCHITECTURAL INTERIOR DESIGNER
(www.b3designers.co.uk)
London.

HELEN GREEN DESIGN LIMITED
(www.helengreendesign.com)
(Residential Design)
London.

HELLMUTH, OBATA + KASSABAUM, INC. (HOK)
(www.hok.com)
London.

INTERIOR BIS
(www.interiorsbis.com)
(Residential Design)
London.

MACKAY AND PARTNERS LLP
(www.mackayandpartners.co.uk)
London.

MARKAM ASSOCIATES
(www.markamassociates.com)
(Residential Design)
London.

Australia

ARTILLERY ARCHITECTURE AND INTERIOR DESIGN
(www.artillery.co.uk)
Melbourne.

Preparing Your First Résumé Worksheet

RÉSUMÉ WORKSHEET

After reviewing this chapter's discussion of résumé writing, complete this worksheet using your own information. You will then be able to complete a résumé using each of the formats described in this chapter.

1. CONTACT INFORMATION:

....

Name

....

Address: Current

....

Address: Permanent

....

Phone, e-mail, and other

2. OBJECTIVE/PROFESSIONAL SUMMARY:

....

Type of position, firm, and a possible brief description

3. EDUCATION:

....

Reverse order

....

Course highlights or related courses

4. WORK EXPERIENCE:

....

Experience: full-time, part-time, summer, and design-related work experience

5. SKILLS:

....

Computer/software knowledge, language fluency, technical skills

6. HONORS AND ACTIVITIES:

....

When applying for an internship, the list of honors and activities will most likely be related to college or academics:

....

Dean's list, honor societies, certification, publication, professional/honorary organization membership, offices held, volunteer work

7. REFERENCES

References available upon request

Source: Kendall, G. T. (2005).

Designing your business: Strategies

for interior design professionals.

New York: Fairchild Books.

Résumé Checklist

Résumé of ....

Rate the résumé on the following points, scoring from a low of 1 to a high of 3 in each of the categories listed. Then score and compare your rating against the highest possible total score of 30. Write comments for each category receiving a score of fewer than 3.

ITEM	SCORE 1	2	3	HOW IT COULD BE IMPROVED
1 **Overall appearance:** Do you want to read it: Is the typeface easily readable?				
2 **Layout:** Does the résumé look professional, well typed and printed, with adequate margins, and so on. Do key sales points stand out? Is it chronological?				
3 **Length:** If it were shortened, could the résumé tell the same story?				
4 **Relevance:** Has extraneous material been eliminated?				
5 **Writing Style:** Is it easy to get a picture of the applicant's qualifications?				
6 **Action Orientation:** Do sentences and paragraphs begin with action verbs?				
7 **Specificity:** Does the résumé avoid generalities and focus on specific information about experience, project, products, and so on?				
8 **Accomplishments:** Has the applicant quantified accomplishments and problem-solving skills?				
9 **Completeness:** Is all important information included?				
10 **Bottom Line:** How well does the résumé accomplish its ultimate purpose of getting the employer to invite the applicant in for an interview?				

Rating Point Total   (maximum of 30)

If peer-reviewed, this question may be asked:

"What are some other ways that you would suggest to improve this résumé?"

Source: Granger, M. (2004). *The fashion intern.* New York: Fairchild Books.

Cover Letter Worksheet

Use this template to draft a résumé cover letter

Your name:

Your address:

Area code and phone number:

E-mail address:

Other contact information as appropriate:

Date:

Title and name of person to whom you are applying:

Name/title of company to which you are applying:

Company/office address:

City, state ZIP code:

Dear Mr./Ms.:

The first paragraph should tell the reader:

1. Why you are writing ("In response to your [advertisement, website posting, etc.], this letter is . . .).

2. What you are seeking (". . . to show my interest in and application for . . .").

3. The specific position you are interested in
   ("the position of [use the specific position title used by employer] . . .").

4. Your ability to practice interior design relevant to the state in which your registration/license will be held.

5. How you heard about the position ("I read of this opportunity . . .").

The body of the letter (two to three paragraphs, unless you have extensive experience to note) should spell out for the reader not only your education and experience, but also how they directly relate to the available position. One way to approach this may be to:

1. Explain how your formal education is appropriate for the position
   ("I have earned a bachelor of arts degree in interior design, as required in the posting").

   Explain further details about your education, such as honors or awards.

2. Explain how your previous internship experiences are appropriate for the position
   ("As an intern with Co. X, I gained experience relevant to this position by doing . . .").

3. Explain how your early formal work experience is appropriate for the position
   ("While working as a [name position], I performed the following tasks
   that enable me to perform this position's tasks of . . .").

4. Explain how your recent work experience is appropriate for the position
   ("As manager of projects similar to those referenced in the position, I . . .").

5. Address any concerns that might be provoked by your résumé or that you otherwise need to address.
   (This may be necessary if there are considerable gaps in your work history, for example.)

The final paragraph should include the following:

1. Thank the readers for their time and interest.

2. Express your availability for an interview, either in person or on the telephone.

3. Add a conclusion, such as "Sincerely" or "Thanking you for your consideration."

4. Leave space for your signature.

5. Write your signature.

6. Type your full name.

Add the following notation when sending a résumé.

Enclosure: résumé

Source: Kendall, G. T. (2005). *Designing your business: Strategies for interior design professionals.* New York: Fairchild Books.

Cover Letter Checklist

Cover Letter of ....

Rate the cover letter on the following points, scoring from a low of 1 to a high of 3 in each of the categories listed. Then score and compare your rating against the highest possible total score of 30. Write comments for each category receiving a score of fewer than 3.

	ITEM	SCORE 1	2	3	HOW IT COULD BE IMPROVED
1	**Organization of cover letter:** Is it in a business-like format?				
2	**Relevance to the design firm:** Can you determine if the firm was researched?				
3	**Source of information regarding the position:** Was the source stated?				
4	**Use key words or phrases to catch the review's attention:** Are key words found that relate to being a valuable part of the team?				
5	**Clarity of employment history:** Is there reference to being part of an important project or position that qualifies s/he for the position?				
6	**Good communication skills:** Does the letter demonstrate good written skills with no spelling and grammar errors?				
7	**Creative writing:** If too creative and wordy, is s/he covering up the truth?				
8	**Achievement:** Does s/he show a proven level of accomplishments?				
9	**Care and thought:** Did s/he state when they are available? Was s/he appreciative of the reader's time? Is there attention to detail?				
10	**Neatness:** Was the cover letter neat and professionally presented when received?				

Rating Point Total   (maximum of 30)

If peer-reviewed, this question may be asked:

"What are some other ways that you would suggest to improve this cover letter?"

Ideas from sources:

Granger, M. (2004). *The fashion intern.* New York: Fairchild Books.

Piotrowski, C. M. (2003). *Professional practices for interior designers* (3rd ed.). Hoboken, New Jersey: Wiley.

Portfolio Checklist

Does your portfolio contain items similar to the following?

An entire project from early sketches to completed renderings, including programming and schematic development references

Freehand sketches showing how you reached specific design conclusions

CAD renderings

Perspective and elevation drawings; isometrics

Furniture-placement floor plans; space-planning drawings

Color boards

Evidence of lettering abilities

A copy of your résumé

Interview Preparation Checklist

INTERVIEW PREPARATION: ASK YOURSELF THE FOLLOWING QUESTIONS.

Have you reviewed the firm?

What is the firm's dress policy?

Where is the interview site? Do you know where the appointment is to take place and how to get there?

What the mode of transportation? Have you arranged for transportation, if needed?

How long it will take to arrive?

Do you have enough money for parking or transportation?

Have you confirmed your appointment with the appropriate contact person?

Have you left your contact information with the individual who will interview you in case there is a change or delay?

Did you make a list of questions to ask for the specific firm?

What are possible interview questions?

What are some illegal questions to be aware of?

PERSONAL PREPARATION

Your Portfolio

Does your portfolio contain your name and contact information in case you have to leave it with the interviewer for later review? (Include a copy of your résumé as well.)

Is your portfolio clean in appearance and neatly organized when opened?

Have you repaired or replaced any damaged exhibits in your portfolio?

Can you explain how each and every portfolio entry has prepared you for future work or how it relates to the position for which you are interviewing?

Can you anticipate a discussion in which you describe your portfolio?

What kinds of questions do you think will be asked about your portfolio, and can you answer them?

Does your portfolio show you to be a problem solver?

Your Résumé

Have you prepared your most recent résumé to take with you?

Are you planning to take additional copies of your résumé?

Can you explain how your résumé items (for example, education and work experience) have prepared you for future work or for the position for which you are interviewing?

Can you explain any problems that may be presented by your résumé?

Your Appearance

Do you have a suit that is appropriate for interviewing and that is comfortable, clean, and well-pressed? (Ask a trusted friend or sales associate for direction; if possible, see what others at the prospective place of employment are wearing.)

Do you have shoes, purse, briefcase (as applicable) that are clean and comfortable? (Both your suit and accessories should be fairly conservative in appearance.)

For men: Do you have a clean, pressed necktie that you can tie so that its tip touches your belt buckle?

Most of the ideas are from this source: Kendall, G. T. (2005). *Designing your business: Strategies for interior design professionals.* New York: Fairchild Books.

Personal Time Schedule

Use the following symbols to organize your time during the internship: IN (Intern Hours); IA (Internship Assignments); PRE (Prepare for Work); PT (Personal Time); LNH (Lunch); DNR (Dinner); SLP (Sleep). Add other symbols appropriate to your situation.

Date:

SYMBOLS:
IN-Intern hours
IA-Intern Assignments
PRE-Prepare for Day
PT-Personal Time
BRK-Breakfast
LNH-Lunch
DNR-Dinner
SLP-Sleep

ADDITIONAL SYMBOLS:
CM-Commute time
CLN-Clean

TIME	Monday	Tuesday	Wednesday	Thursday	Friday	Saturday	Sunday
4 a.m.							
5 a.m.							
6 a.m.							
7 a.m.							
8 a.m.							
9 a.m.							
10 a.m.							
11 a.m.							
12 p.m.							
1 p.m.							
2 p.m.							
3 p.m.							
4 p.m.							
5 p.m.							
6 p.m.							
7 p.m.							
8 p.m.							
9 p.m.							
10 p.m.							
11 p.m.							
12 a.m.							
1 a.m.							
2 a.m.							
3 a.m.							

Week #:   From: To:

Activities Log and Internship Hours

Student: ....

Address of Business: ....

Phone #: ....

Student e-mail address: ....

Hours Worked

WEEK:	1	2	3	4	5	6	7	8	9	10	TOTAL

Activities Log

WEEK 1 DATE: ....

Hour	0–15	15–30	30–45	45–60
1				
2				
3				
4				
5				
6				
7				
8				

WORK SCHEDULE

Day	Date	Time Started	Time Ended	Hours Worked
Mon.				
Tues.				
Wed.				
Thurs.				
Fri.				
Sat.				
Sun.				

WEEK 2 DATE: ....

Hour	0–15	15–30	30–45	45–60
1				
2				
3				
4				
5				
6				
7				
8				

WORK SCHEDULE

Day	Date	Time Started	Time Ended	Hours Worked
Mon.				
Tues.				
Wed.				
Thurs.				
Fri.				
Sat.				
Sun.				

WEEK 3 DATE: ....

Hour	0–15	15–30	30–45	45–60
1				
2				
3				
4				
5				
6				
7				
8				

WORK SCHEDULE

Day	Date	Time Started	Time Ended	Hours Worked
Mon.				
Tues.				
Wed.				
Thurs.				
Fri.				
Sat.				
Sun.				

WEEK 4 DATE: ....

Hour	0–15	15–30	30–45	45–60
1				
2				
3				
4				
5				
6				
7				
8				

WORK SCHEDULE

Day	Date	Time Started	Time Ended	Hours Worked
Mon.				
Tues.				
Wed.				
Thurs.				
Fri.				
Sat.				
Sun.				

WEEK 5

DATE: _____

Hour	0–15	15–30	30–45	45–60
1				
2				
3				
4				
5				
6				
7				
8				

WORK SCHEDULE

Day	Date	Time Started	Time Ended	Hours Worked
Mon.				
Tues.				
Wed.				
Thurs.				
Fri.				
Sat.				
Sun.				

WEEK 6

DATE: _____

Hour	0–15	15–30	30–45	45–60
1				
2				
3				
4				
5				
6				
7				
8				

WORK SCHEDULE

Day	Date	Time Started	Time Ended	Hours Worked
Mon.				
Tues.				
Wed.				
Thurs.				
Fri.				
Sat.				
Sun.				

WEEK 7

DATE: _____

Hour	0–15	15–30	30–45	45–60
1				
2				
3				
4				
5				
6				
7				
8				

WORK SCHEDULE

Day	Date	Time Started	Time Ended	Hours Worked
Mon.				
Tues.				
Wed.				
Thurs.				
Fri.				
Sat.				
Sun.				

WEEK 8

DATE: _____

Hour	0–15	15–30	30–45	45–60
1				
2				
3				
4				
5				
6				
7				
8				

WORK SCHEDULE

Day	Date	Time Started	Time Ended	Hours Worked
Mon.				
Tues.				
Wed.				
Thurs.				
Fri.				
Sat.				
Sun.				

WEEK 9

DATE: _____

Hour	0–15	15–30	30–45	45–60
1				
2				
3				
4				
5				
6				
7				
8				

WORK SCHEDULE

Day	Date	Time Started	Time Ended	Hours Worked
Mon.				
Tues.				
Wed.				
Thurs.				
Fri.				
Sat.				
Sun.				

WEEK 10

DATE: _____

Hour	0–15	15–30	30–45	45–60
1				
2				
3				
4				
5				
6				
7				
8				

WORK SCHEDULE

Day	Date	Time Started	Time Ended	Hours Worked
Mon.				
Tues.				
Wed.				
Thurs.				
Fri.				
Sat.				
Sun.				

Activity Log Code

C	Calculations	Calculations made to determine the amount of fabric, wallpaper, paint needed for client.
Cl	Cleaning	Cleaning up office, putting away samples, reorganization of resource room, etc.
Co	Coordinating	Coordinating fabrics, colors, furniture, etc., for the client—putting the design together.
C S	Checking Stock	Making sure supplies needed are in stock—includes business forms, drawing paper, tools, etc.
D	Discussion	Discussion with supervisor about solutions for client—work in general.
Dr	Drawing/Drafting	Drawing floor plan, elevations, sketches, perspectives.
E	Errands	Running errands.
F	Filing	Filing client information, forms, information on clients.
L B	Lunch Break	Lunchtime does not count as time worked toward internship hours required for the credit.
M	Mail	Daily sorting of mail.
Me	Measuring	Measuring rooms, furniture in client's home or business.
M S	Material Selection	Selection of fabrics, paper, etc.
O	Office	Paperwork done in firm's business office—e.g., common bookkeeping.
Op	Opening	Opening workroom, getting out necessary items for the day.
Or	Ordering	Writing up orders of merchandise to companies, manufacturers, and local workmen who assist us.
P	Pricing	Figuring prices for all materials used for client so that job can be accurately quoted to client.
P D	Professional Development	Reading recent articles, tests, and periodicals pertaining to job and assignments. Attending professional meetings.
P L	Price Lists	Updating prices, destroying discontinued samples.
Ph	Phone	Time spent on phone with clients, vendors, workrooms, and such.
R	Resources	Time spent in resource room reviewing and researching fabrics, wallpaper, etc.—becoming familiar with manufacturers.
Sh	Shopping	Shopping with supervisor and/or client in showrooms and various stores for merchandise needed for client.
Sp	Specifications	Writing up specifications for client.
T	Travel	Time spent traveling to clients' home, showrooms, etc.

Additional activities codes you have created: (write in below)

Note: The word materials in explanations of the code includes all items used in interior design, such as wallpaper, fabric, blinds, installation costs, etc.

Source: Nussbaumer, L. L., & Isham, D. D. (2009). Professional practicum student manual: Interior design. Unpublished manuscript.

Daily Journal Format

Your Name:
....

Name of business organization where employed:
....

Inclusive dates covered in report (*June 7–11, 2010*):
....

Monday, June 7, 2010:
....

....

....

....

....

....

....

....

....

....

....

....

....

....

....

....

....

....

....

....

A minimum one-half page journal entry for each day: double-spaced.

Goal Reporting Format

Your Name: ....

Name of Goal and Type (LE or PD): ....

1 State the goal: ....

2 Describe method: ....

3 Analyze outcome: ....

....

....

....

....

....

....

....

....

....

....

....

....

....

....

....

....

....

Goal Reporting Format

Topic Assignment Format

Your Name:
....

Topic Assignment #:
....

Topic *(Name of assignment)*:
....

....

....

....

....

....

....

....

....

....

....

....

....

....

....

....

....

....

....

....

....

State each question prior to your response.

Activity Log Recap:
An Example of a Summary Chart of the Internship's Activities

ACTIVITIES	WK 1	WK 2	WK 3	WK 4	WK 5	WK 6	WK 7	WK 8	WK 9	WK 10	TOTALS
PL-Price Lists											
Dr-Drawing/Drafting											
R-Resources											
Me-Measuring											
Op-Opening											

Source: Nussbaumer, L. L., & Isham, D. D. (2009). *Professional practicum student manual: Interior design*. Unpublished manuscript.

Employer's/Supervisor's Evaluation of Student Intern

Name of Student:

TO THE EMPLOYER/SUPERVISOR: Please read carefully. In the column on the left, place a check mark next to the phrase that describes this student most accurately. There is space for additional comments on the reverse side. We recommend that you discuss your assessment of the student's performance with him/her.

ATTITUDE—APPLICATION TO WORK

5	Extremely Enthusiastic
4	Very interested and industrious
3	Average in diligence and interest
2	Somewhat indifferent
1	Definitely not interested

ABILITY TO LEARN

5	Learned work exceptionally well
4	Learned work readily
3	Average in understanding work
2	Rather slow in learning
1	Very slow to learn

DEPENDABILITY

5	Completely dependable
4	Above average in dependability
3	Usually dependable
2	Sometimes neglectful or careless
1	Unreliable

INITIATIVE

5	Proceeds well on his/her own
4	Goes ahead independently at times
3	Does all assigned work
2	Hesitates
1	Must be pushed frequently

APPEARANCE

5	Exceptionally neat; dresses appropriately
4	Neat, dressed appropriately
3	Satisfactory appearance and dress
2	Sometimes neglectful of appearance
1	Slovenly; dressed inappropriately

QUALITY OF WORK

5	Superior
4	Above average
3	Average
2	Below average
1	Unacceptable

Employer's/Supervisor's Evaluation of Student Intern

RELATIONS WITH OTHERS

5   Works exceptionally well with others
4   Works well with others
3   Gets along satisfactorily
2   Has difficulty working with others
1   Works very poorly with others

MATURITY—POISE

5   Very poised and confident
4   Has good self-assurance
3   Average maturity and poise
2   Seldom asserts him/herself
1   Timid or brash

JUDGMENT

5   Exceptionally mature in judgment
4   Above average in making decisions
3   Usually makes the right decision
2   Often uses poor judgment
1   Consistently uses bad judgment

QUANTITY OF WORK

5   Unusually high output
4   More than average
3   Normal amount
2   Below average
1   Low output; slow

ORAL COMMUNICATION

5   Always uses good grammar and vocabulary
4   Usually uses proper English
3   Occasionally uses slang or jargon
2   Consistently uses slang or jargon
1   Uses poor English, slang, or jargon; careless

ATTENDANCE

5   Exceptional
4   Above average
4   Regular
2   Irregular
1   Seldom

PUNCTUALITY

5   Exceptional
4   Above average
3   Regular
2   Irregular
1   Always late

Employer's/Supervisor's Evaluation of Student Intern

The student's outstanding personal qualities are:

....

....

The personal qualities that the student should strive most to improve are:

....

....

Additional remarks:

....

....

....

This report has been discussed with the student? Yes / No

Feel free not to discuss this report with the student.
Thank you for your assistance to the practicum student.

Is this student the kind of person you would consider for permanent employment on your staff? Yes / No

(An affirmative answer will not commit you to employ the student at any time.)

STUDENT HAS COMPLETED: ....

DATE INTERNSHIP COMPLETED: ....

Signed: ....

Date: ....

Business Name: ....

Address: ....

Phone: ....

Mail or e-mail to: Academic Supervisor: ....

Address: ....

Fax #: ....

E-mail: ....

The student is to inform the site supervisor of the name of their faculty supervisor
and if report is to be sent to a different address.

Source: Nussbaumer, L. L., & Isham, D. D. (2009). *Professional practicum student manual: Interior design*. Unpublished manuscript.

Intern's Evaluation of Internship Supervisor

1 Describe the way the firm worked (i.e., teamwork, individual efforts, or other):

....

....

....

2 What opportunities were you given to learn and apply new knowledge?

....

....

....

3 Were you able to attend presentations and provide input when asked?
If so, was your opinion appropriate and/or valued?

....

....

....

4 How was professionalism demonstrated within this firm?

....

....

....

APPENDIX W

Self-Evaluation by Student Intern

1 What were the main activities that you participated in during your internships? (See activities log.)

....

....

....

2 What experiences contributed most to the achievement of your goals?
(Refer to goals statements and your individual goal statements.)

....

....

....

3 How did you demonstrate initiative during the internship? What contributions did you make to the firm?

....

....

....

4 What was the most difficult part of the on-site experience?

....

....

....

5 What was missing from your experience that you had anticipated and/or thought would be included?

....

....

....

6 What cultural activities did you attend in the community?

....

....

....

7 In retrospect, what on-campus experiences or classes contributed most to
your preparedness to do the internship?

....

....

....

8 In what distinctive ways did the internship contribute to your education?

....

....

....

9 What grade would you give yourself on your internship? ....

glossary

academic supervisor A professor or advisor at an educational institution who oversees an internship and makes certain the student intern follows academic guidelines.

activity log A log for recording time spent on various tasks throughout the day.

adhocracy A type of organizational culture that is similar to the clan type in its flexibility and discretion but has an external focus. It has a dynamic, creative environment.

American Society of Interior Designers (ASID) A nonprofit professional organization of interior designers and industry partners in the United States.

British Institute of Interior Designer (BIID) Formerly known as the British Interior Design Association (BIDA), a professional organization made up of interior designers in the United Kingdom.

chronological résumé A résumé that lists the education and experience in reverse order, from most recent to earliest.

clan This type of organizational culture has an inward focus; similar to the hierarchical, but has a more open, friendly, and familial atmosphere.

code of ethics A rule or regulation related to moral values of good and bad, right and wrong.

combination or hybrid résumé A résumé that combines features of the chronological and functional résumés. A résumé that places emphasis on skills and abilities and less on education.

Commonwealth of Independent States (CIS) Nations included in the CIS are Russia or Russian Federation, former states that were part of the former Soviet Union, Azerbaijan, and Georgia.

conversational-style interview An interview style that may not seem like an interview. The interviewer may talk about a variety of topics that may not relate to the position; the purpose is to see if the applicant is able to organize and control a random situation. Questions are generally open-ended.

Cooperative Center for Study Abroad (CCSA) A consortium of American colleges and universities that offers study abroad programs and internships in English-speaking regions.

corporation A company recognized by law to act as a single person with its own power and liabilities separate from individual members.

cover letter A letter sent with another document, such as a résumé, or with a package, that provides necessary or additional information.

daily journal A document that describes and reflects upon each day of the internship and is part of the weekly report submitted to the academic supervisor in accordance with each university's requirements.

electronic résumé A résumé that is designed to be sent as an e-mail attachment or displayed on a website.

energy levels Refers to times when a person is more or less alert than other times.

ethics A system of moral principles that govern appropriate conduct for a person or a group; a concern with moral values—good and bad, right and wrong.

etiquette System of rules that regulates social and professional behavior.

European Union (EU) An economic and political alliance of European nations whose goals include a single economic community as well as social and political cooperation.

evaluation The act of considering or examining something to judge its value, quality, importance, and/or condition.

Evidence-Based Design Accreditation Certification (EDAC) An educational and assessment program that tests individual's understanding of how to base healthcare building design decisions on credible research evidence and project evaluation results.

flat organizational structure A type of organization in which the team approach is used and the managers, supervisors, and/or principals of a firm work as part of the team.

Form W-2 (Employer's Wage and Tax Statement) This form shows wages paid and that federal, state, city, and social security (FICA) taxes were withheld. The employer must prepare and send a W-2 to an employee by January 31 of the calendar year following employment.

Form W-9 (Employee's Withholding Allowance Certificate) The completion of this form allows the employer to deduct federal income tax from your wages. The amount of this tax deduction will depend upon the number of exemptions claimed. The employer is required to keep one copy and send the other to the IRS.

functional résumé A résumé that groups education and experience into sections categorized by skills or abilities, which are listed in order of importance rather than by date.

goal reports A document or group of documents that describe intended goals and ways goals were accomplished.

goals An object, a target, or an aim; a plan to do something today or at some future date.

globalization The development of an integrated worldwide economy based on an increasing free flow of trade, capital, and labor.

Guanxi A Chinese philosophy that represents a commitment by one to offer assistance to another.

hierarchical organizational structure See hierarchy.

hierarchy A type of organizational culture in which the chain of command begins at the top and progresses downward. This type of firm has an internal focus. Another term for hierarchy is hierarchical.

Inhwa A Korean philosophy emphasizing harmony between individuals. This includes harmonious relationships among and loyalty to one other. Even unequals, such as a boss and an employee, are included. For example, in the home, the older takes care of the young, and the young are loyal to the older individuals (Wenslow, 2006).

internship A supervised work experience within a profession.

internship supervisor An individual within the firm who oversees an internship.

Interior Design Experience Program (IDEP) A structured method of recording work experience for a transition between formal education and professional practice that recognizes differences between the classroom and workplace. The program develops specific competency in interior design practice.

Interior Designers of Canada (IDC) A nonprofit organization made up of interior designers and industry partners who are primarily Canadian citizens.

International Interior Design Association (IIDA) A nonprofit association made up of interior design professional and industry partners worldwide.

interview A meeting to ask questions of the interviewee when applying for a job, internship, or project.

interviewee The person being interviewed for a job, internship, or project.

interviewer The prospective employer who conducts an interview.

job application A formal written request for work.

Leadership in Energy and Environmental Design (LEED) An international green building certification system that provides third-party verification for all phases of the designing and building of a building or community.

learning experience goal (LE) Something an individual wants to achieve that relates to tasks or activities in order to gain new knowledge in the workplace.

market Similar to a hierarchical or hierarchy type; however, in this type of organization, people are concerned about protecting their reputation from external forces.

National Council for Interior Design Qualification (NCIDQ) A nonprofit organization whose purpose is to protect the health, life safety, and welfare of the public by establishing standards of competence in the practice of interior design.

National Kitchen and Bath Association (NKBA) A nonprofit organization made up of kitchen and bath designers worldwide.

netiquette A set of guidelines for e-mail communication.

networking The process or practice of building or maintaining informal relationships with people whose friendship could bring advantages such a business or job opportunities.

office politics Interrelationships among people within the work environment that involves power and influence or conflict as well as the strategies created for rewards and promotions, competition, retribution, and punishment.

partnership A firm where a legal relationship has been formed between two or more parties who have specified rights and responsibilities.

passport An identification document; a document that provides access into another country.

personal goals Something an individual wants to achieve that relates to one's personal life.

portfolio A case that holds drawings or documents; a set of drawings or documents that represent somebody's creative work.

practitioner A professional within a specific field.

priorities A state of having importance or urgency.

professional conduct The idea that professionals are expected to perform duties in a competent manner.

professional development The ongoing development of skills, abilities, and attitudes that are appropriate to the profession.

professional goals Something an individual wants to achieve that relates to one's profession.

professional development (PD) goal Goals created that will enhance ones skill, abilities, and attitudes.

psychographics Marketing the study of psychological profiles of potential buyers of a product; used to improve marketing of a product.

résumé A summary of an individual's educational and work experience to present to a possible future employer.

self-evaluation The act of examining oneself to determine value, quality, importance, or condition.

site supervisor One who oversees and guides the intern within the design firm during an internship.

situational interview or case study interviews A meeting in which a hypothetical situation is presented and the person being interviewed explains ways to handle the situation.

sole proprietorship A firm owned by a single owner.

stress interview An interview in which the interviewer ask questions to put the interviewee under pressure or make the interviewee feel stressed. The intent is to see the interviewee's reaction under the worst conditions.

summary chart A table or spreadsheet that summarizes data from the internship.

team interview Several individuals from the firm ask questions and evaluate the interviewee.

teamwork Work shared by two or more equal parties.

three Es (education, experience, and employment) Similar to the 3Rs, the 3Es are an interconnected and sequential learning process from education to experience to employment.

topic assignments A task assigned on a specific subject.

visa An official endorsement in a passport that authorizes the bearer to enter or leave, and to travel in or through, a specific country or region.

Wa A Japanese philosophy based on the group and the individual's affiliation. Membership and group loyalty are critical. Loyalty to the group builds consensus and maintains harmony that consequentially benefits the individual.

weekly reports A document or group of documents produced on a weekly basis.

index